China, Oil and Global Politics

China's rapid economic growth has led to a huge increase in its domestic energy needs. This book provides a critical overview of how China's growing need for oil imports is shaping its international economic and diplomatic strategy and how this affects global political relations and behaviour.

Part One is focused on the domestic drivers of energy policy: it provides a systematic account of recent trends in China's energy sector and assesses the context and processes of energy policy-making, and concludes by showing how and why China's oil industry has spread across the world in the last fifteen years. Part Two analyses the political and foreign policy implications of this energy-driven expansion and the challenges this potentially poses for China's integration into the international system. It examines a number of factors linked to this integration in the energy field, including the unpredictabilities of internal policy-making, China's determination to promote its own critical national interests, and the general ambition of the Chinese leadership to integrate with the international system on its own terms and at its own speed.

This highly topical book examines China's international energy strategy, and provides insights into the impact of this on China's growing presence in various parts of the world.

Philip Andrews-Speed is an Associate Fellow of Chatham House and an independent energy policy analyst with twenty years' experience of China's energy sector. He recently edited *International Competition for Resources: the Role of Law, the State and of Markets*.

Roland Dannreuther is Professor and Head of the Department of Politics and International Relations, University of Westminster, UK. Recent publications include *International Security: The Contemporary Agenda* and, as co-editor, *Russia and Islam: Religion, State and Radicalism* (also published by Routledge).

Routledge Contemporary China Series

China, Oil and Global Politics

Philip Andrews-Speed and
Roland Dannreuther

Routledge
Taylor & Francis Group

LONDON AND NEW YORK

First published 2011
by Routledge
2 Park Square, Milton Park, Abingdon, Oxon, OX14 4RN

Simultaneously published in the USA and Canada
by Routledge
711 Third Avenue, New York, NY 10017

Routledge is an imprint of the Taylor & Francis Group, an informa business

British Library Cataloguing in Publication Data
A catalogue record for this book is available from the British Library

Library of Congress Cataloging-in-Publication Data
A catalog record has been requested for this book

ISBN: 978–0–415–60395–9 (hbk)
ISBN: 978–0–203–81789–6 (ebk)

Typeset in Times New Roman by
Florence Production Ltd, Stoodleigh, Devon

110510

Contents

Figures

Tables

Abbreviations

ABM	Anti-Ballistic Missile
APEC	Asia-Pacific Economic Co-operation Forum
ARF	ASEAN Regional Forum
ASEAN	Association of Southeast Asian Nations
CCP	Chinese Communist Party
CEO	Chief Executive Officer
CNOOC	China National Offshore Oil Corporation
CNPC	China National Petroleum Corporation
CTL	Coal-to-liquids
EU	European Union
FDI	Foreign direct investment
GDP	Gross domestic product
GNPOC	Greater Nile Petroleum Operating Company
GW	Gigawatt
IEA	International Energy Agency
IMF	International Monetary Fund
IOC	International oil company
IR	International relations
KOGAS	Korean Gas Corporation
LNG	Liquefied natural gas
MPLA	Popular Movement for the Liberation of Angola
NATO	North Atlantic Treaty Organisation
NDRC	National Development and Reform Commission
NGO	Non-governmental organisation
NOC	National oil company
OECD	Organisation for Economic Cooperation and Development
ONGC	Oil and Natural Gas Corporation
OPEC	Organisation of Oil Exporting Countries
PDVSA	Petróleos de Venezuela S.A.
PLA	People's Liberation Army
PLAN	People's Liberation Army Navy
RMB	Renminbi (the Chinese currency)
SABIC	Saudi Basic Industries Corporation

SASAC	State-owned Assets Supervision and Administration Commission
SCO	Shanghai Cooperation Organisation
SDPC	State Development and Planning Commission
SETC	State Economic and Trade Commission
SLOC	Sea-lines of communication
SPC	State Planning Commission
SSI	Sonangol Sinopec International
TAC	Treaty of Amity and Cooperation
TPAO	Turkish Petroleum Corporation
UAE	United Arab Emirates
UN	United Nations
UNOCAL	Union Oil Company of California
VAT	Value-added tax
WTO	World Trade Organization

1 Introduction

China, oil and global politics

China needs oil and needs oil in ever-increasing quantities. Until 1993, China was an exporter of oil; since then, its demand for oil imports has grown steadily and inexorably. Net imports of oil reached 150 million tonnes in 2004 and 220 million tonnes in 2009, some 55 per cent of the nation's total oil consumption, and are projected to rise to 400–500 million tonnes per year by 2020. China will, in the process, overtake the United States as the largest net importer of oil. Oil is not the only commodity that China is importing in increasing quantities. Gas is another critical energy commodity that is being imported from abroad. But similar markedly upward trajectories for imports are found with numerous other primary commodities, such as timber, minerals, cereals, rice and soybeans. This surging demand for imports reflects the extraordinary growth, particularly during the 2000s, of China's economy. It also reflects the reality that China is emerging as one of the most important power houses of the global economy along with the associated need to meet the increased wealth and levels of consumption of China's 1.3 billion population. This surge in commodity imports, mirrored by the expansion in China's exports of manufactured goods, is one of the most visible and concrete expressions of China's emergent rise to great power status.

Oil does have a particular domestic and global significance compared to other commodities. In the first instance, ensuring that China has sufficient supplies of oil at a reasonable price represents a major domestic challenge for the Chinese government. Certainly, oil is not the only or the most important of China's energy inputs. Here, pride of place goes to coal, which currently still provides nearly 70 per cent of China's overall energy needs and which is still mainly sourced from within China. But oil, its supply and price, is a sensitive popular issue since it remains the principal fuel in the transportation sector and the hopes and expectations of most Chinese, as elsewhere in the world, rest on car ownership and in enjoying the sense of freedom and prosperity that such ownership provides. Oil prices, particularly when they rise as sharply as they did during most of the 2000s, also remain the most visible expression of a more challenging energy security environment. For energy-importing states like China, this becomes a major political test for the government.

A further particularity of oil is its geopolitical dimension. Oil is different from other commodities in the extent to which its production, supply and distribution are marked by geopolitical tensions and sensitivities. This is a function of both the high value that oil has in the global economy and the distribution of much of the world's energy supplies in unstable and geopolitically contested parts of the world. To a degree surpassing other commodities, oil excites considerable strategic nervousness and suspicion. And as China is driven to secure ever-increasing quantities of oil from different parts of the world, so the anxieties and suspicions of other countries about China's intentions and ambitions grow. For those seeking to interpret the meaning and significance of China's rise, China's global search for oil becomes an ever-important factor in the equation. For China itself, the hunger for oil and how this leads the Chinese government to engage more intensively with regions of the world where it hitherto had only limited involvement inevitably brings new foreign policy choices and dilemmas. As China charts its course towards great power status, the vulnerability, both perceived and actual, to oil imports inevitably enforces choices about what sort of great power China wishes to be. That being said, dependence on oil imports need not prevent a country from being a great power though it can constrain its freedom of action, as the case of the United States demonstrates.

Adelphi Paper of 2002

These oil-related geopolitical challenges are not new or newly discovered for China. Indeed, we first explored the strategic implications of China's energy needs in an *Adelphi Paper* that was published in 2002.[1] We believe, as authors tend to do, that most of the conclusions we drew in that earlier study have stood the test of time. However, we admit that we (along with others) failed to predict the extraordinary economic growth of China in the mid-2000s. We similarly failed to predict the rapid rise in oil prices during this period and the way in which China's growing imports contributed to this rise. As such, energy security has gained an increased global salience, which was generally unexpected at the beginning of the decade when many openly predicted that we would be entering an 'era of cheap energy'. Also, though we explored the geopolitical implications of China's search for oil in Russia, central Asia and the Middle East, we failed to anticipate that China's energy drive would become truly global, extending deep into sub-Saharan Africa and Latin America.

The conclusions that we drew from the *Adelphi Paper* in 2002 generally tended to accentuate the positive while recognising the difficulties and constraints. We noted the internal incoherence of domestic energy policy-making, the lack of coordination between the multiplicity of competing actors and the weakness of state capacity, and the tendency to promote more strategic and statist, rather than market-driven and more efficient, solutions. But we also assumed that the general trajectory of China's policy learning was positive and that greater experience and understanding of the policy options, drawing not least from advice and expertise from abroad, would promote a more capable and effective policy framework. On the international front, we tended to position ourselves among the 'liberal optimists', to use the category set out by Friedberg, and which emphasised the generally pacifying impact of China's integration into global energy markets and the implausibility of the more alarmist accounts of how China's international energy strategy would almost inevitably lead to conflict and war.[2]

Although our basic outlook remains positive, we have become notably less sanguine, or perhaps more accurately more uncertain, about the implications of China's energy drive in terms of domestic stability and global security. Domestically, the striking fact that in the mid-2000s China's long-term secular decline in energy intensity – the amount of energy used for overall economic production – was reversed is indicative to us of a wider and more serious set of problems that the government has faced in articulating and implementing an effective energy strategy. The policy urgency of confronting this seemingly inexorable growth in energy-intensive industrial activity has only been heightened by domestic and international expectations for the government to respond to the challenges of environmental degradation and climate change.

The difficulties that the Chinese leadership has faced in meeting these demands presents a picture of a government that is more constrained and less autonomous than our previous study suggested. The fragmented nature of the structures and systems of governance continues to place significant constraints on the leadership's ability to formulate and implement energy policy and other domestic policies in a coherent and sustained manner. Many policies appear to be short term in nature and ad hoc reactions to events or to pressure from domestic interest groups. Many long-term policies encounter obstacles, which constrain implementation or result in unintended consequences. As a consequence, outside observers are frequently taken by surprise by policy announcements, by the success or failure of policy implementation, and by the outcomes of policies. Such is the scale and rate of growth of China's economy and energy sector that relatively small changes from expected trends can cause significant disturbances in both domestic and international energy markets.

On the international and geo-strategic level, we still argue that the pacifying effects of a liberalising and integrationist energy policy agenda remains the most probable potential outcome, which should help to increase trust between China and the West. But we also now recognise that China's strategic orientation includes alternative possible options, such as balancing against the West with, for example, Russia, or seeking a regional hegemony over neighbouring regions such as central Asia and Southeast Asia, or even a neo-imperial option as Chinese companies extend Chinese political interests into parts of the Global South such as Africa and Latin America. Predicting China's foreign policy course, as refracted through its drive for oil, is thus more problematic and complex, dependent on a number of unpredictable interactions and feedbacks, than our earlier study suggested.

Aim and structure of the book

The aim of this book remains, as with our earlier work, to provide an accessible but theoretically-informed account of the global strategic implications of China's international energy strategies, primarily as they relate to oil. Our focus on oil is driven by our belief that oil is a powerful prism through which to understand the dilemmas facing China in terms of formulating and implementing an effective energy policy, and in how to project this internationally. Given the centrality that oil plays in China's foreign policy, it also provides a powerful prism through which to assess China's rise and the potential implications of that rise for global politics. We also address issues relating to natural gas where they impact on China's wider international energy strategies. The book does not dwell on the challenges of climate change, except in so far as China's energy policies reflect such concerns.

In order to carry out an effective analysis of China's international oil and energy strategies, it is essential to start by examining the domestic energy sector and the domestic drivers for an international energy policy. Thus the book has two main parts. The first part focuses on the domestic energy policy context, how oil fits into the general energy-related interests and objectives of the Chinese government, and the reasons why Chinese oil companies are increasingly looking overseas for their markets. We start with the assumption that all politics is ultimately local and that this is arguably even more the case for a country of the size and magnitude of China. The principal domestic challenge for the Chinese government, and for which its legitimacy depends, is symbolised by the need 'to keep the lights on', something that it singularly failed to do in 2004 with numerous outages at that time. Energy supply in sufficient and adequate quantities is vital not only for meeting the basic needs of the population; it is also critical for ensuring China's economic growth and for doing so in a manner, which ensures that this growth is environmentally sustainable. Clearly the fact that China has become increasingly dependent on and vulnerable to energy supplies from abroad is itself a significant and legitimate source of concern for the government. But, ultimately, it is the domestic context and the need to meet the energy demands of the Chinese population that dominates the strategic calculations of the Chinese leadership and the Chinese Communist Party (CCP). The legitimacy of the state and the ruling party depends ultimately on their capacity to deliver this vital input to China's economy.

Chapter 2 provides a systematic account of China's energy challenges and policy priorities, with a focus on the period since 2002 when domestic energy demand started to rise sharply after the slowdown associated with the Asian financial crisis. It shows how the government has sought to maximise domestic production of energy as well as raising imports in order to assure an adequate supply of energy. At the same time, the government has radically strengthened measures to encourage energy efficiency and energy conservation. Chapter 3 seeks to explain the nature of China's approach to energy policy and to the measures employed to implement policy. This chapter identifies the importance of the agenda setting process, it examines how ideas, beliefs and traditions contribute to shaping policy approaches, it explains how the very nature of the energy sector constrains the government's freedom of action and it identifies some of the key parties to the energy policy processes. These considerations provide the basis for an examination of the key features of energy policy-making and implementation in China, which are covered in Chapter 4. We highlight the relative predictability and path-dependency of long-term policies against the unpredictability of short-term decisions, the challenges imposed by such rapid and sustained economic growth, the tensions between different objectives of national energy policy, and the discontinuities between different parts of the energy sector. Taking such factors into account cautions against too literal a reading of the rhetoric of the Chinese government and the corresponding need to test this rhetoric against actual results.

Chapters 5 and 6 provide a link with the second part of the book and give an overview of the historical evolution of China's international oil and gas strategy, identifying the main actors driving this policy, their aims and objectives, the progress made, and the trends and outlook for the future. The particular focus of Chapter 6 is on the corporate strategies of the Chinese oil companies who have been at the forefront of this intense international engagement, and the ways in which the Chinese government have facilitated their foreign economic activities and investments.

The second part of the book shifts its focus away from domestic politics and the perspective of the Chinese oil companies to the foreign and global context and how China's international energy strategy fits into and influences China's foreign policy and how this in turn impacts on external perceptions of China. This part of the book assesses the broader international implications of China's energy-driven expansion and how this is defined by, and helps to define, China's foreign policy. Chapter 7 provides an overview of China's foreign policy towards the West and then addresses the ways in which China's energy needs help to promote integration and its peaceful accommodation as a rising power but also highlights the main constraints and limitations to this integration. This complex relationship with the West, as viewed from the international energy perspective, is then theorised and it is suggested that China seeks to maintain multiple policy dimensions or alternatives in its attempts to ensure its energy security against a potentially antagonistic West – these include the option of 'balancing' against the West, the prospect of asserting a regional hegemony, and the aim of gaining a truly global presence and foreign policy through intervention in far-distant regions such as sub-Saharan Africa and Latin America.

The following three chapters explore whether these various potential strategic options are in fact being pursued by China in its international energy policy. Chapter 8 examines whether China is encouraging an anti-western balancing policy through its development of close energy and foreign relations with a number of energy-rich revisionist states, most notably Russia but also with Iran. Chapter 9 assesses how the drive to secure oil and gas from its immediate region, and the problems of ensuring secure transportation of oil from the Middle East, are helping to consolidate a strategy of regional hegemony, which seeks to exclude or minimise US and western intervention, as well as to limit the influence of the other major regional powers of Japan and India. Chapter 10 examines the remarkable expansion of Chinese oil companies into sub-Saharan Africa and into Latin America and assesses whether this has always been seen to be supportive of China's broader foreign policy goals, particularly as many local actors have begun to criticise the Chinese engagement as 'neo-imperialist'.

The main argument of the book is that China is pursuing all of these strategic options simultaneously and with varying effect, so that it is not possible to provide a simple picture of a China inexorably integrating with the global international economy and the West, nor of a China seeking definitively to balance against the West or to challenge the West through hegemonic expansion. The picture is more complicated and requires an understanding of the complex interaction of domestic energy policies, external perceptions of these policies, and the ways in which these intersect with regional and global politics. However, what certainly is the case is that the drive for gaining access to oil supplies, and the sense of vulnerability due to the need to import ever-increasing quantities of oil, are vital strategic interests, which are independently shaping and directing China's foreign policy and the ways in which China is emerging as a rising power. How China is perceived and understood, as well as its actual behaviour, will be strongly linked to its domestic and international energy policies.

Part 1

Energy policy, the government and China's oil industry

2 China's energy challenges and policy priorities

Introduction

As it formulates national energy policy, any government has to balance four key priorities: the need and cost of securing energy supplies to support economic growth and development; the desirability of raising the technical and economic efficiency of energy production and energy use; the political obligation to address the energy and economic needs of poorer sections of the population; and the growing requirement to invest in measures to protect the environment and improve the manner in which natural resources are exploited.

Only rarely can a government of an energy-importing country enjoy the luxury of having a resource base, an energy sector and an economy that provides for a convergence of these four objectives at a low cost to society. In most countries a tension exists between these priorities. As a result, government has the responsibility to rank the respective priorities and to decide how to manage trade-offs where conflicts exist between the priorities.

The aims of this chapter are to show how security of supply continues to be China's top priority for national energy policy through an examination of the evolving supply and demand balance, to illustrate the nature of the measures that the government has been taking to secure energy supplies and to constrain demand, and to examine the consequences of these measures.

The long-standing challenge of meeting the demand for energy

Ensuring a sufficient and reliable supply of energy to support economic growth and development has been a long-standing challenge for China's government. After Liberation in 1949, one of Mao Zedong's first economic priorities was to expand domestic oil production. This was achieved, first, through the development of the Yumen field in the north-west of the country and, later, by the discovery of the giant Daqing field in the north-east.[1]

The same challenges faced the new government that took power in the late 1970s with the explicit intention of modernising the economy.[2] Indeed, the problems underlying China's energy sector remain almost unchanged thirty years later: namely, to raise the domestic capacity to produce primary energy and transform it into useful energy; to transport that energy to the end-users; to improve the efficiency of energy use; and to limit damage to the environment.

Though these general challenges may be applicable to most developing countries, they are exacerbated in the case of China by its large population and geographic area, by its sustained high rate of economic growth and by the structure of its economy. Of even greater importance is the nature and distribution of its natural resource endowment. Though its coal resources are vast, even by international standards, they are concentrated in the north of the country. The significant but declining oil reserves lie in the north-east and north-west, while the limited resources of natural gas are found mainly in the north, north-west and south-west. Hydro-electricity is concentrated in the centre and south-west of the country. Not only are these primary energy resources probably insufficient to meet the long-term demand, but they lie far from the main centres of economic activity in the south and east of China.

The three decades of China's economic development since reform was launched in the late 1970s can be divided into three main phases from the perspective of energy supply and demand. The period to 2001, which was characterised by falling energy intensity, the years from 2002 to 2005 when this trend was temporarily reversed, and the subsequent years during which the government put in place new policies to drive down energy intensity again.

Energy supply and demand from 1980 to 2001

The period 1980 to 1996 was characterised by sustained high levels of economic growth in China, with only occasional interruptions. The average annual rate of increase of GDP was about 11 per cent.[3] Throughout most of this period the economic growth was driven by the industrial sector, though the tertiary sector expanded greatly.[4] This growth was accompanied by a gradual reform and liberalisation of the industrial sector and of the domestic commodity markets.[5] These measures also affected the energy sector, but to a much lesser extent than most other industries.[6]

As the economy grew, so did energy consumption (Figure 2.1), until the Asian crisis when demand flattened, at least according to official Chinese statistics.[7] The country's primary energy supply continued to be heavily dependent on coal (Table 2.1). The proportion of coal in the energy mix appeared to decline in the late 1990s, but this may be a result of systematic statistical distortions related to false reporting of coal output at this time.[8] Throughout most of this period the proportion of oil in the energy mix increased as its use in transport, petrochemicals and construction grew.[9] The role of natural gas and hydro-electricity remained small.

During the 1980s and 1990s China was largely self-sufficient in primary energy supply. Domestic production of coal, hydro-electricity and natural gas continued to rise, aside from the apparent decline of coal output in the late 1990s (Figure 2.2). The country had always been self-sufficient in coal and, since the

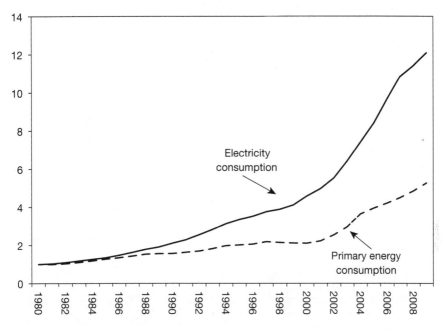

Figure 2.1 Primary energy consumption and electricity consumption in China, 1980 to 2009, normalised to 1980 levels

Sources: U.S. Energy Information Administration, *International Statistics 2010*, for years 1980–2007; supplemented by *BP Statistical Review of World Energy 2010* for primary energy consumption for years 2008–09, and Chinese official data sources for electricity consumption for years 2008–09.

Table 2.1 China's primary energy consumption mix, 1980–2009

	1980	1985	1990	1995	2000	2005	2009
Coal	72.2%	75.8%	76.2%	74.6%	61.4%	69.5%	70.6%
Oil	20.7%	17.1%	16.6%	17.5%	28.6%	21.0%	18.5%
Natural gas	3.1%	2.2%	2.1%	1.8%	2.7%	2.7%	3.7%
Hydro-electricity	4.0%	4.9%	5.1%	6.1%	6.8%	5.8%	6.4%

Source: *BP Statistical Review of World Energy*, various years.

late 1990s, had become a significant net exporter. The story for oil was quite different. Since the mid-1980s the oil industry had struggled to raise production at annual rates of just 1–3 per cent per year, meanwhile consumption was rising at rates of between 5 per cent and 8 per cent per year. After 1993 China became a net importer of oil, and the import requirement grew each year (Figure 2.3). The construction of oil refinery capacity continued at a great pace (Figure 2.4) and so a large proportion of China's oil imports took the form of crude oil, which was then refined in domestic plants (Figure 2.5).

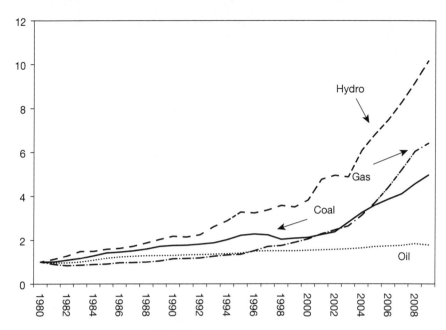

Figure 2.2 Primary energy production in China, 1980 to 2009, for different types of energy, normalised to 1980 levels

Source: BP Statistical Review of World Energy 2010.

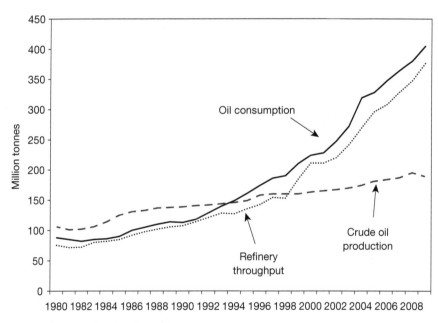

Figure 2.3 Oil production, consumption and refinery throughput in China, 1980 to 2009, in millions of tonnes per year

Source: BP Statistical Review of World Energy 2010.

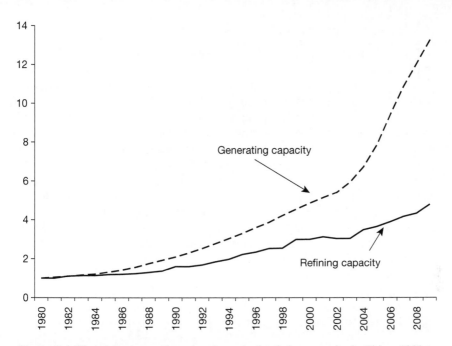

Figure 2.4 Electricity generating capacity and oil refining capacity in China, 1980 to 2009, normalised to 1980

Sources: BP Statistical Review of World Energy 2010, for refining capacity; U.S. Energy Information Administration, *International Statistics 2010*, for generating capacity 1980–2007, supplemented by Chinese official data sources for 2008–09.

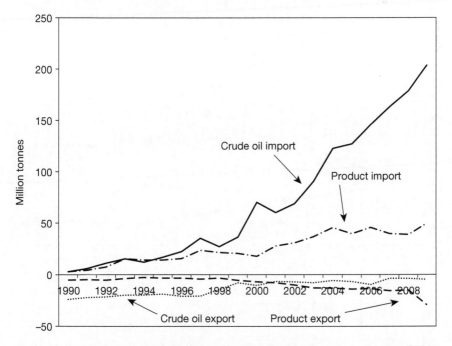

Figure 2.5 China's imports and exports of crude oil and oil products, 1990 to 2009, in millions of tonnes

Source: *BP Statistical Review of World Energy*, various years.

This period also saw the rapid rise of the role of electricity in final energy consumption (Figure 2.1), replacing the direct combustion of coal and oil, and the gradual introduction of nuclear power generation and modern renewable energy such as wind and solar power.

Though the main priority of energy policy during the 1980s and 1990s appeared to be to increase domestic energy production as fast as possible, a very notable feature of the energy sector during this first twenty years of China's economic reform was the consistency with which energy intensity declined (Figure 2.6). This decline occurred for all major forms of primary energy, but was most marked for coal.[10] A consensus has emerged that the steady decline of energy intensity during the 1980s and 1990s can be mainly attributed to efficiency and productivity changes within industries, and that these gains were achieved through technological improvements, research and development, and innovation.[11] In the 1990s efficiency improvements were particularly marked in energy-intensive industries such as metallurgy, cement, paper, textiles, oil and coal processing, and electrical power generation.[12]

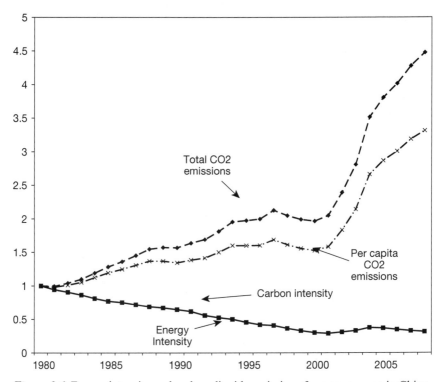

Figure 2.6 Energy intensity and carbon dioxide emissions from energy use in China, 1980 to 2008, normalised to 1980 levels. The plots for energy intensity and carbon intensity lie very close to each other and both are calculated at market exchange rates

Source: U.S. Energy Information Administration, *International Statistics 2010*.

The sustained improvement of energy efficiency within different sectors of the economy may be attributed to systematic policy measures to enhance energy efficiency and to the gradual marketisation of the economy, especially since 1993. The government established energy conservation technology centres throughout the country to provide information. Low interest loans and tax credits were available for investment in energy conservation. As a result the level of investment in energy conservation rose rapidly from 1981 to 1995.[13]

This reduction of energy intensity was paralleled by a decline in carbon dioxide emissions per unit of GDP, although total carbon dioxide emissions and per capita emissions rose as the energy consumption grew (Figure 2.6).

Energy demand from 2002 to 2010

The years 2002 to 2005 were marked by a boom in economic growth and a surge in the output of heavy industry.[14] The national efficiency gains made during the 1980s and 1990s were reversed from 2002. Energy intensity rose, the production and consumption of all forms of energy accelerated, oil imports soared, and levels of emissions of both carbon and other pollutants increased (Figures 2.1–2.6).

The main cause of this rise in energy intensity was the expansion of the role of secondary industry which took place after a decline in the late 1990s, and this expansion was focused on energy-intensive industries.[15] The proportional increases in energy intensity were greater for coal and for electricity, which are the fuels of industry, than for oil, the fuel of transport.[16] Total investment in fixed assets jumped from 36 per cent to 47 per cent of GDP over the period 2002 to 2005.[17] The output of key energy-intensive products rose sharply after the year 2000, and China became firmly established as the world's largest producer of steel (35 per cent of world output in 2006), cement (48 per cent of world output), flat glass (49 per cent of world output),[18] and aluminium (28 per cent of world output). Surplus output was exported.[19] The production of other products also grew markedly during this period, for example building space, motor vehicles and chemical fibre.

At the same time as these industrial developments were pushing energy intensity upwards, technological advances were appearing to be having less impact in the other direction. Overall, at a national scale, the early years of the century were characterised by a slowdown or even reversal in the rate of energy-related technological improvements, and such efficiency gains as there were failed to offset the impact of the structural shift.[20] The overall level of investment in energy efficiency, as a proportion of total investment in energy, remained lower than at any time during the period 1981–95.[21]

The third and final factor underpinning the increase in energy intensity was the slight increase in proportion of coal in the energy mix at the expense of oil and hydro-electricity (Table 2.1).[22]

In 2009 China's total energy consumption was equal to that of the USA, previously the largest energy consumer in the world (Figure 2.7a), though a

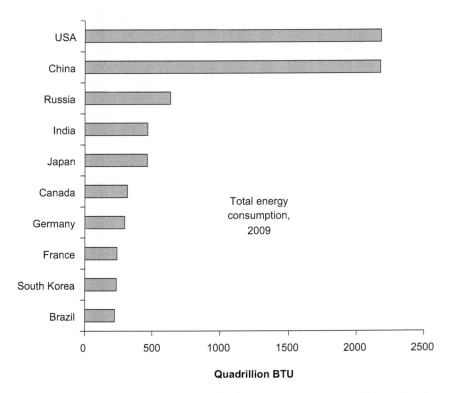

Figure 2.7a Total energy consumption for the top ten energy consuming nations in the world in 2009, quadrillion British Thermal Units

Source: U.S. Energy Information Administration, *International Statistics 2010.*

more benign view of China's energy demand is revealed by examining the demand on a *per capita* basis (Figure 2.7b). Its energy intensity is one of the highest in the world, whether the GDP is measured at market exchange rates (Figure 2.7c) or on a purchasing power parity basis (Figure 2.7d).

Projections of energy demand in China have generally been proven to be rather inaccurate. To a great extent this is because the government has retained the power to constrain or stimulate growth in the economy at short notice, and such decisions appear to outsiders to come quite suddenly. But never have the forecasters been so utterly wrong-footed as they were by the surge in energy demand seen in the first few years of the twenty-first century.[23] The International Energy Agency (IEA), for example, in 2004 projected a average annual rate of increase of demand between 2002 and 2010 of 4.0 per cent. The actual rate of increase for the period 2002–9 was more than 10 per cent per year. More recently forecasts have tried to make amends for these misjudgements. Most notable is the change of the forecasts made by the IEA

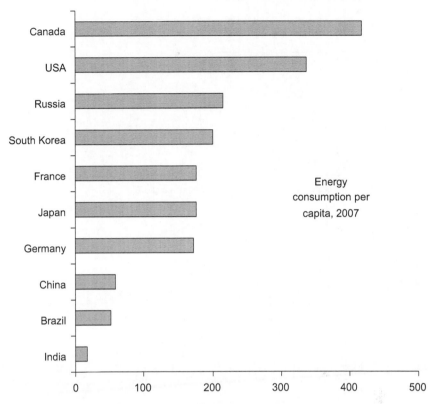

Figure 2.7b Energy consumption per capita in 2007 for the top ten energy consuming nations in the world in 2009, million British Thermal Units

Source: U.S. Energy Information Administration, *International Statistics 2010.*

from a 3.4 per cent rate of growth of demand to 2020 made in 2004 to a rate of 4.6–5.1 per cent for the period 2005–15 made in 2007 (Table 2.2, see p. 20). These forecasts compare to a mean rate of growth of demand of 5.8 per cent over the period 1980–2009, and 9.4 per cent from 2000–09. But it still appears that forecasters consistently underestimate China's consumption of energy, most probably because of errors in the underlying assumptions.[24]

The sudden rise of energy intensity resulted in widespread shortages of almost all types of commercial energy across China, starting in 2003. As a consequence, the new government directed considerable efforts to regaining control over the energy sector, under the leadership of Premier Wen Jiabao. Though the production of domestic energy remained a priority, much greater emphasis was placed on energy efficiency and energy conservation than had been seen before.

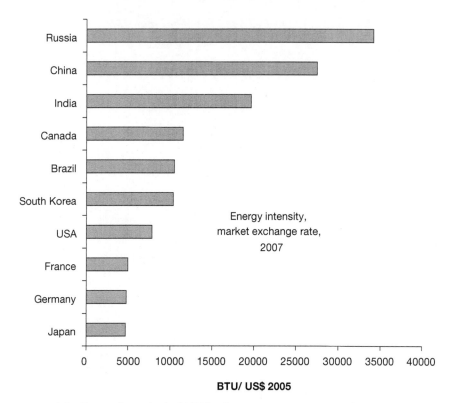

Figure 2.7c Energy intensity in 2007 for the top ten energy consuming nations in the world in 2009, at market exchange rates, British Thermal Units per US$ (year 2005)

Source: U.S. Energy Information Administration, *International Statistics 2010.*

Future energy demand and strategies for energy production

Economic growth rates of 5–10 per cent will continue to drive a rising demand for energy for many years to come. Despite the rising level of energy imports, China still possesses substantial resources of primary energy, in many forms. Successful exploitation of these resources will help China constrain the level of imports. This section presents some projections for future energy demand, examines the potential domestic supplies of coal, oil and liquid fuels, gas and electricity, and identifies key elements of government strategy since 2005 to secure future energy supplies.

Coal

China is pre-eminent in the world's coal industry. In 2009 it accounted for 47 per cent of the world's consumption of coal and 46 per cent of the production. Coal is likely to remain China's single most important primary

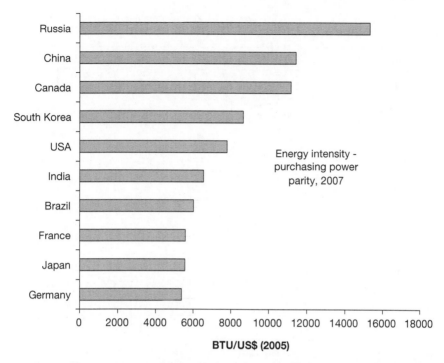

Figure 2.7d Energy intensity in 2007 for the top ten energy consuming nations in the world in 2009, at purchasing power parity, British Thermal Units per US$ (year 2005)

Source: U.S. Energy Information Administration, *International Statistics 2010.*

source of energy for the foreseeable future, though its use will be progressively restricted to power generation, and eventually to clean power generation.[25] With the third largest reserves in the world China should be able to remain self-sufficient or almost self-sufficient in coal or nearly so for many years to come. Conservative estimates place the remaining reserves at 115 billion tonnes, with more generous assessments of as high as 190 or 320 million tonnes (Table 2.3). At present rates of consumption the proven reserves should last fifty years, and new deposits continue to be discovered. The annual rate of growth of demand for coal fell from 19 per cent in 2003 to about 11 per cent in 2004 and 2005, then progressively down to 7 per cent in 2008 before rising to 9.6 per cent in 2009. Even if this slows to an average of 3–4 per cent, the annual demand for coal is set to rise from about 3.0 billion tonnes in 2009 to as much as 5.0 billion tonnes in 2030.[26] Other projections suggest that annual coal consumption may reach this level by the year 2020,[27] and these tend to be supported by the rebound of annual demand to levels close to 10 per cent in 2009.

Table 2.2 Projections for rates of growth of energy demand in China, and recent historical trends

Projections	2010	2015	2020	2030
IEA, 2004	4.0% (2002–10)	(2002–20)	3.4% (2002–30)	3.0%
DRC, 2004			3.3–4.75% (2000–20)	
Chen Zhongtao, 2006	8.3% (2006–10)			
IEA, 2007		4.6–5.1% (2005–15)		2.5–3.2% (2005–30)
Sheehan and Sun, 2007		5.9–7.9% (2005–15)		4.6–6.4% (2005–30)
EIA, 2007				3.1–3.9% (2004–30)
IEA, 2009				2.9% (2007–30)
EIA, 2010		3.1–3.5% (2007–15)	3.2–3.8% (2007–20)	2.9–3.6% (2007–30)
Recent trends	*1980–90*	*1990–2000*	*2000–09*	*1980–2009*
BP, 2010	5.1%	3.5%	9.4%	5.8%

Sources: IEA, *World Energy Outlook 2004, 2007 and 2009*; Development Research Centre, *Overview of the National Energy Strategy*; Z. Chen, 'Study on estimating demand and supply in China's energy market in the 11th Five-Year Plan period'; P. Sheehan and F. Sun, *Energy Use in China: Interpreting Changing Trends and Future Directions*; U.S. Energy Information Administration, *International Energy Outlook 2007 and 2010*; BP Annual Review of World Energy 2010.

Table 2.3 Estimates of primary recoverable energy reserves in China

	Coal billion tonnes	Oil million tonnes	Natural gas billion cubic metres
BP, 2010	114	2,000	2,460
EIA, 2010	114	2,160	2,240
IEA, 2007	115–92	2,160	3,720
MOLAR, 2007	184	2,439	2,663
World Bank, 2009	320		

Sources: IEA, *World Energy Outlook 2007*; U.S. Energy Information Administration, *International Statistics 2010*; BP Annual Review of World Energy 2010; Ministry of Land and Resources (MOLAR), unpublished data, 2007; World Bank, *Economically, Socially and Environmentally Sustainable Coal Mining Sector in China*.

Massive and continuous investment is required to identify new deposits and to bring new mines into production. Restructuring and modernisation of the coal industry needs to be continued in order to improve coal recovery rates and commercial efficiency.[28] Transport has long been a key concern for China's coal industry, for most of the large reserves lie in the north of the country, far from the centres of demand in the south and east. More than 50 per cent of coal moves by rail, and this uses nearly 50 per cent of the country's rail capacity. The balance travels by road, river and sea.[29] Investment in these transport networks has to keep pace with production, though the construction of power plants in the coal mining areas continues to alleviate this bottleneck to some extent.

New discoveries of large deposits of coal continue to be made in the north-west of the country, but huge effort and investment is needed to sustain the ever-increasing levels of investment in extraction and transportation infrastructure. Failure to anticipate a surge in demand over the last few years caused a dramatic change in China's status on world coal markets. In 2001, before the economic growth started to accelerate after the Asian crisis, China was a net exporter of coal, delivering a net 88 million tonnes onto world markets, about 9 per cent of total internationally-traded coal.[30] In 2007 and 2008 China's coal exports and imports were approximately in balance. By 2009 China had become a net importer of just over 100 million tonnes of coal per year, equivalent to about 20 per cent of sea-borne, internationally-traded coal and about 3.5 per cent of China's annual consumption of coal. The country is likely to remain a significant net importer of coal for several years,[31] though Chinese sources suggest there may be an over-supply of coal in 2011 and 2012 on account of the massive ongoing investment in new mines.[32]

Oil and liquid fuels

China was, in 2010, the world's fifth largest producer of oil, after Saudi Arabia, Russia, the USA and Iran, and accounted for about 5 per cent of world production. Yet existing proven reserves will provide for barely more than ten years of present-day consumption. Demand has been rising at an annual rate of 7–9 per cent, despite government moves to restrict the use of oil to transport and petrochemicals,[33] while domestic production has been growing by just 1–2 per cent per year. Indeed, 2009 saw a decline in domestic crude oil production of 2.8 per cent, the first annual decline since 1981.[34] Already imports account for more than 50 per cent of consumption (Figure 2.3).

With the exception of a few offshore areas, China has been well-explored for oil over the past fifty years. Onshore exploration has been carried out almost entirely by the Chinese NOCs. In the early 1980s China's government was keen to explore for domestic offshore oil and gas reserves. Realising that its own companies lacked the expertise, it invited foreign oil companies to participate, in collaboration with the state oil company China National Offshore Oil Corporation (CNOOC). In later years, onshore regions were progressively opened for foreign companies. Though some discoveries were made by the foreign companies offshore, overall the results have been disappointing, primarily for geological reasons, but also on account of administrative challenges onshore.[35]

Estimates of remaining reserves of oil range between 2.1 and 2.5 billion tonnes (Table 2.3). New discoveries will continue to be made, but they seem to be barely replacing ongoing production rather than adding to the remaining reserves. Most projections for future levels of crude oil production show a decline from current levels of about 190 million tonnes per year, which may accelerate after 2015 (Table 2.4).

In order to maximise its security of supply and the economic benefits to be derived from refining, China continues to invest heavily in upgrading and expanding its refining capacity (Figure 2.4). Upgrading has been necessary to cope with sour crude oils imported from the Middle East, and expansion is required to keep pace with the rising level of demand for oil products.[36] On account of this construction, the relative gap between oil consumption and refinery output is diminishing (Figure 2.3) and thus the net import of oil products is being constrained (Figure 2.5). The recent involvement of foreign

Table 2.4 Projections for growth of liquid fuel production and demand in China, including crude oil, CTL and biofuels, in millions of tonnes

	2009 Actual	*2010*	*2015*	*2020*	*2030*
PRODUCTION					
Crude oil					
BP, 2010	189				
IEA, 2007			192		135
EDRC, 2008		177–98	182–200	220–40	
EIA, 2009			170–85	150–80	125–55
CTL					
IEA, 2007			9.2		37.5
EIA, 2009			0–10	0–15	5–30
Biofuels					
IEA, 2007			5.7		
EIA, 2009			5–10	10–15	20–25
DEMAND					
BP, 2010	405				
IEA, 2007			518–43		653–808
EIA, 2007		430–50		520–600	660–820
EDRC, 2008		407	480	563	
IEA, 2009			490	522–57	664–758
EIA, 2010			470–525	530–630	630–840

Sources: IEA, *World Energy Outlook 2007, 2009*; U.S. Energy Information Administration, *International Energy Outlook 2007, 2009 and 2010*; BP *Annual Review of World Energy 2010*; Energy Development Report of China 2008.

companies, both international companies and NOCs from Saudi Arabia and Kuwait, should help accelerate the construction of new refineries, and the IEA has projected that refining capacity will reach the level of demand from the year 2012. But the challenge will remain to match the demand in terms of product type and product quality. In the past China's refineries have produced too much gasoline and not enough diesel, and in recent years have struggled to raise the quality of output to meet ever rising technical specifications driven by environmental policies.[37] The continuing construction of new refining capacity should successfully address these shortcomings, though the result may be massive overcapacity.[38]

Even the most optimistic projections for domestic crude oil production show that the trend of rising import dependence is set to continue unabated. As a consequence, and in the light of its security of supply fears, the government has supported the development of two sources of alternative supply of liquid fuels for transportation and petrochemicals: biofuels and CTL.

Official documents have given targets as high as 20 million tonnes of annual biofuel output by 2020, though this level is likely to depend on the level of international oil prices with higher prices leading to higher levels of biofuel production, as well as on China's ability to produce biofuels from non-edible crops.[39]

The government and the major Chinese coal companies have also invested large amounts of money in the development and initial commercialisation of CTL technology, in order to produce liquids that can be used for transport and petrochemicals. But enthusiasm for this technology waned in 2007 as the environmental costs became increasingly apparent.[40] Official targets and projections suggest that the production of liquids from this technology may reach 10 million tonnes by 2015 and more than 35 million tonnes by 2030 (Table 2.4).

These sources of liquid fuels may provide a useful supplement to China's domestic supply of crude oil. Yet demand for liquid fuels is set to continue rising over the period to 2030, though the rate of rise will depend on domestic economic growth rates, on international oil prices and on measures to constrain the use of liquid fuels. Net imports of oil are likely to rise from 220 million tonnes in 2009 to possibly more than 300 million tonnes by 2015 and to as much as 500 million tonnes by 2020. Import dependency could reach 70–80 per cent by 2030, up from 54 per cent in 2009.

As a result of these projected trends, the government made the decision in 2003 to construct emergency oil storage facilities in order to enhance its ability to react to short-term interruptions to supply or to price spikes. Though construction started in 2004, the high level of oil prices rendered filling the tanks unviable until international crude oil prices fell in the summer of 2008. China then took advantage of the low prices to fill its existing tanks, taking its reserve to 15 million tonnes or 2 weeks' supply.[41] The second phase of the programme should add 25 million tonnes to the storage capacity by the end of 2011, and a third phase will add a further 28 million tonnes by 2020.

By then total storage would amount to some 70 million tonnes or about six weeks' supply.[42]

A final dimension to China's oil supply strategy has been to support the internationalisation of China's NOCs, a topic explored in some detail in Chapters 5 and 6 of this book.

Natural gas and coal-bed methane

The period since 1997 has seen a concerted attempt by the government and by the state companies to raise the level of use of natural gas. Three considerations have underpinned this policy: the desire to use domestic primary energy sources, to introduce a cleaner fuel to replace coal, and to diversify the energy supply mix.[43] Despite annual increases of 15–20 per cent in the domestic production of natural gas that have allowed China to raise its domestic production of natural gas from 19 billion cubic metres in 1997 to about 85 billion cubic metres in 2009, gas continues to provide less than 4 per cent of the country's energy supply, up marginally from 2 per cent in the mid-1990s (Figure 2.8; Table 2.1).

The long-term future of the domestic gas supply industry is quite uncertain as systematic exploration for gas only started in the 1990s. Major new discoveries continue to be made, especially in the Ordos Basin of north China, in the Tarim Basin of north-west China and in Sichuan Province, and these

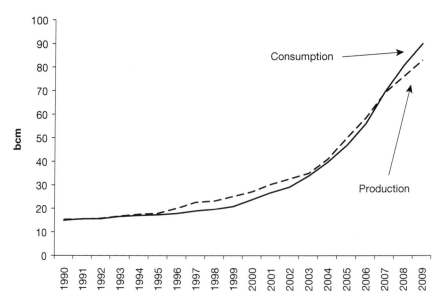

Figure 2.8 Natural gas production and consumption in China, 1980 to 2009, in billions of cubic metres per year

Source: BP Statistical Review of World Energy 2010.

should allow gas supply to continue growing rapidly over the coming years.[44] The delivery of this gas to the energy consuming regions of eastern China has required the rapid construction of a completely new network of domestic gas pipelines. The most impressive of these is the 4,000 km West-to-East pipeline, which brings natural gas from the Tarim Basin of Xinjiang to Shanghai and which has a annual capacity of 17 billion cubic metres.[45] Exploration also proceeds offshore, including in the East China Sea where China and Japan have overlapping claims.[46] Projections show domestic supply of natural gas rising to levels in the range 120–170 billion cubic metres in 2020 (Table 2.5).

The second strand of China's natural gas strategy relies on imported gas both through pipelines and on ships as liquefied natural gas (LNG), for domestic production will not be able to keep pace with demand (Table 2.5).[47] Total imports of natural gas are projected to rise from 1 billion cubic metres

Table 2.5 Projections for growth of gas supply and demand in China in billion cubic metres

	2009 Actual	2010	2015	2020	2030
PRODUCTION					
BP, 2009	85.2				
EDRC, 2006		80		100	
IEA, 2007		76	103	118	111
EIA, 2007		70	87	98	120
EDRC, 2008		90	140	150	
CNPC in Higashi, 2009				160–70	
Higashi, 2009				120–40	
DEMAND					
BP, 2009	88.7				
EDRC, 2006		100		200	
IEA, 2007			120–40		222–59
EIA, 2007		78–81		123–34	180–213
Jackson and Jiang, 2007			55–95	75–65	
EDRC, 2008		110–20	170–210	220–60	
CNPC in Higashi, 2009				210	
EIA, 2009			104–9	129–43	173–204
IEA, 2009			132	151–63	184–224
Higashi, 2009				180–200	
EIA, 2010			134–7	168–80	235–50
Xinhua, 2010				200	300

Sources: *Energy Development Report of China, 2006 and 2008;* IEA, *World Energy Outlook 2007 and 2009*; U.S. Energy Information Administration, *International Energy Outlook 2007, 2009 and 2010*; BP *Annual Review of World Energy 2010*; M.P. Jackson and B. Jiang, *Natural Gas in the Energy Futures of China and India;* N. Higashi, *Natural Gas in China. Market Evolution and Strategy*; 'Chinese agency: natural gas market on fast track', Xinhua News Agency, 29 March 2010.

in 2006 to 60 billion cubic metres or more in 2020 and to more than 100 billion cubic metres by 2030. Pipelines are seen as being more secure because the flow of gas is not open to interruption on the high seas. LNG is more cost-effective over very long distances and, as regional LNG markets develop, LNG can be more flexible because a buyer of gas can have a number of suppliers. The first imports of gas arrived in Guangdong in 2006, as LNG, accounting for less than 2 per cent of China's total gas consumption that year.

Price continues to be a concern for LNG imports.[48] By chance, China's first LNG plant in Guangdong was able to secure a very low price for a supply of gas from Australia in 2002. This was on account of a temporary excess of supply over demand in the global LNG market. Encouraged by this low price China's oil companies announced a number of LNG terminals along the east coast of the country.[49] However, the low price achieved by the Guangdong project could not be repeated in the following years as demand for LNG grew throughout the world.[50] By late 2007 the Chinese companies and the government had conceded that the higher prices had to be paid. Current plans would add three more LNG terminals to the currently operational plants in Guangdong, Fujian and Shanghai, bringing a total of six plants onstream by 2012 with a total capacity of about 25 billion cubic metres per year, and a further growth of import capacity to more than 40 billion cubic metres per year by 2020. By 2010 the volume of LNG contracted on a long-term basis by Chinese companies from the year 2014 had exceeded 30 billion cubic metres.[51]

Central Asia and Russia both contain substantial proven and potential reserves of gas that could be imported through pipelines and make a major contribution to China's gas supply.[52] In 2006 China and Turkmenistan signed agreements that gave CNPC rights to explore for and produce gas in Turkmenistan and to construct an export pipeline to China with a planned capacity of 40 billion cubic metres per year. This pipeline was commissioned at the end of 2009. It connects to the new, second West-to-East gas pipeline within China, which brings the gas to southern and eastern parts of the country.[53] In Russia, progress to develop gas resources and export them to China has progressed rather slowly, despite planning and discussion since the late 1990s. Progress has been delayed by changes of gas policy priorities within Russia and a failure to agree a price acceptable to both parties.[54]

Despite these projections of rising domestic production and rising imports, it is clear that what is called 'conventional natural gas' is only likely to provide a modest proportion of the national energy supply, and that little of this gas will be cheap. As a result, the last ten years have seen significant efforts in China to identify and exploit domestic sources of 'unconventional gas' and these are now starting to bear fruit.

Such is the poor quality of many gas reservoirs in China that the boundary between conventional and unconventional gas is rather blurred. 'Tight gas' is already being exploited in the Ordos Basin of northern China and in the Sichuan Basin. Indeed, these accumulations already provide some 15 per cent of the nation's domestic natural gas production, a proportion that may rise to 30 per cent by 2020. Collaboration with foreign companies such as Shell and Total has been and will continue to be crucial for this success.[55]

The country's energy companies have been working jointly with foreign companies since the early 1990s to develop coal-bed methane reserves that are abundant in some of the major coal basins of northern China. Progress has been slow as the companies struggle to overcome technical challenges. Current production is about one billion cubic metres per year. The government is aiming for coal-bed methane production to reach 3.5 billion cubic metres per year by 2015.[56]

Exploration for shale gas is only now starting in China and the government has committed to funding the assessment of these reserves. BP and Exxon have already shown an interest in participating. Provisional reports suggest that the marine shales in the southern part of the country may offer the greatest potential. Offshore, Chinese companies are also exploring the potential to produce gas from hydrates on the sea-floor.

Electricity

Electricity plays a key role in any modern economy, and thus electricity consumption in China has risen at twice the rate of that of total energy demand (Figure 2.1). Total generating capacity rose fourteen-fold from 62 gigawatt (GW) to 874 GW from 1980 to 2009, and doubled over the five-year period following each of the years 2001, 2002 and 2003.[57] Projections from the IEA suggest that total capacity and output is expected to continue growing at an average of nearly 7 per cent per year to the year 2015, but slowing down after that to give an average of closer to 4 per cent for the period 2007–30.[58] This implies a near tripling of capacity and output from 2006 to 2030 (Table 2.6) and an incremental output over the period, which would be equivalent to the entire electricity generated in the USA and Canada in the year 2006.[59] These projections may still be too conservative. Shealy and Dorian (2007) have suggested that the rate of growth of demand for electricity may be twice as large as estimated by the IEA and by the U.S. Department of Energy.[60]

Both the quantity of electricity consumed and the energy mix within the power supply will depend on the rate of growth of the economy and on the success of the government's policies to enhance energy efficiency and the use of clean energy.[61] Coal will continue to play a predominant role in China's power generation, though in the event that government policies are successful the proportion of coal in the mix may decline from 80 per cent in 2007 to as low as 50 per cent by 2030 (Table 2.6).[62] A key government objective is to radically raise the unit capacity and the thermal efficiency of new plant. At the same time the government has been forcing small-scale and inefficient plants to close.

Natural gas is seen as an important clean fuel for the future, as discussed above, but policy decisions and pricing structures have led to a relatively low

Table 2.6a Forecast of total electricity generation in China in terrawatt hours and of shares of different fuels

	Actual	Reference scenario		Alternative scenario	
	2007	2020	2030	2020	2030
TWh	3,318	6,692	8,847	6221	7022
Percentage shares					
Coal	80.9%	76.5%	75.0%	67.6%	50.1%
Oil	1.0%	0.6%	0.4%	0.6%	0.4%
Gas	1.2%	2.3%	2.9%	2.1%	2.8%
Nuclear	1.9%	4.8%	5.5%	8.1%	13.6%
Hydro	14.6%	12.4%	11.8%	14.3%	17.5%
Wind	0.3%	2.5%	2.5%	5.9%	9.0%
Other renewables	0.1%	0.6%	1.8%	1.5%	6.6%

Table 2.6b Forecast of total electricity generation capacity in China in gigawatts and of shares of different fuels

	Actual	Reference scenario	
	2007	2020	2030
Coal	502	970	1275
Oil	20	19	16
Gas	24	88	125
Nuclear	8	40	60
Hydro	145	255	316
Biomass and waste	1	4	21
Wind	6	74	95
Geothermal	0	0	1
Solar	0	9	27
Tide and wave	0	0	0
Total	**706**	**1460**	**1936**

Source: IEA, *World Energy Outlook 2009.*

level of supply of gas to power stations. In particular, natural gas has been directed to cities for commercial and household use rather than power stations.[63] As a result, natural gas accounted for only 1 per cent of power generation in 2007 (Table 2.6), which contrasted with its 3 per cent share of generating capacity. Sustained and coherent government direction will be needed if the optimistic projection made by the IEA in 2007 of a 6 per cent contribution to power supply by natural gas by 2030 is to be achieved.[64] More recent projections place the contribution at just 3 per cent by 2030 (Table 2.6).

Hydro-electricity has been the main source of primary electricity supply in China for many years, yet its share of electricity supply has declined from nearly 20 per cent in 1990 to 16 per cent between 2006 and 2009.[65] The government continues to boast of the country's vast potential for hydro-electricity,[66] but a range of obstacles may result in a continuing decline in the relative contribution of hydro-electricity unless great efforts are expended by the government, as required in the IEA's alternative scenario (Table 2.6).

Meanwhile the government is pushing forward with plans to rapidly expand the capacity of nuclear power. As of March 2010, China had eleven operating nuclear power plants with a total capacity of about 8.5 GW. At this time twenty-one reactors were under construction, with a total capacity of about 21 GW. Most of them are due to come into commercial operation by 2015. A further thirty-six plants with a total capacity of about 40 GW are being planned. Estimates of the capacity of nuclear power generation available by 2020 range from 60 GW to 80 GW.[67]

Renewable energy, aside from hydro-electricity, continues to account for a negligible proportion of China's power generation capacity and output (Table 2.6). The Renewable Energy Law passed in 2005 marked a new determination by the government to substantially enhance the role of renewables in the national energy supply. Of particular importance is the role of wind power in electricity generation.[68]

At the end of 2005, total installed wind power capacity was about 1 GW. Since then the rate of growth has been dramatic. Total capacity reached 12 GW by the end of 2008 and is set to reach 20 GW by the end of 2009. During 2009, China's wind power capacity took it to fourth in the world, behind the USA, Germany and Spain. In 2007 the target set for the year 2020 was 30 GW. By 2010 the target for 2020 stood at 100 GW and might be raised yet again.

In addition to the feed-in tariffs introduced in 2009, a further potential incentive for the construction of renewable energy capacity is the Clean Development Mechanism, the instrument established by the Kyoto Protocol to encourage financial support from developed economies for investment in clean energy in developing economies. Administrative obstacles and policy ambiguity have prevented rapid implementation within China to date.[69]

Strategies for energy conservation and efficiency

The strong emphasis on maximising energy production from domestic sources has been a long-standing preference for China's government. In contrast, the political weight placed behind the new strategy for energy conservation and energy efficiency is quite new. For the first time, energy conservation could be said to lie at the heart of China's official energy policy.[70] This section describes a few of the measures taken since 2004.

Key strategic measures

The new strategy was encapsulated in the Medium and Long-Term Energy Conservation Plan issued in 2004. The overriding goal of the plan was to reduce energy intensity by 20 per cent between 2005 and 2010, an annual average rate of 3.6 per cent per year, and to continue this decline at the same rate until 2020. This Energy Conservation Plan and subsequent documents set targets for energy consumption per unit of output for the years 2010 and 2020 for individual energy intensive industries such as electrical power generation, steel, non-ferrous metals, oil refining, petrochemicals, chemicals, cement and plate glass, as well as providing proposals for technological, process or management improvements needed to achieve these targets. By 2010, standards for major energy-using appliances were to be raised to international levels, and the systems for policy, regulation and technical support for energy conservation were to be dramatically improved. Many of the same targets, objectives and policies appear both in the Five-Year Plan for Energy Development and in the China National Climate Change Programme, both published in 2007,[71] and a revised Energy Conservation Law was issued on 28 October 2007, for implementation on 1 April 2008.

These key policy and legal documents were backed up by a significant increase in financial support. Investment in energy efficiency by the central government was planned to rise to RMB Yuan 21.3 billion in 2007, which is thirteen times the level in 2006,[72] and a massive increase from the RMB Yuan 1 billion per year of the early 2000s.[73]

Industry

Industry remains the key focus of energy conservation efforts in China, for this is where substantial gains can be made in both the short and the long term. Of greatest importance is the Programme for 1000 Enterprises. These companies together account for about one-third of the total national consumption of energy and nearly 50 per cent of industrial energy demand, and the aim was to save 100 million tonnes of coal equivalent of coal equivalent by 2010.

The details of the 1000-Enterprise programme were announced in April 2006.[74] A total of 1008 enterprises were identified. They were charged with setting up management groups, establishing targets for all units within the enterprise, establishing procedures for energy audits, drawing up energy saving plans, investing in energy saving technologies, and introducing internal incentives to save energy. The programme allocated specific roles to different government departments.

The programme documents also provided for a range of supporting measures to be taken, including financial and fiscal policies such as providing income tax deductions for enterprises making energy saving products or reductions of VAT on specified energy saving technologies, equipment or products. Progress in implementing these proposals has been slow.[75]

In addition to this 1000-Enterprise programme, the government drew up a range of measures to address the challenges posed by the energy intensive industries. These include raising energy prices, establishing voluntary agreements, closing small and outdated plants, and a number of specific measures in the power sector.[76]

Transport

Great potential exists for future energy savings in the transport sector through further raising fuel efficiency standards in vehicles, replacing old vehicles, changing the structure of the road fleet, by encouraging the use of diesel and hybrid cars, and by investing in urban transport systems.[77] But efficiency of oil use is not yet as critical an issue as the efficiency of coal and electricity use, though it will become progressively more important as the use of oil in transport continues to grow.[78]

Since 2006 the government has taken a number of steps to constrain the rise of oil use in the transport sector. It has raised the level of purchase tax on large cars, raised the fuel economy standards for vehicle manufacturers, increased state funding for research and development in alternative-fuelled vehicles, and ordered that government departments use vehicles with higher fuel efficiency standards and that departmental vehicles not be available for private use by employees.[79] Further, it has gradually raised the end-user price for oil products, as discussed below.

Buildings

Buildings have been another priority target for government policies on account of the large amount of energy wasted in heating or cooling them once they are occupied. In addition to exhorting local governments to implement more effectively the existing building codes and to encourage the retrofitting of older buildings, a new state regulation has been issued banning the use of certain building materials, and also banning the import of energy-inefficient building materials and techniques.[80] Further measures have been taken to curb the ostentatious and wasteful construction practices of local governments[81] and to apply tighter control over new construction in order to constrain levels of investment.[82]

The government is also seeking to reduce the amount of energy expended in existing buildings for heating and cooling, especially in public and government buildings. The Ministry of Construction and Ministry of Finance has established a nationwide system to monitor the energy consumption of such buildings[83] and city governments have raised the permitted levels of summer temperatures in public buildings and offices.[84]

Energy pricing

The pricing of energy is one area of policy that the government has been cautious to address in a robust manner. As international prices for coal and crude oil rose during the early 2000s, so did China's domestic prices paid to producers of coal and crude oil. The government has allowed coal prices to react to supply and demand. So border prices for steam coal rose from about US$40 per tonne in 2004 to US$110 per tonne in July 2008 in line with international prices and were close to this level in July 2010.[85] Inland, near the areas of production, coal prices were at lower levels but had also risen by a similar proportion. The government has sought to constrain the price of coal sold to power stations but otherwise does not generally seek to directly cap coal prices. Domestic prices for crude oil rose sharply between 2002 and 2008 as the government allowed them to follow trends in the international markets.

In contrast, in its concern to protect private citizens and, to a lesser extent, industrial and commercial enterprises, the government has proven reluctant to raise end-user prices for oil products, for electricity and for natural gas. Over the period 2005–07 the government raised the factory gate and retail prices for oil products by 5–10 per cent on a number of occasions, in the spring of 2005, in March 2006 and November 2007.[86] Together these represented an increase of about 30 per cent, which compared with a doubling of product and crude oil prices on international markets. Though producer prices for electricity and natural gas were also raised by similar proportions, residential customers were protected from most of these increases. A reluctance to raise energy prices further was enhanced during 2007 by rising domestic inflation.

By June 2008 China's government could no longer resist the pressure for further substantial tariff adjustments and it announced a round of price rises for energy products. Retail prices for diesel, gasoline and jet fuel were raised by 17–18 per cent with immediate effect, taking gasoline to about 75 US cents per litre.[87] Freight rates on the railways rose by a similar proportion. At the same time the government put in place a range of measures to ensure that the poorer sections of society were not unduly affected. Subsidies to farmers, payable by unit area of land, were raised, as were payments per person to poor families in both urban and rural areas. Passenger fares for rail, for urban and rural public transport and for taxis went unchanged.

From 1 July 2008 wholesale electricity tariffs were allowed to rise by 5 per cent. The burden of these tariff increases was borne mainly by the industrial and commercial sectors, as rural and urban households were protected.

The summer of 2010 saw the government torn between raising energy prices to satisfy the energy industry and holding prices steady to constrain rising inflation. In June, gas prices for onshore producers were raised by 25 per cent, and these increases were passed on to industrial and commercial users, but not to households. At the same time the National Development and Reform Commission (NDRC) announced that the price for coal should be capped and appeared to postpone long-planned rises in retail power tariffs.[88]

This manner of managing energy pricing has had two negative consequences. First, while coal mining companies and crude oil producers have been making large profits, those enterprises involved in the transformation of energy, power generators and oil refiners, have been sustaining substantial financial losses. The government has been granting partial compensation to the major oil refiners, Sinopec and PetroChina, but not to power generators. Second, the impact of rising energy prices on end–user behaviour has been dampened, especially for households and rural communities, and this almost certainly undermines the energy efficiency strategies.

The sudden fall of international oil prices in the summer of 2008 gave the government the opportunity to start bringing domestic prices for oil products in line with international levels. In January 2009 taxes were raised five-fold for gasoline and eight-fold for diesel. These were followed by further price rises and by the introduction of a mechanism that allowed for an automatic adjustment of domestic prices for oil products in line with fluctuations of international prices, though the government reserved the right to constrain price rises in extreme circumstances. The government also gave assurance to oil refiners concerning their profit margins.[89]

Progress to date and the stimulus package

These strategies to constrain the rate of growth of energy demand met with some success. A slow start resulted in a decline in energy intensity of just 1.79 per cent in 2006. But this accelerated to 4.04 per cent and 5.2 per cent in 2007 and 2008 respectively, putting the country on track to achieve the goal of a 20 per cent reduction between 2005 and the end of 2010, provided improvements continued in 2009.[90]

The economic slowdown that emerged during 2008 triggered a substantial decline in China both of economic activity and of the rate of growth of demand for energy. Indeed, demand for electricity declined sharply. Many steel and cement plants lay idle. This may have been bad for the economy, but such a slowdown could have provided a chance for the government to further consolidate the energy efficiency gains already made. More inefficient plants could have been closed. Mergers and acquisitions would have allowed better companies to improve the energy performance of the less efficient ones. The uncontrolled construction and operation of inefficient industrial plant would have ceased.

This outlook changed on 10 November 2008 when the government announced its economic stimulus package. The ten priorities identified in the package were welfare housing, rural infrastructure, key public infrastructure projects, social services, environmental services, promotion of new industrial sectors to change the structure of the economy, economic reconstruction in areas hit by natural disasters, and income assistance for the poor, VAT reform, and increased lending by banks. These plans included some 6,000 km of rail to be laid by 2010. According to the Chinese press, the prime minister made special mention of the need to boost the production of iron, steel and cement.

This approach was entirely consistent with the need to stimulate economic growth and to address pressing social concerns, which is why the package has received such a welcome from around the world. But the contents of the plan appeared to indicate that energy conservation and energy efficiency had dropped down the list of government priorities. Provisional data for the year 2009 showed that the rate of decline of energy intensity had indeed slowed to a mere 2.2 per cent.[91] This trend worsened further in the first quarter of 2010, as provisional data indicated that the nation's energy intensity had increased by 3.2 per cent over this period.[92] This rise partially offset the decline of 14.8 per cent achieved between 2006 and 2009. Unless there is a substantial revision of the economic or energy statistics for 2009, this setback calls into doubt the country's ability to meet its self-imposed target for 2010.

The consequences of these policies

Since 1949, the main priority of China's government in the energy sector has been to raise domestic production of energy and thus to enhance security of supply. The government may be congratulated on the considerable achievement of expanding energy supply at a sufficient rate to support an economy that expanded about fifteenfold over the period 1978 to 2009. Over this period energy consumption grew fivefold and doubled over the eight years 2001–2008.[93] In 1980, China's energy demand was just one quarter of that of the EU in today's configuration and barely larger than that of Japan. The country accounted for just 6 per cent of world energy use. By 2006 China was consuming the same amount of energy as the EU. In 2009 China was on a par with the USA as the world's largest consumer of energy and it accounted for nearly 20 per cent of global energy demand.[94] Despite this soaring requirement, 90 per cent of China's energy demand in 2009 was satisfied from domestic supplies.

This success in supporting economic growth has also been accompanied by an effort, unprecedented in developing countries, to supply electricity to all households. It is estimated that 99 per cent of China's population now has access to electricity.[95] This compares to less than 60 per cent in India in 2006.[96]

The cost of this success has taken various forms. Trillions of Yuan have been required in investment in infrastructure for the production and transmission of energy, and nearly all of this has had to come from China's government, state-owned companies and state-owned banks. Foreign involvement in China's energy sector has been very modest. As primary resources are extracted from more remote locations and more testing geology, so the unit cost of energy supply has risen. Likewise the cost of oil imports has increased as the import requirement has grown.

Despite this vast and continuing expenditure, supply disruptions for different forms of energy persist. The period since 2003 has seen shortages of coal, electricity, oil products and natural gas, at different locations at different times. Though some of these shortages have been caused by unusual weather, or by time lags in investment in extraction, transformation or transmission infrastructure, other shortfalls in supply have resulted from the gaming behaviour of energy companies as they seek to take advantage of or to reduce the negative impact of pricing anomalies in the domestic market.

The most serious negative long-term consequences of the government's single-minded focus on energy production rather than energy conservation have been on the environment. The production and consumption of energy in China has resulted in serious pollution at local, regional and global scales. At local level, land has been destroyed where coal mining has not been accompanied by land rehabilitation, rivers have been poisoned by mine effluent, solid waste and oil spills, and the air in China's cities is among the worst in the world.[97] Sulphur dioxide emissions from power stations continue to create acid rain across China and neighbouring countries, and at a global level China is estimated to have been the world's largest emitter of greenhouse gases through energy use since 2006.[98]

The production of energy in China has had other negative impacts on different segments of society. These have included millions of people displaced by large dam projects, thousands of coal miners killed or injured each year in accidents, and entire communities abandoned as oilfields or mines reach the end of their life without any plans having being drawn up for future economic development in the locality.[99]

Only since 2003 has the government made real efforts to switch the focus on energy policy from the supply-side to the demand-side, bringing in a wide range of measures to promote energy conservation and energy efficiency. Inefficient industrial plants have been closed, new standards have been established for appliances, targets have been set for large companies and for local governments, and end-user prices for energy have been raised. These strategies are intended to have positive impacts not just on the energy sector but also on the environment, at national and global levels.

The future trajectories of China's energy demand and energy import requirement will depend to a significant extent on the degree of sustained success achieved by these energy efficiency strategies as they are rolled out over the coming years. Short-term success may not necessarily lead to long-term achievement. The reasons for this lie in the wider context in which energy policy is formulated and implemented in China, as will be discussed in the following chapters.

3   The wider context of China's energy policy

Introduction

Energy policy is not created in a vacuum and the nature of energy policy is not dependent solely on the current prevailing circumstances in the energy sector. The very importance of energy to modern industrialised societies results in energy policy being intimately linked to most other aspects of the society, of the economy and of the natural resource endowment of the country concerned. Further, current attitudes to the management of natural resources may have their roots deep in the historical past of the national culture.

For these reasons, the nature of the prevailing energy policy in a country like China with its large size and population, with its profound socio-economic challenges and with its long history of civilisation, will be highly constrained both by conditions in the country today and by beliefs and values shaped by thousands of years of history. Further, incentives to take active steps to formulate a clear energy policy or to modify an existing policy may be diminished if the government of the day has other priorities. But no society and no policy is static. Events may force a government to address challenges and opportunities in the energy sector, and new ideas may encourage it to take new approaches to solving new or long-standing problems.

This chapter examines a number of factors outside the core of the national energy sector that may shape the development path of the China's energy policy, as a prelude to examining specific features of energy policy-making and implementation in Chapter 4. We start by looking at what drives energy up the political agenda in China, before moving on to examine, first, certain long-held ideas and beliefs that determine a degree of path-dependency in China's energy policy and, second, a number of new ideas and concepts that have provided impetus for the government to experiment with new policy approaches. The chapter concludes with a section that shows how changes in a modern energy sector, whether in China or elsewhere, are tightly constrained by the resource endowment and the energy infrastructure, and by the links between the energy sector and many other aspects of government policy.

What drives energy up the political agenda?

Despite the importance of energy to a modern economy and to daily life, the sector is rarely at the top of the policy agenda for national governments for long periods of time. Exceptions are those countries which are major exporters of energy and which are highly dependent on revenues from these exports to support national development. In other countries, energy supply is commonly taken for granted, and the government devotes its attention to other economic or political objectives which are considered to be more important at the time.

It takes a crisis, an impending crisis or an apparent crisis to bring energy to the attention of most governments. Such crises tend to take the form of events or sudden changes of trend which in themselves create a threat, enhance an existing threat, or create or enhance the intensity with which a threat is perceived. This may take the form of an increased probability of the threatened event materialising, an increased scale of impact from such an event, or a reduced ability to react to the threat should it materialise.[1]

Most commonly it is a threat to security of supply that pushes energy up the government agenda. The source of the threat may be domestic or international. In the case of China, it has been both. Increasing dependence on imported oil since 1993 and high levels of international oil prices between 2003 and 2008 saw oil rise steadily up the agenda. But the continued ability of the international markets to supply these imports and of the country to pay for them consequently meant that this increasing vulnerability did not bring security of oil supply all the way to the top of the agenda.

In contrast, the realisation by China's government in 2004 that the country faced a major shortfall in *domestic* energy supplies, particularly of electricity, brought energy security right to the top of the agenda. Immediate and radical action was needed to ensure that the economy and people's livelihoods were not seriously damaged by a shortfall in energy supply. Attention switched from the production of energy to its consumption, and to the challenge of reducing waste in all parts of the energy supply chain, as discussed in Chapter 2.

The new importance attached to energy security by China's government was enhanced by renewed worldwide concern during the first decade of the twenty-first century relating to the future availability of energy supplies and to the governance of international energy markets.[2] This concern comprised three factors. The first derived from the perception that the level of investment in new oil and gas supply capacity in major exporting countries was inadequate to meet medium-term demand. The second was a resurgence of the belief, widely held in the 1970s and early 1980s, that primary energy resources were close to depletion. Third, the early years of the century demonstrated that the liberalisation of energy markets had created a range of systematic risks that had not been adequately addressed.

Two further issues have brought energy up the agenda around the world. The most prominent of these relates to the environment and, particularly, to global climate change. Within China, the negative environmental impacts of the country's dependence on coal have long been recognised by the Chinese government. Though action has and continues to be taken to constrain these impacts, environmental concerns alone have not been sufficient to raise energy up the government agenda. Indeed, even the recently enhanced enthusiasm for addressing climate change builds mainly on the energy efficiency programmes, which themselves are driven by security of supply objectives.[3]

The second issue relates to the need in developing counties to supply inhabitants with modern and clean supplies of energy. China has achieved remarkable success in this respect. As a result, the physical supply of modern energy to all segments of the population is not now a major policy concern, though the appropriate pricing of this energy remains an important priority.

The power of long-held ideas, beliefs and traditions

Events may bring the energy sector to the attention of government, but it is ideas, beliefs and traditions that to a great extent determine the way in which government and society perceive a challenge or a problem, how they analyse it and how they formulate strategies to address the problem. Though academic theories and concepts relating to economic policy may evolve, their formulation and implementation in the policy sphere are likely to be constrained to a greater or lesser extent by long-held beliefs and traditions prevailing in society.[4]

Constantin examined the relevance of 'ideational frames' to understanding the evolution of China's energy policy.[5] He identified three such frames: a strategic frame that emphasises self-sufficiency and national security; a market frame that focuses on prices, costs and markets; and an environmental frame that highlights the need to address challenges relating to the management of depletable resources and the environment.

Here we develop further the relevance of ideas, beliefs and traditions to China's energy policy, but distinguish between, on the one hand, the long-held beliefs and traditions, many of which were explicitly sustained in the early decades of the communist regime and, on the other hand, ideas that have been expounded and adopted to varying degrees in more recent years. One of our aims is to show the extent to which the long-held beliefs and traditions lie in tension with some of the more recent ideas.

Two long-held attitudes that have great relevance to the management of energy in China are the preference for self-reliance and a belief in man's ability to master nature. A third factor has been the stoical acceptance of austerity.

China's attitude to external economic relations has varied greatly during its history. The wealth and variety of its natural resources rendered a policy of self-reliance more viable than in many other countries. Yet the nation was a significant participant in international trade during some of the periods when its economic power was greatest; for example in the Later Han (first and second centuries AD), Song (eleventh to thirteenth centuries), Tang (seventh to ninth centuries) and Qing (eighteenth and nineteenth centuries) dynasties. Much of this trade was carried out by foreigners, from the Middle East, east Asia and Europe. Only in the Song period did Chinese traders themselves become a powerful force. It was this dominance of trade by foreigners and their unsavoury practices that led the rulers of the late Qing dynasty to take a strongly negative approach to international trade.[6]

After the communists took power in 1949, a high degree of self-reliance became an immediate necessity as the West failed to recognise the new regime. The Soviet Union stepped in to provide technology and skills that had the potential to play a key role in the development of the energy and mineral sectors. But China was left on its own when the Soviet Union withdrew its support in 1960.[7] The search for self-reliance in the energy and mineral sectors was accentuated by the belief that these sectors should drive growth in the rest of the economy.[8] The rapid development of the Daqing oilfield in Heilongjiang Province during the 1960s became emblematic of the 'heroic' self-reliance of the New China.[9]

China's distrust of the outside world took a new turn during the world energy crisis of the 1970s and early 1980s. The shortage of oil and the high prices were seen as part of a conspiracy hatched by the rich nations in order to further subjugate the Third World, thus further confirming the need for self-reliance. The crisis was interpreted as a Marxist struggle between the rich and the poor, and as a consequence China welcomed the shift in the balance of power towards the oil-rich states.[10]

Though the open-door policy introduced in the 1980s did result in foreign involvement in the economy, participation by foreign companies in the domestic energy sector remained restricted to those activities for which foreign technologies and skills were absolutely necessary.[11] These included offshore oil exploration, offshore and onshore gas production, nuclear power generation, liquefied natural gas importation and the manufacture of large-scale turbines.[12] Indeed, the main objective for the government in inviting foreign involvement in China's energy sector was to maximise the country's ability to be self-reliant in energy supply. This preference for self-reliance was exacerbated during the 1990s after China became a net importer of oil, and has been reflected not just in government policy but in the attitudes of citizens, even of university students.[13]

An important component of the self-reliance approach was the direct involvement of the government in managing the energy sector, initially through Ministries for Petroleum, for Coal and for Electrical Power and, more recently, through state-owned energy companies. Despite recent commercialisation, these companies remain under relatively tight government control with respect to strategic concerns, especially those enterprises owned at central government level. This contrasts with the situation of enterprises in most other sectors of the economy that have been largely released from government control and, in many cases, fully privatised. Energy, other natural resources and rail transport remain the exceptions to this general trend of liberalisation.[14]

A second factor that plays an important role is China's approach to natural resource management. The country's main ancient philosophical traditions explicitly addressed the relationship between man and nature and emphasised the close interdependence between them. While both Confucianism and Taoism highlighted the need for a balance between man and nature, both strands of belief included adherents who believed that man had the power and, indeed, the obligation to control and conquer nature.[15]

More convincing than any arguments based on philosophy is the evidence from history itself. Indeed, the very seeds of Chinese civilisation germinated on the realisation that man needed to control water. Four thousand years ago, the Emperor Yu was the first ruler to systematically carry out extensive large-scale projects for flood control, irrigation and inland water transport.[16] Thereafter, the constant struggle to gain political power and then to retain it led to an environmentally destructive cycle of warfare and economic development. Warfare required the provision of weapons made from wood and metal to equip armies of hundreds of thousands of men, as well as systems to deliver supplies to the armies. Thus were ore deposits mined, forests cut down and canals constructed. The intervening periods of peace required the new government to centralise its power through economic development, infrastructure construction, population growth and intensive agriculture. Respect for nature remained subordinate to the call of power.[17] This was not a feature of China alone, but also lay at the heart of the rise of other early 'hydraulic societies' in which the control of water lay at the heart of political power, for example Sumer, Assyria, Egypt and India.[18] Such an approach to the management of water, of the environment and of other natural resources lay in stark contrast to and in tension with the collective decision-making processes that typified local communities in the very same societies and which showed greater awareness of the values of sustainable development.[19]

The governance of natural resources in imperial China displayed three specific characteristics that are of great relevance today: the importance of engineers, the key role of the state in major projects, and the lack of systems to regulate the use of natural resources. Though engineers were rarely admitted to the social and political elite, they have played an important and respected role in imperial China for three thousand years. Many became bureaucrats and a few became senior officials. This in turn reflected the close involvement of the state in projects crucial to its power, such as hydraulic engineering, manufacturing weapons and other military hardware in imperial workshops, and the mining of raw materials critical for weapons, for currency and for daily life such as copper, iron, lead tin, zinc and salt.[20]

Where the state was not itself directly involved, it tended to take a very relaxed view of natural resource exploitation. This was especially notable in the case of mining. Officials tended to dislike unofficial mining operations as they could distract labour from more important agricultural tasks. At the same time, though noting the poor working and living conditions of the workers, they took few steps to address them. Likewise, the state took few steps to create systematic procedures to manage the nation's mineral resources. This contrasts sharply with the body of mining law that had been established in late medieval Europe.[21]

The pre-eminence of communist theory and practice in the governance of China since 1949 has, if anything, accentuated such an approach to natural resources and the environment. The early decades of the communist regime saw explicit statements to the effect that natural resources were boundless, and what was required was a greater ability to mobilise society to exploit them. Further, economic development should be pursued regardless of the cost to natural resources and the environment.[22]

This approach has expressed itself in various forms, from the unquestioned desirability of building very large dams, to the subordination of environmental concerns to energy production, and to the relatively low priority attached until recently to energy efficiency. Indeed, it has been argued that Mao took historical traditions to new extremes in his calls to conquer nature.[23] Though many countries and cultures may be accused of taking such an approach to nature at some periods in their economic development, China would appear to be exceptional in the duration and the intensity with which this belief has been held. Such a view should, however, be moderated by consideration of more nuanced analyses of the actual practices of natural resource management in the early years of communist rule that show that efforts were made to constrain or reverse the negative environmental impacts of agricultural development.[24]

Though no major war took place, Mao's 'Third Front' strategy, implemented during the late 1960s and early 1970s, at the same time as the Cultural Revolution, is a modern analogy for the ancient periods of militarisation. Fearing attack from either the USA or the Soviet Union, China undertook a massive and rapid relocation of people and productive assets such as factories and mines to south-western and western China. This immense undertaking resulted in further widespread environmental destruction and waste of natural resources.[25]

The final belief or attitude relevant to energy policy was also long-standing but has been further emphasised by the Communist Party. Centuries of poverty had left the majority of China's citizens accustomed to austerity. An acceptance of austerity and a sense of responsibility to society at large was encouraged and even imposed throughout society by the government after Liberation in 1949. All commodities and supplies were scarce, including energy, and everything obtained by individual households would be valued and used with care. Despite improvements in health care and significant alleviation of rural poverty, the 1960s and 1970s saw little growth in average per capita energy consumption.[26] The scope for wasteful consumption was limited.

It was against this long history of widespread poverty that China's Communist Party developed its strategies to promote economic development and social equity. The key instruments were to be planned production and consumption, controlled prices and, within the cities, a relatively high degree of equality in access to goods and services.[27] Within the energy sector these priorities remain evident even today in the close involvement of central government in many strategic aspects of energy production and consumption, and in the continuing efforts to constrain energy prices, especially for private citizens.[28] More recently, the social dimension of the government's energy policy has been exemplified by the hugely successful rural electrification programme that has resulted in some 99 per cent of the population having access to electricity – an unprecedented level of electrification for a developing country.[29]

The role of new ideas and approaches

Against this background of long-held beliefs and values, a number of new ideas relevant to energy and natural resources policy have started to enter the thinking of the Chinese government since the 1980s. While they have not caused the abandonment of the earlier beliefs they have variously created tensions in the policy making and implementation processes or have caused adaptations to existing policies. Not surprisingly, most of these new ideas have their source either in the growing internationalisation of the country or in its rising wealth.

The first idea of direct relevance to the energy sector entered into the thinking of China's government during the 1990s through the World Bank and other providers of economic advice. The belief that market forces could and should be introduced to the domestic energy sector, even to electrical power, was still relatively new even in the West, and became part of the tide of advice flowing into China.[30] Zhu Rongji, in his position at the head of the State Economic and Trade Commission and later as prime minister, was a supporter of this approach. As a result, steps were taken during the 1990s and into the early 2000s to restructure the energy industry, to reduce the extent of government intervention in operational management, and to start to introduce market forces to the energy sector.[31]

These steps towards liberalisation were constrained by the government's desire to retain ownership and control over key sectors of the economy, such as energy. Thus government at central or provincial levels continues to maintain majority ownership and control over most large energy companies in China, despite steps to commercialise and to list these companies on domestic and international stock exchanges.[32] In this way have the 'old ideas' constrained the implementation of the 'new'. Given the recent shortages of energy in China and the dubious experiences of energy markets in some other countries, this cautious approach is probably appropriate at this stage of China's development.[33]

An idea that has been embraced with greater enthusiasm has been the need for international economic engagement. Again, this was pushed by Zhu Rongji, and China's accession to the World Trade Organization (WTO) is emblematic of his achievement.[34] However, its application to energy has been pursued with a higher degree of selectivity than in other sectors of the economy. Foreign investment in China's energy sector faces numerous constraints and remains at a low level, including in the wholesale and retail of oil products that have been newly opened under the WTO accession agreement. Long-standing obstacles include policy and legal ambiguity, the market power of incumbents and the pricing systems for oil products and electricity.[35]

China has pursued international energy engagement in a number of fields. These relate to overseas investment by state-owned energy companies, the increasing import of energy products, bilateral energy diplomacy with energy exporters, and active participation in international organisations relating to energy.[36] To a great extent this engagement has been driven by the growing dependence on external supplies of oil and, to a lesser extent, of natural gas. Thus the power of necessity has overwhelmed the power of old ideas of self-reliance and isolation in the field of energy.

Two further sets of ideas relating to energy that have been prevailing around the world have made an impact in China to different degrees. As mentioned earlier in this chapter, the resurgence of the fear of an imminent depletion of certain energy resources has found resonance with the government, and has underpinned its support for overseas investment by NOCs as well as the growing scope of its energy diplomacy. In contrast, the prerogative to protect the environment, both locally and globally, was not initially embraced by government with the same enthusiasm. Rather, such concerns appear to have been subordinated to the need to maximise economic growth.

Nevertheless, the 1990s and first decade of the twenty-first century have seen the government show a greater willingness to recognise the environmental challenges created by thirty years of rapid and poorly regulated economic growth, and a growing willingness to invest political and economic capital in addressing these challenges. This trend has been exemplified by the emergence of new political slogans such as the 'conservation society' and 'scientific development'.[37] Despite these efforts and the elevation of the State Environmental Protection Agency to ministerial status in 2008, many fundamental deficiencies lie at the heart of China's systems for regulating the environment.[38]

Switching our attention to Chinese society, especially to urban middle-class society, the acceptance of and respect for austerity would seem to be disappearing.[39] It has been replaced by a wasteful materialism, which does not yet appear to be greatly tempered by consideration of the wider impacts of this behaviour on the environment. Certainly the last two decades have seen a growth of environmental awareness across society of the extent of and the consequences of damage to the environment, one of the symptoms of which has been the expansion in numbers and degree of activism of domestic environmental Non-governmental Organisations (NGOs).[40]

That being said, China has yet to experience the rebellious, environmentally conscious, 'back-to-nature' movements that swept through Europe and North

America in the 1960s and 1970s and which, despite their eccentricities, provided an important impetus for the development of today's appreciation of global warming and other environmental threats. Instead, the growing middle classes in China, as in many countries today, enjoy and expect plentiful energy supplies at low prices. Though they may have some appreciation of or concern for the longer-term costs in terms of security of supply and environmental damage, their perception of the importance of the environment and their willingness to adapt their behaviour voluntarily appear to be limited.[41] However, some evidence exists that a significant proportion of Chinese university students are indeed aware of the environmental and energy challenges facing China and are willing to take certain steps in their own lives to address these challenges.[42]

The underlying framework for energy policy-making

New ideas cannot easily be translated into new policies. Not only is this process constrained by the older values and beliefs, but the formulation of a realistic new energy policy is constrained by the nature of the energy sector itself and by its links to all aspects of the national economy. As a result, the making of energy policy takes place within a tightly defined framework that rarely allows for sudden and radical shifts; or if such shifts are made, then the costs and risks may be be high.

The most immutable aspects of a country's energy sector are the scale, nature and geographic distribution of its primary energy resources. In the case of China, as examined in Chapter 2, these comprise an abundance of coal resources and only modest oil and gas resources, which mainly lie in the north of the country, far from the current centre of economic activity in the south and east. Though efforts have been made to encourage the diffusion of economic activity to the west and north, for example through the Develop the West Strategy, and to develop new and renewable forms of energy, the country is condemned for the foreseeable future to rely on an essentially inefficient and dirty fuel (coal) and on the need to transport energy over large distances.

Investment in new infrastructure to produce, transform and transport energy has continued at a prodigious and accelerating rate. For example power generation capacity doubled from 357 GW to 713 GW over the period 2002 to 2007, and some 90 per cent of this growth was in coal-fired plants.[43] Investment in rail networks to transport coal, in electricity transmission lines and in oil and gas pipelines has also been massive.[44] Though such investment is clearly necessary in order to supply the energy required to support economic growth, the nature of this investment is such that it perpetuates and 'locks in' the country to the existing system of energy supply. Given how much of China's energy infrastructure is relatively new and given that its working life should be in the order of decades, these recent investments provide a tight constraint on future government energy policy.[45]

Likewise, at the other end of the energy supply chain, the nature, the energy properties and the location of new factories and of civil, commercial and residential buildings will play a strong role in determining the scale and nature of energy demand for many years.[46]

Energy is linked to almost every sector of the economy. The manner and rate in which energy is consumed is dependent on the size, rate of growth and structure of the national economy, and on the state of technology applied in the consumption of energy in the industrial, commercial and household sectors. The manner in which investment is made in energy production and consumption varies according to the way in which finances are made available, for example through banks or directly from the government, and the systems for pricing energy products, commodities and manufactured goods. In turn, the pricing of energy is itself linked to the nature of the social welfare systems, for if these systems are not well developed it may be essential to use energy subsidies as an instrument for poverty alleviation. If energy is imported or exported, this energy trade is likely to be supported by actions in the field of diplomacy and security. As a consequence, energy policy is intimately linked with many other national policies.

National economic development policies will set out the desired rate of economic growth, the overall structure of the economy, and the role of exports or imports. In the case of China, the desire for a sustained high rate of growth, continuing investment in heavy industry and infrastructure, and the drive to maximise exports have all contributed to the size and structure of demand for energy and have constrained the scope for changes in energy policy.[47] The industrial policy of retaining majority state ownership over large energy companies and of promoting their internationalisation plays an important role in both the way in which the domestic energy industry is structured and operated, as well as in the manner of overseas investment by these companies, as will be examined in later chapters.

China's social policies, as discussed earlier, have played a key role in determining the high degree of availability of energy across society, and at relatively low prices for most users. The same attitude to promoting social welfare accounts for the government's keenness to maximise the level of employment in the few remaining large state-owned enterprises, of which the energy companies are key examples. This concern played a significant role in the way in which the oil companies were restructured in 1998. The productive and potentially profitable assets were collected into the commercialised entities that were later listed on international stock markets. The service enterprises were kept in the non-listed, wholly state-owned holding companies. These service companies were able to retain large numbers of employees by continuing their operations within China and by rapidly expanding their activities overseas, both in support of the investments made by the NOCs and on their own account.[48]

Transport policy has a direct relationship to energy policy in any country. In the case of China, the argument for an energy efficient and environmentally friendly transport policy seems to have been subsumed beneath an industrial policy that has championed automobile manufacturing, an urban design policy that has favoured multi-lane highways as the main transport network, and a social policy that, intentionally or otherwise, has highlighted car ownership as a legitimate expectation of the growing urban middle classes.[49] Only belatedly have a small number of Chinese cities started to invest substantially in modern mass transport systems such as metro and light rail. Indeed the abundance of cheap taxis in the cities has created a further class of citizen requiring protection from rising oil prices: the taxi drivers.[50]

Energy policy may also be subservient to monetary, exchange rate and fiscal policies. Energy is one of the few items the price of which remains, to a greater or lesser extent, under the control of China's government.[51] Thus, in times of rising inflation the government will tend to use energy prices as an instrument to constrain inflation, holding prices down rather than letting them rise along with international energy prices. China's exchange rate policy has been predicated on the perceived need to maximise exports of manufactured goods and thus the government has artificially restrained the rise of the Yuan against the American dollar by buying dollars.[52] This has had the effect of encouraging the export not only of manufactured goods but also of energy intensive materials such as steel, plate glass and cement. The volume of such exports has been further stimulated by tax rebates.[53] Indeed this policy results in exports accounting for as much as one-third of Chinese energy consumption and carbon dioxide emissions.[54]

Looking overseas, it is clear that much of China's diplomacy is driven by concerns related to security of energy supply. Conversely, energy is being used as an instrument of diplomacy to build or enhance bilateral relations both close to home, with countries in the former Soviet Union, as well as further afield in Africa and Latin America. These issues will be explored further in subsequent chapters.

This chapter has examined a range of factors that act to constrain the path of China's energy policy, such as long-standing ideas, beliefs and traditions, the nature of the modern energy industry itself, and the intimate links between energy policy and many other national policies. We have also shown the potential power of new ideas on energy policy. In the next chapter we focus more closely on the processes of energy policy-making and implementation in China today.

4   Inside China's energy policy

Introduction

Such is the overwhelming requirement to provide additional energy to fuel continuing economic growth and thus to maintain the legitimacy of the Communist Party, that security of supply remains the first priority of energy policy at all times in China, along with social equity. Other objectives, such as economic competitiveness, the efficient use of resources and environmental protection remain subordinate. Yet, despite the consistency of this prioritisation, China's energy sector is characterised by internal contradictions, by short-term policy measures, by 'campaigns', and by sudden changes of direction.

Observers of China's energy sector have long been drawn to a common set of conclusions relating to energy policy-making and implementation:[1] that the agencies of government are fragmented and uncoordinated; that they lack the capacity for well-informed policy-making; that special interest groups, particularly state-owned energy companies, have undue influence over policy content; and that, as a result, the policies that emerge are inadequately formulated, fragmentary, contradictory, and tend to focus on ambitious and often unrealistic quantitative targets. Further, effective implementation is obstructed by special interests either within local governments or state-owned enterprises, by rivalry between parallel lines of government, as well as by a shortage of manpower in the relevant departments at all levels of government.

China is not unique in lacking coherent energy policy-making and effective implementation, for few countries can boast great success in this field.[2] But the nature and origins of deficiencies in policy are specific to each country. The aim of this chapter is to examine the factors that appear to determine the nature of energy policy-making and implementation in China within the wider framework outlined in the previous chapter.

We start by examining the main actors in the energy sector, before identifying the key features of economic policy-making and policy implementation. Taken together with the previous chapter, these lines of evidence show that China's energy policy is characterised by continuity, path-dependence and incremental change, but yet is also subject to short-term and highly unpredictable shifts in policy that tend to have unexpected consequences. The chapter concludes by explaining why oil, the main subject of this book, is of such critical importance to China and its energy policy.

The actors in the energy sector

Policies arise from the need to address specific challenges and these policies are framed in the context of long-lived beliefs and traditions, of prevailing political values and of recent economic ideas. But these challenges are identified and the policies formulated within component organisations and groups that form the institutional structures of government, industry and society, and which have their owns sets of priorities and interests.

Three sets of actors can be identified that directly or indirectly affect the development of energy policy in China: the government, industry and civil society.

Government

Such has been the importance of the energy sector that, as in most other countries, key policy initiatives or decisions rise to the very apex of power in China's government. Here the State Council lies at the top of the government structure, the membership of which is very similar to that of the other key institution, the Politburo, which oversees the running of the Communist Party of China.[3] Such was the importance of oil to China at the time that members of the 'petroleum clique', who were drawn from the oil industry, played a crucial role in China's economic policy-making during the 1960 and 1970s.[4] Alongside the State Council and the Politburo, and yet distinctly subordinate, the National People's Congress forms the legislature. Despite the high degree of concentration of power in these bodies, authority over the energy sector is highly diffuse below this level.

China's energy sector has long been characterised by a lack of a strong and well-resourced agency at central government level. During the 1980s and beforehand, each individual energy industry (coal, power, petroleum, petrochemicals) was itself a ministry within government. Each reported to the State Planning Commission (SPC) and the State Council. Other than the SPC, which coordinated all economic activities in the country, no other agency existed to develop a coherent policy for the energy sector. As a result, energy policy consisted mainly of the summation of the individual industry plans.[5]

The Ministries for Petroleum and for Petrochemical Industries were abolished in the 1980s, and replaced by two corporations, China National Petroleum Corporation (CNPC) and Sinopec respectively.[6] A Ministry of Energy was created in 1988 to oversee these companies and the remaining Ministries for Coal and for Electrical Power. But the new Ministry of Energy lacked the status, the authority and the resources to impose itself on the individual industries, and it itself was abolished in 1993.[7]

This disaggregated structure persisted through the reforms of 1998. At that time, the Ministries for Coal and Electrical Power were abolished, and replaced by provincial level coal companies and by a State Power Corporation respectively. The State Economic and Trade Commission (SETC) took responsibility for overseeing the operations of the state-owned energy companies, while the newly renamed State Development and Planning Commission (SDPC) retained authority over medium and long-term plans, pricing and energy efficiency.[8]

With authority split between these two high level commissions, the degree of coherence in energy policy-making deteriorated rather than increased, not least because of bureaucratic competition. One symptom was the progressive decline of central government control over the energy sector that was highlighted by the energy crisis that faced the new government in 2003.[9]

Two key priorities for the government at this time were to regain and centralise control over the energy sector and to provide for more coherent policy-making. Three institutions were established in order to achieve these objectives. The Energy Bureau was created within the NDRC (which replaced the SDPC) in March 2003. This brought together many, but not all, of the energy functions, which had been scattered across the previous SDPC and SETC, the latter having now been abolished. The functions of the Energy Bureau included formulating policy and drawing up plans for sector reform, as well as routine oversight of the country's energy sector.[10] It soon became clear that this small bureau with a staff of less than thirty could not possibly fulfil its mandate. Two years later, in 2005, the government set up an Energy Leading Group within the State Council, supported by a State Energy Office. Their role was to set strategic directions and to improve policy coordination.[11]

The ten years of government restructuring since the mid-1990s, rather than improving governance, seem to have led to a progressive loss of control by central government and a decline in the quality of governance within the energy sector.[12] In the build-up to the plenary session of the National People's Congress in March 2008, it was anticipated that a new and powerful energy agency would be established. This did not happen. Instead the reforms to those agencies managing the energy sector were rather modest in comparison with reforms to other parts of government. The existing Energy Bureau was renamed the National Energy Administration, and a National Energy Commission was created from the pre-existing National Energy Leading Group.[13]

The National Energy Commission retained the overall roles of coordinating energy policy and setting strategic direction that were previously held by the Leading Group. Meanwhile the National Energy Administration took on the functions of the former Office of the Energy Leading Group, the NDRC's Energy Bureau and Department for Energy Efficiency, and the former China Commission of Science, Technology and Industry for National Defence. Its functions were to develop energy strategy, to draft plans and policies, to make proposals for energy industry reform, to oversee the country's oil, natural gas, coal and power industries, to manage the strategic oil reserves, to formulate policies for renewable energy and energy conservation, and to carry out international energy cooperation. The responsibility for energy pricing remained with the NDRC's Department of Price Administration. The level of staffing was set initially at 112.[14]

Other government agencies at or close to ministerial level also continued to have a role to play in the energy sector. The Ministry of Land and Resources continued to manage resource extraction and exploitation, and the environmental protection of the land. The newly created Ministry for Environmental Protection was responsible for controlling the pollution of air and water. The State-owned Asset Supervision and Administration Commission (SASAC) took the ownership role for government over the large state-owned enterprises. In addition, the Ministry of Science and Technology, the Ministry of Commerce, the Ministry of Foreign Affairs, the Ministry of Finance, the Ministry of Transport, the Ministry of Railways and the Ministry of Housing and Urban-Rural Development all retained significant roles in the energy sector.[15]

Each ministerial organisation has the authority to issue regulations relating to its sphere of activity. Of these the most powerful in the energy sector is the NDRC, which, as the successor of the State Planning Commission, has nationwide and sector-wide responsibility. Above all these ministerial organisations sit the three key bodies in which the top leadership of the country are represented, as described above: the State Council, the Politburo and the National People's Congress. The military also have a role to play in energy policy formulation, but this is probably rather limited.[16]

Each of these organisations is supported by one or more think tanks that provide advice. The leading research centres in the field of energy are the State Council's Development Research Institute and the NDRC's Energy Research Institute.[17] Despite the growing number and variety of these think tanks, they nearly all owe their loyalty to the government and often to a specific government department or state-owned enterprise. The exceptions are the universities.

Though China's government is unitary according to the constitution, substantial economic power was delegated to successive levels of government at provincial, city and district levels, especially in the early years of reform.[18] Unlike a truly federal state, these subordinate levels of government have no rights over natural resources, except for those powers delegated to them by the central government. Indeed, in most aspects of energy policy, the major responsibility of sub-national governments is to adapt national polices, laws and regulations to local conditions and to enforce them.[19] All the ministries and most government agencies have equivalents at lower levels of government.

Industry

China's energy sector continues to be dominated by Chinese state-owned enterprises, albeit that they are now commercialised and partially privatised.

Three companies dominate the oil industry, each comprising a wholly state-owned holding company and a listed subsidiary.[20] CNPC/PetroChina and Sinopec are very large, vertically integrated corporations, with the former focusing on upstream and the latter on downstream. In terms of reserves, production, refining output, revenue and profits, these two corporations rank alongside the largest international oil companies (IOCs) in the world, as well as some of the larger national oil companies (NOCs) (see Table 4.1). The smaller CNOOC is predominantly an offshore exploration and production company, and is equivalent in size to medium-sized IOCs and NOCs such as BG from the United Kingdom and India's Oil and Natural Gas Corporation (ONGC). A large number of smaller companies play a minor role in China's domestic oil refining and distribution sectors.

In the electricity industry the State Power Corporation has been progressively commercialised and broken up into two grid companies and five large, listed national power generating companies. These account for more than 50 per cent of China's power generation capacity.[21] In addition there are countless smaller power generation companies owned by a wide range of entities at local government level. The coal industry is even more highly

Table 4.1 Comparative data for Chinese NOCs, IOCs and other NOCs, for the year 2008

	Oil and gas production (mmtoe)	Reserves (mmtoe)	Refinery Output (mmtoe)	Revenue (million US$)	Profit (million US$)
Chinese NOCs					
CNPC	227	5,025	125	185,839	19,679
PetroChina Ltd	161	4,665	74	156,372	18,489
Sinopec Group	49	n/a	173	213,495	3,854
Sinopec Ltd.	47	933	169	211,986	3,550
CNOOC	43	344	0	28,438	9,898
CNOOC Ltd	26	343	0	18,391	8,450
IOCs					
Exxon	195	9,819	270	477,359	45,220
Shell	162	1,487	169	458,361	26,476
BP	191	2,475	107	365,700	21,666
Chevron	126	1,077	92	264,958	23,931
Total	117	1,426	118	253,719	19,524
BG	31	1,790	0	18,474	7,941
Other NOCs					
Saudi Aramco	570	41,627	79	n/a	n/a
Gazprom	582	36,012	79	85,050	30,384
Petrobras	119	2,059	98	113,111	14,002
Petronas	89	3,685	22	63,980	27,387
ONGC	48	1,322	3	13,084	4,824

Note: mmtoe = million tonnes of oil equivalent.
Sources: company websites.

fragmented with a small number of large companies and a very large number of private and locally-owned mining companies.[22]

Despite this apparent diversity and the number of partially-listed companies, the majority of enterprises operating in China's energy sector are owned mainly by the state, at central or local level.[23] With the exception of the upstream oil and gas industry, foreign investment in China's energy sector has been very limited, despite official encouragement. This situation can, to a great extent, be accounted for by policy ambiguities, regulatory weaknesses and the power of the state-owned incumbents.[24]

Civil society

The power and ability of local communities and social groups to participate actively in policy-making continues to be relatively weak in China. The last thirty years of economic reform has not seen the development of a strong civil society independent of the state.[25] Despite the recent growth in the number of protests against government or company policies[26] and the rise in the number of rural and urban civil organisations,[27] neither local communities nor more widespread social organisations appear to play a significant role in policy-making at national and sub-national levels.[28] Despite this general lack of influence, civil society organisations do seem to be exerting greater influence in certain policy fields, for example environment, health and social justice.[29]

Chinese and foreign NGOs, together with the media, play an important role in raising awareness of environmental issues, in identifying alleged malpractice in state-owned energy companies and in attempting to block certain policy proposals.[30] Many of the projects that such groups try to block on the grounds of environmental or social impact relate to energy, and include thermal power stations and dams. However the NGOs are rarely involved formally in the policy-making process.

An apparent exception to the lack of willingness to engage with the public includes the practice of publishing drafts of certain laws on the internet in order to stimulate public discussion and to elicit views.[31] In early 2008, a draft of the Energy Law was placed on the internet in order to stimulate comments from the public. Some 5,000 responses were received.[32] Meetings with foreign energy specialists were also organised.

The characteristics of economic policy-making

Policy decision-making in China under the leadership of Chairman Mao tended to be confined to a small elite and was highly personalised around Mao himself, especially for decisions relating to political issues but also for strategic decisions relating to economic development. Power was highly centralised. Mao succeeded in building up a substantial government infrastructure to formulate and implement the economic plans, but then destroyed this structure during the Cultural Revolution.[33]

This wilful destruction of the systems of government laid the foundations for a renewal of local self-reliance across China as communities and localities took steps to protect themselves from the economic chaos and ensure their own economic survival. Indeed, even the previous years of communist rule had been characterised by successive phases of centralisation and decentralisation.[34]

After Mao's death in 1976, his successor Hua Guofeng tried to recentralise control and to launch a new centrally-planned economic leap forward. This approach was short-lived. When Deng Xiaoping took over the reins of power in 1978, he built on the earlier unintentional delegation of power to the localities by encouraging economic activity at the lowest level of the administrative structure, in the townships and villages. Decisions concerning the overall direction of economic development remained in the hands of the elite, but power over economic management was progressively ·delegated to individual enterprises and to local governments down to village level. Thus the 1980s and 1990s saw an incremental release of state control over the economy.[35]

Over the same period, the political system itself underwent a gradual evolution. Key trends included the decline of the role of personality, a growth in numbers and diversification of the members of the political elite, a formalisation of the political institutions and processes, a reduction of the intensity of factionalism and an expansion of the role of the legislature, the National People's Congress.[36] Progressive pluralisation has been accentuated by the growing role of think tanks and of advisers outside the central government.[37]

Unlike in Russia where reform led to the demise of the Communist Party, China kept its Party but embarked on a concerted attempt to adapt its focus away from political ideology to economic development and to change its mode of operation. At the same time steps were taken to professionalise the bureaucracy of government at all levels.[38]

Despite these changes, a number of features remained constant. The top leadership retains its role in setting overall policy directions and in setting the conceptual frames for formulating policy. In this they may be assisted by think tanks such as the State Council's Development Research Centre.[39] The role of ideology remains important, but it is less radical than before.[40] 'Campaigns' continue to be a favoured instrument of policy implementation[41] and feigned compliance has returned as the favoured response by lower levels of government, as will be discussed in the next section.[42] But above all else, policy-making continues to be characterised by bargaining. As policy-making has become more pluralised so the role of bargaining has become more intense as specialist bureaucrats and state company officials protect and promote the interests of their agencies and as government officials negotiate upwards, downwards and laterally in the hierarchy.[43] Such bargaining can often lead to solutions that do not match or even address the policy problem, but such solutions have the advantage that risks relating to implementation may be reduced.[44]

This gradual decentralisation, pluralisation and bargaining has resulted in a system of policy-making that has been characterised as 'fragmented authoritarianism'.[45] The key to this interpretation lies in the balancing of the forces of fragmentation just described by the forces for unification. These unifying forces include the power of the Communist Party, the role of personal relations and of informal institutional networks, and the traditional preference for decision-making by consensus.[46]

Though formulated more than twenty years ago, this concept of 'fragmented authoritarianism' is still applicable to China today. More recent analyses have added insightful nuances to this understanding. The term 'pluralistic elitism' recognises the enhanced pluralisation of the policy-making process while ultimate power is retained by the political elite.[47] This tense pairing of forces has been referred to as 'Consultative Leninism'.[48] A symptom of this retention of power by the elite is that policy proposals that are aligned with the key priorities of the top leadership tend to be agreed relatively rapidly, while those proposals that may not address these key concerns and yet at the same time threaten the interests of other key actors may take years to be enacted.[49]

Many of these general features of policy-making can be seen in China's energy sector, for example: a lack of strong leadership over the energy sector; the disproportionately high degree of influence over policy-making held by state-owned energy companies; a delight in the use of ambitious targets; the prevalence of bargaining in policy-making; and marked contrasts between some policies that are launched within a few weeks or months of their inception and others that remain under debate for ten years or more.

As described above, China's energy sector has consistently lacked a well-staffed and authoritative agency to formulate and implement energy policy, and to provide overall leadership of the energy sector. Instead the structure of government has led to policy proposals related to energy arising from individual line ministries or, latterly, state-owned enterprises. These individual entities champion their own proposals, which might take the form of targets for five-year plans, of laws and regulations covering their specific activities or of ideas for industry restructuring or price reform. In cases where these policy proposals were limited to the specific industry or activity, then the proposal might be accepted and implemented with little obstruction from other parties. In this way energy policy and plans for the energy sector tended to resemble a summation of individual industry strategies and targets, which together may be inconsistent or even contradictory, rather than a coherent package of policies designed to address the wider energy, economic and environmental challenges facing the country.[50] The restructuring of government agencies carried out in 2008 does not appear to be sufficiently profound to effect any great change in these patterns.[51]

The prime examples of this fragmented policy environment are the five-year plans for energy, which continue to be characterised by specific targets for each component of the energy industry, but by only vague statements relating to measures and mechanisms that would apply across the energy sector and provide some coherence. Formal laws and regulations show the same features.[52]

Disjointed policy is also exhibited by the contrasting approaches to pricing for crude oil and coal, on the one hand, and for electricity supply and oil products, on the other hand, as described in Chapter 2. These fundamental pricing discontinuities continue to cause major difficulties in a progressively commercialised energy sector.[53] Likewise, laws and regulations applying to a single activity, such as township and village coal mines, have tended to emanate from a number of different sources and tend to be inconsistent and contradictory.[54]

The period of restructuring of the energy industry in the mid and late 1990s saw a number of occasions in which the newly commercialised state-owned energy enterprises were able to influence government policy to their direct advantage. In both the coal and oil industries, the interests of the major state-owned enterprises were potentially threatened by smaller enterprises. In the coal sector, the large mines, in which the state had invested billions of Yuan, were threatened by the township and village coal mines in 1998. At that time, demand for coal in China greatly exceeded domestic supply and the smaller mines, with their lower operational standards and lower costs, were able to undercut the larger mines in the market. The ensuing campaign to close the township and village mines was ostensibly driven by concerns for safety and the environment, but the timing of the campaign was decided by the short-term need to protect the interests of the larger mines.[55] Thus, when demand picked up again, output from the smaller mines was allowed to grow again, until a further campaign to close them was launched in 2004.[56]

In a similar manner, the restructuring of the petroleum industry in 1998, far from leading to an enhancement of competition, resulted in the further consolidation of the market position of the newly commercialised companies, PetroChina and Sinopec, as the government enforced their takeover of a large number of local wholesalers and retailers in the late 1990s.[57]

The fragmentation of policy was further enhanced by the tendency of the top leadership to issue edicts or launch campaigns directed at a specific activity or industry, without apparent consideration for the wider or longer-term consequences or requirements of these policy actions. Two recent examples concern the construction of power stations and of the West-to-East gas pipeline. The year 1998, as mentioned above, was characterised by an oversupply of energy, and this affected the electrical power industry. Partly in response to this, the central government banned the construction of large new power stations from 1999 in order to prevent over-investment and a waste of resources. This edict created the background for the nationwide power shortages that emerged in 2003, once economic growth picked up again, and which lasted through 2008.[58]

The decision to build the West-to-East gas pipeline from Xinjiang to Shanghai was made in a relatively short period in 2001.[59] The decision was driven by the wider Develop the West programme that was being formulated by the political elite in order to enhance the economic development of western

China. By chance a new gas field had just been found in the Tarim Basin. While the decision to build the pipeline may indeed have been justifiable in terms of energy policy, it was made in the absence of a wider policy for natural gas.[60] Indeed such a policy was only formulated and published in 2007.[61] Investors in the pipeline and in gas-using infrastructure had no policy framework to guide their investments. As a consequence, all the foreign companies invited to participate in the pipeline project withdrew and, at the other end of the supply chain, gas-fired power stations were built which, even in 2008, were receiving no gas supply.

Further, as a relic of the Mao era, individual industries in the past appeared to revel in setting themselves extremely ambitious targets and deadlines, most of which were quite unachievable. For example, in the late 1970s the government set long-term production targets for the oil and coal industries for the year 2000 of 200 million tonnes and 2,000 million tonnes, representing a doubling and trebling of output respectively.[62] The target for oil was missed by a long way, but thanks to soaring demand and massive investment, the coal target was met in 2005. Recent commercialisation has dampened this tendency for setting ambitious targets for individual industries. However, the government in 2005 was bold enough to set the objective of reducing energy intensity by 20 per cent between 2006 and 2010, as mentioned in Chapter 2.

In the case where initiatives had wider ramifications, the policy proposals would be subject to bargaining between the various parties and would tend to result in final policies that resulted from a consensus. In such consensus building, a single entity could protect its interests by vetoing a proposal that threatened its vital interests, and thus reform measures intended to produce radical change would be substantially diluted or even stalled completely.

While internal debate and bargaining are characteristics of government decision-making in most political regimes, the structure and nature of China's energy sector has granted considerable bargaining and veto power to the individual ministries and state-owned enterprises.[63] In recent years, efforts to make substantial changes to the energy sector that have a clear policy logic have foundered, with the end result being a compromise, a step of little significance, or a further postponement of the decision. Examples are numerous, and all relate to key aspects of the energy sector.

The 1998 reforms to the petroleum industry were initially intended to create five or more oil companies that would compete with each other in the domestic market, in the same way as the State Power Corporation was later broken up in 2002. Instead, CNPC and Sinopec just underwent an asset swap and retained their de facto duopoly over the domestic markets.[64]

Likewise have the energy companies and the NDRC continued to prevent the re-creation of the Ministry of Energy, a topic that has been on the agenda since at least 2003. These parties succeeded in rendering the Ministry of Energy powerless in the early 1990s. In the same way they have ensured that steps to create a new and powerful energy agency have been reduced to very modest bureaucratic adjustments, as discussed above.[65]

The introduction of a consumer tax, or rather a significant increase of existing taxes on oil products such as gasoline and diesel, has been debated in the National People's Congress since the early 1990s. The aims of the tax were said to be to encourage energy saving, to promote stability in the oil sector, and to assist economic reform. The move was consistently blocked by delegates of the National People's Congress concerned for the impact of this tax on the poorer members of Chinese society. Fuel tax was eventually increased on 1 January 2009, at a time that allowed the government to take advantage of a relatively low level of international oil prices.[66]

A final example concerns the draft Energy Law. The idea of creating an Energy Law came firmly on to the government agenda in 2005 as part of the leadership's drive to constrain energy use and improve the management of the energy sector. The draft itself covers all conceivable aspects of energy production and consumption. It is so ambiguous or self-contradictory on the key points, such as ownership, pricing and access to infrastructure, that it would not appear to be of much value as a tool for charting the future development of the energy sector. The end result of extensive bargaining and compromise is likely to be a document that fails to achieve its intended objective of providing a clear framework for the future development of the nation's energy sector.[67] As of July 2010, there is no sign of the Energy Law being enacted.

Problems in policy implementation

The implementation of a policy can fail for a number of reasons: the concept behind policy itself may be inappropriate or misguided, in particular it may fail to take into account other major policies or certain circumstances that lie in contradiction to the new policy; the details of the policy may have been inadequately thought through before implementation; the consultation during policy-making may have been insufficient to win the support of all key parties; the systems and resources to support policy implementation may be inadequate; or circumstances may change to render the new policy irrelevant.[68]

Within the energy sector, all these types of obstacles may be found. They are exacerbated by a number of other factors specifically, though not uniquely, related to energy. The first is the 'lock-in', which is underpinned by the high capital costs and long lifetimes of much energy infrastructure, as mentioned in Chapter 3. The second is the framework of ideas and beliefs within which energy policy is formulated. This may constrain the development of appropriate policies that may be implemented with ease and success. A third is that the prevailing systems of discourse and governance may not be suited to the implementation of certain energy policies. Finally, energy policies that require the entire population of a country to radically change its behaviour may face profound obstacles if these required new behaviours contradict prevailing aspirations and beliefs.[69]

Energy policy in China suffers from various combinations of these deficiencies. The most prominent derives from active resistance from local governments. This resistance has two sources. First, local governments, even provincial governments, are generally not formally involved in the formulation of national policy, or only marginally. They may push for national policy changes or they may be recipients of national policy initiatives, but unless the policy goes through the National People's Congress, representatives from lower levels of government do not formally draft national policies or have the chance to debate them in an open forum. Second, in the case of energy, natural resources and the environment, the interests of local governments are often diametrically opposed to policy initiatives from the central government. The latter seek to effect long-term management of energy, natural resources and the environment, while the local governments tend to be focused on short-term economic growth. The implementation of national policy is further constrained by the fact that the local bureaus of the ministries report to and are paid by the local governments, not by the central government.[70]

Poor implementation at local level is enhanced by the involvement of local officials in the very businesses they should be regulating, by shortage of trained staff in certain areas, and by the low level of penalties for certain offences. Further, the immaturity of the legal system has the effect of protecting local state-owned enterprises and local governments from prosecution by private parties.

As a result, any measures introduced by the central government that have the effect of reducing local economic activity are highly likely to be resisted by local governments unless the central government employs what would appear to be a disproportionate degree of effort to enforce the new measures, in the form of a campaign.

The production and consumption of energy continues to be a major source of pollution, and environmental protection remains a long-standing problem in China. Despite extensive environmental legislation and despite the progressive upgrading of the status and staff of the Environmental Protection Agency to a ministry, a lack of regulatory resource and authority, weak penalties and local resistance continue to ensure that China has some of the world's most polluted skies and rivers.[71] Likewise, the government has carried out repeated campaigns to close the township and village coal mines. The weakness with such campaigns is that local authorities feign compliance through false reporting. Further, the mines reopen as soon as the campaign ceases, especially if demand for coal is rising, which was the case after the 1998–2001 campaign.[72]

When the Energy Conservation Law was introduced in 1997, it had almost no impact. A few provinces passed local regulations that were just slightly modified from the national law, but little effort was expended in enforcement.[73] The current nationwide programme to enhance energy efficiency appears to have succeeded in overcoming obstruction at provincial level, but is still meeting resistance from lower levels of government and state-owned enterprise, as has been discussed in Chapter 2.

That being said, it would be incorrect to assume that all policy initiatives in the field of energy are doomed to fail. This is clearly not the case, and for one important reason – the authority of the Communist Party. The Party is all pervasive, at all levels of government, in state-owned enterprises and also in the private sector. The Party is the glue that holds the fragmented system together, along with networks of relationships between individual officials and managers.[74] The importance of the Party and of loyalty to national interests is best illustrated by the career progress of officials both in government and in state-owned enterprises. The Party retains tight control over career progression within government and across the wider public sector. Successful and loyal officials at lower levels of government may be promoted to higher levels of government. Thus, the top leadership has tended to be drawn from those who were previously governors or Party Secretary Generals of provinces, or mayors of major municipalities such as Beijing, Shanghai and Tianjin.[75]

Although the most senior leaders tend to have emerged from a career in the Party apparatus, in the ministries or in provincial-level government, a number of senior officials from the state-owned energy enterprises have also been promoted to high government positions. Before he became prime minister in 1987, Li Peng had been Minister for Electrical Power. More recently Zhou Yongkang moved from his position as president of CNPC to be Minister for Land and Resources, then Party Secretary General of Sichuan Province and later Minister for Public Security. As of July 2010, Mr Zhou was on the Politburo Standing Committee, was a state councillor and was Chairman of the Party Central Political Legislative Committee.[76]

The prospects for promotion to the highest levels from all streams of government and state-owned enterprise combined with the near essential requirement to be a Party member in order to rise through the ranks, ensures that policies critical to the survival of the Party and to the security of the state are likely to be decided relatively quickly, are likely to be supported by substantial resources and will be implemented with at least some degree of success. It is because the inadequacy of the energy supply is now seen as a serious threat to the economic interests of the country, and therefore to the interests of the Party, that the government is expending so much effort in implementing the new energy efficiency policies.

The path of China's energy policy

The context in which policy is formulated and the process of policy-making in China results in the overall national energy policy being characterised by, on the one hand, continuity and path-dependency and, on the other hand, by incremental, short-term adjustments.

The path-dependency in China's energy policy arises from a range of constraints in the society, in the institutions of government and in the nature of the energy sector, as discussed in Chapter 3. In the absence of a major economic or political crisis, a sudden and fundamental change in the manner in which the energy sector is managed in the long term is most unlikely. Indeed, the same can be said of all industrialised or industrialising countries. Thus, the general paths that China's energy policy and energy consumption will follow over the coming two decades are relatively predictable, and the most important determinants will be the scale and nature of economic growth. Setting aside the possibility of major domestic crises, it is to be expected that China's demand for energy will continue to grow, albeit at a rate that gradually declines, and the net import requirement for oil, natural gas and possibly coal will also continue to rise.

Set against this path-dependency is a tendency for sudden minor changes. Many policy measures in China are short term in focus, are reactive in character and are liable to rapid reversal or modification. These features, combined with the difficulties associated with policy implementation, render the path of China's energy policy and the outcomes highly unpredictable in the short term. Further, the unwillingness of the government to keep energy policy at or near the top of the agenda for sustained periods of time renders even the long-term impact of major policy initiatives uncertain. This has consequences for those observing energy phenomena within China, as well as for those engaged with China's activities overseas.

In addition, the rapid and sustained growth in China's energy demand taking place in such a policy environment creates and sustains a number of fundamental tensions and contradictions within the energy sector. For example, the problem of keeping up with the rate of growth of demand for energy and trying to keep each link in the energy supply chain expanding rapidly at the same pace and in a coordinated manner distracts policy makers from longer term energy considerations. Second, policy proposals generally fail to address in a satisfactory and sustainable way how the fundamental tensions between the requirements of security of supply will be reconciled with those of social equity, with those of economic competitiveness and efficiency and with those of environmental protection. In the context of China's overseas activities, tensions may be developing between the commercial objectives of the NOCs and the diplomatic goals of the government, as will be discussed in Chapter 6.

The path-dependency of, and the internal inconsistencies within, China's energy policies are not unique, neither is the failure to react to new challenges in a coherent and sustained manner. The energy crises of the 1970s may have succeeded in persuading the governments and societies of OECD countries to radically adapt their energy consumption patterns over just a few years, but many initiatives were reversed after energy prices fell in the mid-1990s.[77]

In recent years, almost without exception, OECD governments have been very slow to adapt their energy policies to address the twin challenges of security of supply and climate change. The complexity of the challenges, the costs of policy implementation and an unwillingness to move ahead of the pack have combined to produce a collective paralysis.[78]

That being said, the path of China's energy policy has more impact on the rest of the world than any other energy importing country, with the exception of the USA. This arises from the scale of its energy sector and of its NOCs, from the sudden short-term changes in its energy and economic policy, and also from the lack of transparency in the policy-making process. These features of scale and unpredictability are exacerbated by a distinct set of ideas, beliefs and traditions that frame the policy-making processes.

The special place of oil in China's energy strategy

Despite these ambiguities and unpredictabilities in policy priorities, policy-making and policy implementation, it is undeniable that oil holds a special position in China's energy strategy, as it does in most other countries.

In an international context, oil's speciality derives from a number of features: its physical properties make it a liquid fuel with a high quantity of energy per unit of volume and of weight, and ideally suited to past and current technologies for transport; conventional geological resources of crude oil are becoming increasingly concentrated in a small number of countries, principally in the Middle East, North Africa and the former Soviet Union; and its fungible nature and the relative ease with which it can be transported around the world have resulted in a market for oil that is essentially global in nature, though with regional hubs. As a consequence, all modern economies rely on oil products to provide transport fuels and vital petrochemicals, and those countries that depend on imported oil are, to a greater or lesser extent, dependent on flows of oil from a few major exporters and on volatile prices set in this global market.

In these respects, China is like any other oil-importing country. What distinguishes China from many other oil importers is the speed with which its status changed from being a major net exporter of oil to becoming the world's fastest growing net importer of oil. In the 1970s and 1980s, oil provided a major source of foreign exchange revenue for the country as well as being a source of energy for domestic industry and power generation.[79] There was even talk of substituting oil for coal. By the late 1990s China's net imports of oil reached the same level as its net exports ten years before, and by 2007 the country was dependent on imports for 50 per cent of its oil consumption. This increasing import dependence has arisen despite great efforts on the part of the NOCs to raise domestic oil production

In the case of China, such a level of import dependence exists for no other form of energy, despite the growing level of natural gas imports and the intermittent periods in which China is a net importer of coal. This loss of self-reliance exposes the country to the vagaries of international markets, with risks relating to price fluctuation and supply interruption, and to rising import costs. Further, it draws the government firmly into the whirlpool of international oil politics. No longer can the country stand aloof from tensions and crises in the international oil arena, as it did in the 1970s. China is now, through necessity rather than choice, a major player. In 2009, the country was the world's second largest consumer of oil, accounting for 9.3 per cent of global demand, and the third largest oil importer, accounting for 7.5 per cent of internationally traded oil. [80]

For these reasons, China's strategy for securing oil supply contains a substantial component that is international in nature, and includes trade, aid, overseas investment, and bilateral and multi-lateral energy diplomacy. This is the subject of the next chapter.

5 China's growing presence in the international oil and gas arena

Introduction

The previous chapters have examined the nature and extent of the energy policy challenges facing China, have identified some important features relating to the formulation and implementation of energy policy in China, and have demonstrated that the country is becoming increasingly dependent on overseas supplies of oil and, to a lesser extent, of natural gas.

The aim of this chapter is to trace China's growing presence in the international oil and gas arena since the 1950s, in order to provide a foundation for an examination of the drivers of the internationalisation of the country's oil in industry in Chapter 6, and for the global political analyses in subsequent chapters.

Early involvement in the international oil and gas arena

The story of China's overseas investment in oil and gas assets may begin in 1992, but the country's involvement in international oil markets started long before that. The year 1957 was a memorable one for China's oil industry. Indeed it could be said to be the year in which the nation's modern oil industry was born, for this was the year in which the giant Daqing oilfield was discovered in Heilongjiang Province of north-east China, with recoverable reserves of about two billion tonnes. Further major discoveries followed in 1962 of the Shengli oilfield in Shandong Province and in 1964 of the Dagang field in Hebei.[1]

Crude oil production rose rapidly from less than one million tonnes per year before 1958 to 14.5 million tonnes by 1966, and 100 million tonnes by 1978.[2] In that year China was the sixth largest producer of oil in the world, only marginally below Iraq, Kuwait and Venezuela.[3]

Having previously been dependent on small oilfields in the far north-west of the country and on imports from the Soviet Union, from the early 1960s to 1992 China produced more oil than it consumed and was a net exporter. From 1975 these net exports amounted to more than 10 per cent of domestic oil production.[4] During the 1980s the level of these net exports consistently exceeded 20 million tonnes per year and in 1985 and 1986 reached 35 million tonnes per year. This latter amount is equivalent to the current annual production of countries such as Egypt, Oman or Argentina, meaning that China in the mid-1980s exported more oil than Norway. The main destinations for this oil were Japan, the USA and Singapore.[5]

The realisation that China was becoming a major producer and exporter of oil coincided with the energy crises of the 1970s, and led to a short-lived period of hysteria concerning the possible emergence of yet another oil exporter capable of holding the world to ransom.[6] Further, as China sought to explore the waters of the South and East China Seas it could threaten the security of east Asia.[7] Some US commentators projected China's output reaching 150–200 million tonnes per year by 1980, with exports of 50 million tonnes per year, and production rising to 350–400 million tonnes per year by 1990. Though such forecasts were quickly shown to be fanciful, China's government itself continued to be optimistic.[8] In the five-year plan for 1985–90 they foresaw oil production rising to 150 million tonnes per year in 1990, only marginally in excess of the 138 million tonnes actually achieved that year.[9]

Though the primary motivation for bringing this new oil discovery into production as fast as possible was to provide China with a source of energy to supplement its domestic coal supply, a secondary but still vital objective was to export the oil in order to earn much needed foreign exchange.

The foreign exchange earned by the export of crude oil and of oil products was used not just to support the petroleum and petro-chemical industries themselves, but also to pay for other critical imports to support industrialisation. Of particular importance within the oil industry was the replacement of outdated Soviet technology and techniques with modern western technologies and approaches. Between 1973 and 1977 China imported more than US$360 million worth of petroleum industry equipment and hosted about three thousand foreign technical experts from western companies.[10] By the mid-1990s revenues from oil exports amounted to US$5–6 billion per year. Even after massive expenditure on imported fertiliser, chemicals and investment on imported plans and equipment, the surplus of foreign exchange available for other sectors still exceeded US$2 billion per year.[11] Of particular importance were the large flows of oil to Japan that provided the foreign exchange to pay for major projects like the Baogang steel plant.[12]

Though the domestic oil industry possessed the technology and skills to further explore and develop the onshore areas, it lacked experience offshore. Thus, in the early 1980s they invited the IOCs to participate in the exploration and development of offshore oil and gas, a policy that continues to the present day. This initiative was soon followed by invitations to cooperate with the NOC in onshore areas.[13]

During the late 1980s the level of China's net exports of oil declined steadily. Not only were exports falling, but imports were rising. Great efforts were being expended to explore the Tarim Basin in the far west of the country for new reserves, supported by Japanese loans, but to little avail. Despite optimistic official announcements that national oil production would reach 200 million tonnes by the year 2000, it was evident to most observers that, in the absence of major new oilfield developments, the rising demand for oil would exceed domestic supply at some time in the early 1990s.

From 1977 to 1987 the annual quantity of crude oil imports fluctuated between 50,000 and 650,000 tonnes, but this rose to 3.3 million tonnes in 1989 and 11.3 million tonnes in 1992. More than half of these crude oil imports came from Southeast Asia, principally from Indonesia, and most of the balance from the Middle East, mainly Oman. Singapore was an important source of oil products, mainly diesel and fuel oil.[14]

From this it is evident that by 1992 China was already a player in the international oil arena, but predominantly in the fields of trading in crude oil and oil products, attracting inward foreign investment, and purchasing foreign technology and skills. The year 1992 saw the start of a new era in China's behaviour. Not only was it the last year in which China was a net exporter of oil, it was the first year of investment in overseas oil reserves by a Chinese company. For the first time China's government and NOCs found themselves having to address risks relating to security of oil supply from overseas. Later in the 1990s, as the government sought to increase the role of natural gas in the country's energy mix, security of supply of international natural gas also became a concern.

Enhancing security of international oil and gas supply

As the country has become progressively more dependent on imports first of oil and then of natural gas, the government has paid increasing attention to the international dimensions of security of supply. Indeed, it can be argued that China expended excessive effort during the late 1990s and early 2000s on international security of supply while ignoring the domestic threats to supply.[15]

The threats that face countries that are dependent on imported oil and gas have been well documented. They fall under two headings: an interruption to or a reduction in the physical flow of energy, and a rise in the price of this energy.[16]

Sources of threat to the physical supply of energy are numerous. Some are short term in their impact, while others are long term. They include: a lack of investment in infrastructure to produce or transport the energy; an embargo on an exporting state; a deliberate withholding of supplies by one or more exporting states; domestic conflict or political instability within an exporting state; and physical disruption of a supply line by terrorism, piracy, armed conflict, political action, accident or technical failure. The twenty-first century has seen the realisation of several of these threats. Investment in oil and gas infrastructure has remained well below what might be considered as adequate levels.[17] Domestic disruption of crude oil supplies has been seen in countries such as Venezuela and Nigeria. Iraq's production remains well below its potential. Piracy off north-east Africa has blossomed. Gas supplies from Russia to Europe have been interrupted.[18] Domestic political action has seen supplies from refineries temporarily curtailed in some European countries. Though we may be far from the days of concerted OPEC action seen in the 1970s, the threats to international flows of oil and gas are significant, varied and sometimes unpredictable.

Likewise, the early years of the twenty-first century have seen fluctuations in the price of crude oil that are unprecedented, even by the standards of the 1970s. Between the beginning of 2002 and the July 2008, international prices for crude oil rose seven-fold from US$20 per barrel to a peak of US$145 per barrel. Allowing for inflation, this peak was 50 per cent higher than that reached in 1979.[19] Over the same period, international prices for natural gas also rose by two- to three-fold. During July 2008, as the significance of the impending financial and economic crisis was becoming apparent, oil prices underwent a rapid slide to US$90 per barrel by September and to a low of US$40 per barrel in at the end of the year. By June 2009 they were up at US$70 per barrel.

Price fluctuations on this scale place great pressure on the governments of energy-importing states. The demand on foreign exchange reserves soars, domestic industry struggles to maintain profits, inflation rises, and the risk of political unrest increases. For the latter three reasons, governments of many developing countries protect their citizens from the impact of rising international prices by constraining domestic price rises. This in turn puts pressure on the government's budget. Developed countries tend to be better equipped to cope with such price rises, through the greater wealth of their governments and citizens, and because the tax imposed on oil products dampens the impact of changes in international prices. However, the industries and citizens of even these developed countries were significantly affected by the price rises seen between 2002 and 2008.

Since the 1970s, importing states have developed a range of measures to address the risks relating to physical supply and price. They fall under two headings: those measures intended to reduce the probability of a risk event and those intended to reduce the negative impact of a risk event should it occur.

Measures aimed at reducing the probability of a risk event may be directed either at wider energy markets or at purely national actions. OECD governments take political steps to enhance the effective operation of international markets in oil and gas, and the IEA is one vehicle for this approach. Political or even military action may be taken in an attempt to enhance supplies from a particular country. Likewise political or legal initiatives may be pursued in an attempt to promote investment in oil and gas producing countries. Short-term disruptions, such as to interruptions to gas supplies from Russia and piracy off north-east Africa, may trigger concerted political or military action.

On a narrower front, governments and companies of energy importing states seek to diversify their sources of supply, to build good relations with their suppliers and to promote the construction of energy transport infra-structure, both domestic and international, which addresses their needs.

Measures to cope with a major risk event and to minimise the negative impact on the economy and on the livelihoods of the citizens are rather more limited in scope, for most of them have to be implementable with short notice. The two most effective instruments are cash and strategic stocks. The government or the oil companies need funds to pay for the increased import bill, and the government can use its budget to pay subsidies to the suppliers or to the users of oil and gas. In addition, the government can construct large stocks of oil and gas that can be drawn down in an emergency, either to supply energy in the instance of a physical disruption of supply or in an attempt to reduce the price. Such stocks may be constructed and managed on an individual country basis or cooperatively, as in the case of the IEA.[20] Finally, the government can invest or require the main energy-intensive industries to invest in fuel switching capacity – that is to say the ability to switch between different fuels at short notice.

Governments may also take longer-term measures to reduce a nation's vulnerability to external supply events. On the supply side, they may encourage production of energy from domestic resources. The traditional approach to raising domestic energy production has been to focus on non-renewable energy resources such as oil, gas and coal. But the gradual depletion of these resources in most OECD countries and elsewhere, together with growing concerns about climate change and other environmental impacts, has driven many governments to decide that the future lies with renewable sources of energy, as they can provide apparently secure domestic energy supply with minimal environmental damage. Likewise, on the demand-side, governments may draw up tough domestic policies to promote greater efficiency in the use of energy that, likewise, may simultaneously address both security of supply and environmental concerns.[21]

Steps taken by China to secure international supplies of oil and gas

Since the early 1990s China's government has taken a number of steps to enhance the nation's security of supply of oil and gas. The measures relating to domestic production of oil and gas and to emergency oil stocks have been outlined in Chapter 2. The steps taken to secure supplies from overseas to a great extent follow the internationally accepted practices outlined in the previous section.

The key priority has been to raise the level of imports of oil and to diversify the sources of these imports.[22] Between 1990 and 1997 imports of crude oil rose from 3 million tonnes to 35 million tonnes and of oil products from 3 million tonnes to 20 million tonnes. At the same time, the level of both crude oil exports and oil products exports was kept constant at about 20 million tonnes and 5 million tonnes a year respectively. Over the ensuing decade, crude oil imports rose at an average annual rate of 8 per cent to reach 200 million tonnes in 2009, while imports of oil products doubled to 40 million tonnes (Figure 2.5).

In order to source these new imports, China sought out new suppliers. Southeast Asia soon lost its importance for oil supply, with the exception of oil products. First the Middle East and then Africa became progressively more important (Figure 5.1). Since 1999, these two regions have consistently accounted for 75–80 per cent of China's crude oil imports, up from 50–60 per cent in the early and mid-1990s. The roles of Russia and Kazakhstan as oil suppliers have also grown. They accounted for 14 per cent of China's imports of crude oil in 2007, though infrastructure capacity constrained their share to just 10 per cent in 2008. In contrast, the proportion of crude oil imports supplied by the Asia-Pacific region declined from 55 per cent in 1994 to 3.5 per cent in 2007. Despite these changes, the sources of supply have remained relatively concentrated, with three countries accounting for nearly 50 per cent of China's crude oil imports in 2008: Saudi Arabia, Angola and Iran with 20 per cent, 17 per cent, and 12 per cent respectively.[23]

China's gas imports are at a relatively low level and, until December 2009, were limited to liquefied natural gas (LNG). Though Australia has been the

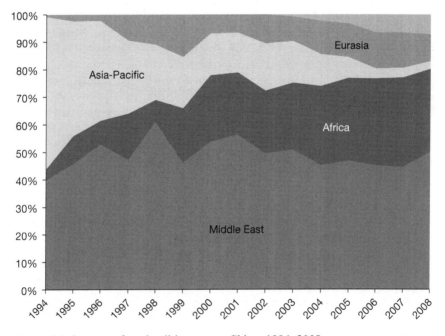

Figure 5.1 Sources of crude oil imports to China, 1994–2008

Sources: C. Tian, 'Review of China's oil imports and exports in 1999'; C. Tian, 'Review of China's oil imports and exports in 2004'; C. Tian, 'Review of China's oil imports and exports in 2008'.

main source of these imports since China's first LNG terminal opened in Guangdong in 2006, two years later China was also drawing on other suppliers such as Oman, Algeria, Egypt, Equatorial Guinea, Nigeria, Ecuador and Malaysia for nearly 20 per cent of the 4.4 billion cubic metres of import requirement in 2008.[24] China's second LNG import terminal opened in Fujian Province in July 2009, taking gas from Indonesia's Tangguh field, and the third terminal, in Shanghai, received its first gas in October 2009, from Malaysia. China's first cargo from Qatar arrived in September 2009, and supply agreements with Qatar and Iran will see an increasing volume of LNG coming from the Middle East.[25] Additional future supplies of imported natural gas are due to come by pipeline from central Asia, Russia and Myanmar.

These supplies from major oil and gas producing states are underpinned by both long-term supply agreements and, as will be discussed below, by wider economic and diplomatic engagement. A further tactic employed in recent years by China's government to secure oil supplies has been to provide financial loans to the NOCs of the producing state. Russia has been the main beneficiary.

After the bankruptcy of Yukos, its assets were sold by auction. In 2005, Rosneft succeeded in acquiring for US$9.3 billion Yukos's most valuable subsidiary, Yuganskneftegaz, through a company called Baikalfinansgroop. As Rosneft was unable to raise this amount of cash from domestic sources, CNPC agreed to lend Rosneft US$6 billion as an advance payment for the future deliveries of 48.4 million tonnes oil between 2005 and 2010. CNPC passed the US$6 billion credit through China's Eximbank to the Russian Vneshtorgbank, which in turn gave the credit to Rosneft. In October 2008, CNPC signed a Memorandum of Understanding in which it agreed to provide Rosneft with an additional loan of US$15 billion and Transneft with US$10 billion, in return for a guarantee that a planned pipeline to China would be completed and that shipments would reach 15 million tonnes per year by 2011.[26]

In February 2009, two other deals were concluded. The China Development Bank agreed to lend Brazil's NOC, Petrobras, US$10 billion in return for supplying between three and five million tonnes per year of crude oil to Sinopec, China's main state-owned refiner, and between two and three million tonnes per year to PetroChina. In Venezuela, China added to the joint fund, which is to be used to finance oil industry projects, bringing the total value of the fund to US$12 billion, of which China has contributed US$8 billion. In return, exports of oil from Venezuela to China are set to rise from 15 million tonnes per year to 50 million tonnes by 2015.[27]

Later in 2009, China's government lent Kazakhstan US$10 billion with two explicit aims. The first was to secure future oil supplies. The second was to allow the Kazakh state company, KazMunaiGas, and CNPC to jointly purchase the independent Kazakh oil producer, MangistauMunaiGas.[28] In the case of Iraq, China did not make new loans but in November 2009 it did agree to forgive 80 per cent of the country's US$8.5 billion of debt, though there does not appear to be a direct connection with the oil deals signed and this debt forgiveness.[29]

A second priority for China has been to construct new infrastructure to deliver imports of oil and gas to China. This has included rail capacity to bring oil from Russia, port capacity to receive marine oil tankers, re-gasification facilities to receive seaborne LNG, and its own oil tanker fleet. But the most important and costly measure has been to embark on the construction of an extensive network of oil and gas import pipelines: from Russia in the north, from central Asia in the west, and from Myanmar in the south-west. These pipelines have three objectives: first to bring oil and gas from key neighbouring suppliers to China by a direct route; second to reduce China's dependence on seaborne imports and thus its vulnerability to disruption of shipping anywhere in the world; and finally, in the case of the pipelines through and from Myanmar, to reduce dependence on the sea lanes off south and east Asia, especially the Malacca Straits through which some 80 per cent of China's oil imports flow.[30]

Negotiations on the construction of oil and gas pipelines between Russia and China have been going on for more than twenty years, but started in earnest in 1994 with the establishment of a 'strategic partnership between' the two countries.[31] The initial ideas related to bringing gas from the Kovytka field in Eastern Siberia to China, but the first concrete plan was drawn up by Yukos and CNPC in 2001 to bring oil from Siberia to China. The subsequent nationalisation of Yukos assets and a dramatic change in Russian domestic energy policy delayed agreement over an oil pipeline. As a result nearly all oil imports to date from Russia have been by rail. A small proportion has come by ship from Iran and Sakhalin. The first direct oil imports by pipeline are planned for late 2010 or 2011, but the construction of a gas pipeline continues to be postponed despite continuing discussions on the subject.[32]

As a result of the delays to the construction of the oil pipeline from Russia, the Chinese government decided to switch its focus from Russia to Kazakhstan. In 2003 it made the decision to construct a pipeline to bring oil from Kazakhstan to western China. This was completed in 2005, with an initial capacity of 10 million tonnes per year, which will rise to 20 tonnes per year by 2011 or 2012.[33] A second pipeline is now under construction. As mentioned in Chapter 2, a gas import pipeline from Turkmenistan was completed at the end of 2009 with an initial annual capacity of 4.5 billion cubic metres. This should rise to 30 billion cubic metres by the end of 2013.[34]

To the south-west, the governments of Myanmar and China signed an agreement in March 2009 to construct two pipelines, for oil and for gas. The oil pipeline will carry crude oil to China, which has been shipped from Africa and the Middle East to the port of Kyaukpyu in Myanmar. Construction started on the oil pipeline in October 2009. The initial capacity will be 12 million tonnes per year, rising to a maximum of 20 million tonnes The gas pipeline is planned to bring 12 billion cubic metres per year by 2012 from gas fields in Myanmar operated by CNPC.[35]

The third component of China's international oil and gas strategy has been the investment in overseas oil and gas assets by the NOCs. Such a measure is not considered to be a normal part of security of supply policy in OECD countries, not least because most national oil companies have been privatised. But also there is strong scepticism that access to oil and gas reserves and production in remote countries can indeed contribute to national security of supply in the event of an international supply crisis.[36]

Notwithstanding this scepticism, China and a number of other oil-importing states in Asia, such as India, Japan and South Korea, continue to pursue the policy of encouraging such investment. In the case of China, the scale and scope of these investments has been quite unprecedented in the history of world oil. These investments, rather than the imports of oil and gas and the construction of pipelines, have been the major source of concern for governments around the world. For this reason, the remainder of the chapter is devoted to examining the progressive expansion of China's global investment in international oil and gas reserves.

China's overseas investment in oil and gas: 1992–2008

The period 1992 to 1995 saw CNPC make small investments in existing oilfields in Canada, Thailand and Peru, as well as in exploration acreage in Papua New Guinea.[37] At the same time CNOOC bought shares in a producing field in Indonesia. These were all small projects with investment commitments of a few million or tens of millions of dollars, and, with the exception of the project in Papua New Guinea, were all directed at fields with proven reserves. In addition, none of these countries are or were among the world's leaders in terms of oil reserves or exports. This could be seen as a phase of experimentation and learning, with low risk.[38]

The years 1996 and 1997 saw a sudden surge in the level of investment, with major commitments being made by CNPC in three countries that were seen to have the potential to produce substantial quantities of oil: Kazakhstan, Venezuela and Sudan. The largest commitment was in Kazakhstan where the company bought a share of two producing fields, Aktyubinsk and Uzen, for several billion dollars. In Venezuela and Sudan CNPC spent several hundred million dollars buying in to proven oilfields as well as the opportunity to explore for new reserves. At the same time deals were struck in Iraq and Nigeria, and CNPC's service companies were entering major contracts in such countries as Kuwait, Egypt, and Turkmenistan.[39]

By 1998 this surge had waned. International oil prices had fallen from an average of US$18 per barrel in 1996 and 1997 to just US$12 per barrel in 1998, and at home the Chinese NOCs were going through a major restructuring. Though incremental deals were signed in Nigeria, Sudan and Venezuela, almost no initiatives to access reserves in new countries were taken between 1998 and 2001. One exception lay in the initial steps taken by both CNPC and Sinopec to establish a position in Iran through undertaking service and construction contracts, both upstream and downstream.

The next five years, from 2002 to 2006, saw a rapid growth of levels of outward investment by China's oil industry and this, in part, paralleled the rise in international oil prices. An estimated twenty billion dollars were committed in many tens of projects in more than 30 countries, and 75 per cent of this was contracted in the two years 2005 and 2006.[40] Such a level of overseas investment by a single country's NOCs was quite unprecedented. The destination countries included major oil and gas producers in the Commonwealth of Independent States, in the Middle East and in Africa such as Russia, Kazakhstan, Iran, Saudi Arabia, Libya, Algeria, Angola and Nigeria. In addition to these potential major sources of oil and gas, target countries were spread across the African and South American continents, as well as south and east Asia and Australia

This phase was distinguished from the previous ten years not just in terms of the scale of investment and its geographical spread, but also by the wider scope of activity as well as by the bolder means for acquiring assets.[41] Earlier investments had been directed principally at known oilfields. This new phase saw more exploration acreage being acquired and a greater interest in natural gas. After years of discussion, plans to construct pipelines to bring oil and gas into China from neighbouring countries were firmly back on the agenda. Further, China's companies started to engage in projects requiring technologies with which they were quite unfamiliar, for example deep-water exploration off West Africa, tar sands in Canada and LNG in Iran. But despite this diversity of geographic location and project type, the large majority of investments continued to flow into oil production in Kazakhstan, Sudan and West Africa.

The second distinguishing feature of the period 2002 to 2006 was the increased boldness displayed by China's oil companies in pursuit of corporate acquisitions.[42] The year 2002 saw success in the acquisition of clusters of fields in Indonesia through purchases of the local assets of Devon Energy by PetroChina and of Repsol-YPF by CNOOC. The same year saw CNPC fail in its attempt to take over Russia's Slavneft.

In 2003 Sinopec and CNOOC together made a bid of US$1.2 billion to buy BG's 16.7 per cent share of the giant Kashagan field in Kazakhstan. This was blocked by BG's partners who invoked their pre-emption rights. Two years later CNPC took over PetroCanada's assets in Syria and Encana's fields in Ecuador. But the highlight of 2005 was CNOOC's failed attempt to buy Unocal on account of obstruction by Congress.[43] Despite these setbacks, Sinopec purchased Ominex Resources' assets in Colombia and in Kazakhstan, CNPC acquired the Canadian company PetroKazakhstan and, in 2006, the CITIC Group bought Nations Energy, also from Canada.

The period 2007 to 2008 saw a lull in major new investment commitments. This was probably on account of the companies' needs to fulfil existing commitments and the very high level of oil prices that drove up the price of assets. CNPC was the most active, as usual, building on existing positions in countries such as Canada, Sudan, Niger, Uzbekistan, and Venezuela. CNPC's Russian joint venture, Vostok Energy, won its first exploitation and development licence.

The most important achievement was the signing of a contract for the Al-Ahdab oilfield in Iraq, a project that had lain in abeyance since an initial signing in 1997. Likewise Sinopec was awarded a contract to develop Iran's Yadavaran gas field and purchased a share of some oilfields in the Timor Sea, off Australia. Though CNOOC had failed in completing major acquisitions, it had used its funds to build on its strong position in gas production in Australia. In July 2008, CNOOC's subsidiary, China Oilfield Services, spent US$2.5 billion to buy the Norwegian oilfield service company, Awilco Offshore.[44]

A resurgence of activity since 2009

The early months of 2009 were dominated by negotiations over pipelines and by loans-for-oil deals, as discussed above. But the rest of 2009 and the first half of 2010 saw China's NOCs spend more than US$20 billion in major acquisitions and licence deals. Most of these deals gave the NOCs access to proven oil and gas reserves, rather than to exploration acreage. This resurgence in investment was not kept secret. Indeed it was well-publicised, especially by CNPC/PetroChina. In August 2009, CNPC announced its intention to accelerate overseas acquisitions and by September it had secured a US$30 billion, five-year, low-interest loan from the China Development Bank.[45] In May 2010, PetroChina claimed that it would spend US$60 billion over the following decade to boost its overseas businesses.[46] Sinopec, CNOOC and Sinochem have also taken part in this spending spree. The principal geographical targets for these investments have been the Middle East and Latin America, with Canada playing a smaller role.

CNPC succeeded in boosting its position in Iran, having been a marginal player. The company signed separate agreements giving it the right to develop the North and South Azadegan fields, which together have a potential to produce 20 million tonnes of oil per year. Iran also chose CNPC to replace the French company, Total, as the main foreign participant in the development of Phase 11 of the South Pars gas field. This field has the potential to produce up to 17 billion cubic meters of gas per year. It remains to be seen whether CNPC is more successful than other Chinese NOCs at turning agreements into actual production. CNOOC and Sinopec both face delays in executing their plans to develop the North Pars and Yadavaran field respectively. China's presence in Iran's oil sector is further enhanced by the engagement of its oil companies in the upgrading and expansion of the country's oil refineries, and in supplying the state with a supply of oil products in defiance of international sanctions.[47] Despite these apparent successes, the ability of China's NOCs to implement these projects continues to be neutralised by the ongoing UN sanctions on Iran.

Chinese companies have also gained assets in Iraq and these are more likely to be productive than those in Iran. In June 2009, the Swiss oil company, Addax, revealed that its board had agreed a takeover of the company by China's Sinopec and that the deal would include some 42 million barrels of oil in the Kurdish region of Iraq.[48] This deal pales in comparison to those struck by the other Chinese NOCs later that year. In the first formal bidding round for fields in southern Iraq, CNPC in partnership with BP won the rights to develop the giant South Rumaila oilfield, which holds about 17 billion barrels of oil-in-place and should yield about 50 million tonnes per year. In the second round, at the end of 2009, CNPC signed an agreement to develop the 4 billion barrel Halfaya field in collaboration with Total, Petronas and Iraq's South Oil Company. In the same round, CNOOC was granted the rights to develop the 2.5 billion barrel Missan oilfield in partnership with the Turkish Petroleum Corporation (TPAO).[49] Meanwhile, Sinopec seems to be prohibited from doing deals in Iraq's heartland after its venture in the Kurdish region.[50]

In Latin America, China's NOCs took steps to establish themselves as major players in Argentina, Brazil and Venezuela over a period of just three months. In March 2010, CNOOC paid US$3.1 billion for a 50 per cent share of the Argentine company, Bridas Corporation, which has assets across Latin America. The following month, in Brazil, Sinopec signed a strategic agreement with Petrobras and the China Development Corporation that might lead to Sinopec gaining shares in two deep-water exploration blocks. At the same time, PetroChina signed an agreement with Venezuela to cooperate and provide the finance for the development of the Junin-4 heavy oilfield, which is believed to contain nearly nine billion barrels of recoverable reserves. In May, Sinochem purchased from Statoil a 40 per cent stake in the Brazilian heavy oilfield, Peregrino for US$3.1 billion.[51]

In Canada, both PetroChina and Sinopec established themselves in the oil sands play. In September 2009, after years are dithering over Canada's oil sands, PetroChina paid US$1.7 billion for a 60 per cent stake of two new projects owned by the Athabasca Oil Sands Company. In the second quarter of 2010 Sinopec paid US$4.65 billion to ConocoPhillips for its 9 per cent share of the Syncrude project and boosted its share in the Northern Lights project by 10 per cent to 50 per cent.[52]

In the USA, CNOOC bought from Statoil a share of four oilfields in the deep-water Gulf of Mexico position, marking the first arrival of Chinese NOCs in this basin. In the southern hemisphere, Shell and PetroChina teamed up to buy the Australian company, Arrow Energy, in order to gain access to the country's coal-bed methane resources.[53]

CNPC further strengthened its position in Kazakhstan during 2009, by joining with the Kazakh state oil company to buy MangistauMunaiGas from an Indonesian company. The sovereign wealth fund, China Investment Corporation, appeared on the oil and gas scene for the first time in 2009 signing a deal with Nobel Oil to gain access to three oilfields in Russia and buying an 11 per cent stake in KazMunaiGas of Kazakhstan.[54]

This period also saw CNPC/PetroChina take a major step towards increasing its overseas refining and trading assets. In May 2009, PetroChina spent US$1 billion to buy from the Keppel Corporation a 45 per cent stake in the Singapore Petroleum Corporation, and was expected to buy the remaining shares. In

Sudan CNPC agreed to expand its refinery at Khartoum. Further afield, CNPC was for a short time reported to be seeking to take over Ineos, a British refining and petrochemical company, and received agreement from the Venezuelan government to build a large refinery in the country in partnership with PDVSA, the Venezuelan NOC.

Conclusions

In this chapter we have reviewed the last fifty years of China's engagement with international oil markets. Having been an importer of oil in the 1950s, China became a significant net exporter of oil during the 1960s, even to the extent of creating a fear in some quarters in the West during the 1970s that it was about to become as important as the main OPEC oil producers. This threat never materialised as China's domestic demand for oil was growing too fast. Instead, China remained a significant net exporter of oil until the late 1980s when the rate of growth of domestic production started to fall behind the rate of growth of domestic demand.

By 1993 China was a net importer of oil and within fifteen years the country was relying on imports for 50 per cent of its annual consumption, despite continuing efforts to raise domestic oil production and to seek savings in oil consumption.

The government progressively embarked on a wide range of strategies to enhance security of oil supply, including the diversification of sources of supply, building strategic oil stocks, engaging in energy diplomacy and enhancing the capabilities of its navy. But none of these measures has captured as much attention from the international community as the massive surge in investment in international oil and gas assets by Chinese NOCs.

As a result of eighteen years of expansion of their overseas activities, by the year 2010 Chinese oil companies had a stake in more than 200 projects in about fifty countries (Table 5.1). The value of these projects was estimated at more than US$60 billion, as of September 2009.[55] By the middle of 2010 additional investments may have added 30 per cent to this aggregate value. Though this appears to be a large amount of money, it should be compared to the annual investment in exploration and production of the major international oil companies in 2008 alone, which amounted to US$20 billion or more for each of ExxonMobil, Shell and BP. China's NOCs have some way to go before they are big players on the international scene, but they are making rapid progress.

The data available at March 2009 shows that sub-Saharan Africa and the former Soviet Union each accounted for 30 per cent of the Chinese overseas upstream investment, with the Middle East and North Africa amounting to just 25 per cent, and the Americas just 5 per cent.[56] The successes of 2009 and 2010 have probably placed the Middle East and North Africa ahead of the other regions, and have greatly enhanced the relative importance of the Americas for the Chinese NOCs.

Table 5.1 Destinations of direct overseas investment in upstream assets by Chinese NOCs

C.I.S.	Middle East and North Africa	Sub-Saharan Africa	S, SE and NE Asia, Australia	Americas
Azerbaijan	Algeria	Angola	Australia	Bolivia
Kazakhstan	Chad	Cameroon	East Timor	Brazil
Kyrgyzstan	Egypt	Congo Brazzaville	Indonesia	Canada
Russia	Iraq	Cote d'Ivoire	Mongolia	Colombia
Turkmenistan	Iran	Equatorial Guinea	Myanmar	Costa Rica
Uzbekistan	Libya	Egypt	Pakistan	Cuba
	Mali	Ethiopia	Papua New Guinea	Ecuador
	Mauritania	Gabon	Philippines	Peru
	Morocco	Kenya	Thailand	USA
	Niger	Madagascar		Venezuela
	Oman	Mozambique		
	Qatar	Nigeria		
	Saudi Arabia	Sao Taome		
	Somalia	Sudan		
	Syria	Tanzania		
	Tunisia			
	UAE			
	Yemen			

Sources: Bo Kong, *China's International Petroleum Policy;* FACTS Global Energy, *China's Overseas Oil and Gas Investment: Recent Developments*, China Energy Series, Gas edition, December 2009.

The production of equity oil from the overseas investments of China's top three NOCs (CNPC, Sinopec and CNOOC) in 2007 amounted to 42 million tonnes, or some 18 per cent of the total oil production of these companies.[57] This rose to 45 million tonnes in 2008.[58] By 2009, the overseas equity production for CNPC alone amounted to 34 million tonnes of oil and 5.5 billion cubic meters of gas, 25 per cent and 7 per cent respectively of its total output.[59] Overseas equity oil and gas production as a share of total company production in that year is estimated at 20 per cent for CNOOC and 12 per cent for Sinopec.[60] Total overseas equity oil production for Chinese NOCs could reach 100 million tonnes per year by 2020.[61]

The scope of activities of China's oil service and engineering companies is even wider than those of the exploration and production companies, for the service and engineering companies operate not just alongside the exploration and production companies but also in countries where the oil companies have no investments. In 2007 alone, CNPC had fifty-five seismic crews and 174 drilling rigs operating outside China, with completed engineering and construction contracts worth US$3.6 billion and exported technology and equipment worth US$1.2 billion.[62]

In the next chapter we examine in more detail the driving forces behind this internationalisation of China's oil industry.

6 Strategies and driving forces behind the internationalisation of China's oil industry

Introduction

This chapter could have been entitled 'China's international oil and gas strategy', but that would have given the impression that a single coherent strategy was formulated to which all actors subscribe and that this strategy has continued relatively unchanged since the early 1990s. Such an impression would be false, for two reasons. First, there are multiple actors with differing interests. These actors lie within the government and in industry. Second, their interests have evolved in response to domestic and international events and trends, and as the actors' understanding of international energy markets and investment has developed.

The aim of this chapter is to examine the strategies and driving forces behind the expansion of overseas activities described in Chapter 5. A key focus for this analysis is the investments made by China's oil companies in overseas assets, and the degree of convergence or divergence between the interests of China's government and those of its NOCs. We will argue that the 1990s and possible the early 2000s were characterised by a strong convergence of interests, but that recent years have seen a growing divergence as the government seeks to respond to wider diplomatic challenges, while the NOCs press on with their commercial agendas. At the same time, a number of foreign governments that initially welcomed China's investments in their oil and gas sectors are tempering their enthusiasm in response to political or commercial concerns.

The corporate actors and their strategies

The growth of overseas investment has been so rapid and so diverse that it would be easy to conclude that no coherent corporate strategy lay behind it. While individual corporate strategies may indeed have been incomplete and opportunistic, a number of patterns can be seen in the eighteen years 1993–2010 concerning the geographic location, and the nature of the projects.

Though investments are spread across nearly sixty countries, four considerations would appear to lie behind the relative emphasis placed on different countries at different times.[1] First, China's oil companies, like all oil companies, want to own assets where the reserves of oil and gas are largest. Thus they have been patiently seeking opportunities in such countries as Iran, Saudi Arabia, Iraq and Russia, which between them hold 45 per cent of the world's conventional oil reserves and 40 per cent of the gas reserves. Second, they have directed considerable effort build current and future production in areas that can deliver oil and gas directly to China by pipeline or by rail. These mainly lie in the adjacent and nearby countries of the former Soviet Union. Kazakhstan and Russia are the prime examples, but gas also flows from Turkmenistan and Uzbekistan to China. To the south, CNPC is involved in building oil and gas import pipelines from Myanmar.

The third feature is the apparent preference for countries where competition from other oil companies, particularly the IOCs, is small. Most notable among these are countries where the international companies are barred by sanctions or discouraged on the grounds of corporate reputation, for example Sudan, Iran, Myanmar, Syria and Iraq under Saddam Hussein. Other examples include countries where most international companies consider that the rewards do not justify the political risk involved, or where the geological prospectivity is perceived to be poor. Thus Chinese oil companies have been active in such countries as Ethiopia, Kenya, Cote D'Ivoire, Thailand and the Philippines

Finally, Chinese oil companies have been drawn to areas that have high quality, light, sweet crude oils. China's own crude oil is sweet and thus its older domestic refineries were constructed to take this type of feedstock.[2] 'Sour' crude oils, which have a high sulphur content and which are highly corrosive, require refineries built to a much higher specification. Thus in the 1990s most of the country's imports came from Southeast Asia and from Oman and Yemen where the crude oils are sweet. In the late 1990s, China embarked on a programme of upgrading existing refineries and building new refineries in order to be able to take the sour crude oils from the major Middle East exporters such as Saudi Arabia and Iran.[3] Despite the enhanced capabilities of the domestic refineries, China's NOCs show similar preferences to the IOCs when they seek to exploit high value, sweet crude oils, notably from West Africa. This explains the particular interest of Chinese companies in Nigeria and Angola, as well as Equatorial Guinea, Gabon, and Sao Tome.

The three major Chinese oil companies have distinct patterns of investment that build on their pre-existing experience and expertise, at least until recently.[4] CNPC and its subsidiary PetroChina have a long experience of exploration and development of onshore oilfields. They have particular expertise in the development of marginally economic fields and in enhancing production from fields from which production is declining. Much of this expertise lies in CNPC's service companies. These companies also have experience in constructing oilfield facilities and pipelines. This capacity, along with a high level of profits from its operations in China at times of high oil prices, has allowed CNPC to expand rapidly into major international onshore field operations and to undertake massive and complex construction projects in a timely manner, for example in Sudan. The company has been slower to take on refinery projects, except where they are associated with its oil production, for example in Sudan, Algeria, Nigeria, Kazakhstan and Chad. The acquisition of Singapore Petroleum in 2009 marked a new determination by PetroChina to become involved in downstream activities away from its centres of production. The scale and experience of CNPC and its relationship with IOCs has given it a strong advantage to compete successfully for very large opportunities when they become available.

Sinopec, with its downstream focus and with a lower level of profits in China, has necessarily been slower, more cautious and more selective in its internationalisation. Only since 2004 has Sinopec has entered into significant upstream commitments in countries such as Angola, Russia, Iran, and Algeria. In the case of Angola, it was the first Chinese oil company to engage in deep-water exploration and production. Sinopec was also one of the few companies to win exploration rights for gas in Saudi Arabia, in 2004. Even in refining, the company is only active in Iran.

CNOOC has a history and culture quite different from that of CNPC and Sinopec, for it was created relatively recently, in 1983, with the specific aim of cooperating with international companies. Thus, by the mid-1990s the staff had already gained a substantial understanding of international practices and technologies. It was also much smaller and had a less bureaucratic management system. Yet CNOOC's experience was limited in scope to the exploration and production offshore, and then only in relatively shallow waters.

Of the three major NOCs, CNOOC has had the most tightly defined scope of activities. Southeast Asia has formed the core area for investment, right from the start and, in line with its involvement in LNG imports into China, the company has succeeded in expanding its involvement in the region's gas production, notably in Australia and Indonesia. More recently it has become increasingly active in offshore Africa, West and East. Its greatest upset was the failure to acquire Unocal in 2005. Its greatest success may prove to be negotiating the rights to the North Pars gas field in Iran. The years 2009 and 2010 saw CNOOC take decisive steps to establish itself in the Americas, especially with its 50 per cent stake in Bridas.

These three oil companies have slightly differing forms of corporate involvement in overseas investment. In the cases of CNPC and Sinopec, the overseas assets may be held by either the fully state-owned holding company or by the listed subsidiary, or jointly. Generally, assets in politically sensitive countries are managed by the holding company and the listed arm holds the others. In contrast, it is the listed arm, CNOOC Ltd, which owns all the overseas investments of the CNOOC.

The other significant Chinese oil company investing overseas is Sinochem. This company was created in 1950 with the sole purpose of carrying out international trade in oil and chemicals, and with monopoly powers. As all the other oil companies in China now have the right to trade, Sinochem is acquiring overseas oil and gas fields in order to assure itself a future. Its focus has been on North Africa and the Middle East. The purchase, in 2009, of Emerald Energy and, in 2010, of a share of the Peregrino field saw it take a strong position in Latin America.

One common component of the strategies of all four companies is that of opportunism, and at no time has this been more evident than in the period 2009 to 2010. The financial crisis that started in July 2008 left the Chinese NOCs and the Chinese state banks relatively unscathed. The scale of the financial resources available to the Chinese oil companies was vastly greater than the IOCs could draw on, reliant as they were on western banks that were struggling to rebuild their balance sheets. At the same time, most host country governments were themselves also short of funds for urgently needed investments to raise domestic oil or gas production. This combination of circumstances was ideal for China's NOCs to go on a spending spree from the middle of 2009.

This recent period has also seen CNPC and Sinopec make bold moves to take significant stakes in unconventional oil and gas reserves; in the Canadian tar sands and in Australian coal-bed methane.

As impressive as this year of activity, to mid-2010, has been, with some US$20 billion of investment in new projects and acquisitions, it may only be the start of a new phase of internationalisation of the China's oil and gas industry.

Corporate tactics for securing deals

A wide variety of options exist for China's NOCs to acquire the rights to explore for oil and gas or to develop and produce from proven fields: participating in a open tender, possibly in a licensing round; buying a share of a field from an owner seeking to reduce their share or to sell out completely; buying an entire field or suite of fields from a company, or buying a local subsidiary from a multinational company; buying shares in an oil company in order to gain access to assets in a specific country; forming a joint venture with a local company; negotiating directly with the host government or the NOC to gain rights to assets or acreage; and, finally, acquiring a whole company.

Chinese oil companies have pursued every one of these tactics in their overseas expansion, and which option they have chosen has depended on the nature of the opportunities and on the local conditions. It is not by chance that some of the biggest deals have been done away from the public eye, in direct negotiation with host governments or NOCs, for example, in Sudan, Iran, Kazakhstan, Russia and Angola. Even some smaller deals, such as those in Myanmar, have been concluded in this fashion. In such cases the Chinese companies tend to receive direct and explicit political support from their government that may also be backed by loans from the one of China's development banks. Of these the most active is the China EXIM Bank. This makes loans available both for specific projects, for example, in Sudan and

Nigeria, or for the construction of infrastructure by the host government, as in Angola.[5]

Though some of the largest and most strategically important projects do receive such political support, in most cases the Chinese companies are purchasing on the open market in the same way as other oil companies. On some such occasions, especially when the prize has been substantial, the Chinese company has won the bid only to find that its bid was far in excess of that needed to secure the asset. Such overbidding is deemed to have occurred in Venezuela, Kazakhstan, Angola and Saudi Arabia, as well as in the failed bids for Slavneft and Unocal.[6] Such aggressive behaviour may be attributed to a mix of inexperience and undisciplined desperation. It may also result from a different view of future oil prices, lower commercial thresholds, a lower cost of capital, and a recognition that more has to be paid by latecomers to the international oil arena. But overbidding is also just part of the experience of any oil company operating internationally and, overall, the Chinese NOCs have probably paid no more per barrel of oil than their international counterparts.[7]

Such a bidding strategy, if it be so, is assisted by their strong financial positions. The high level of crude oil prices since 2003, both internationally and in China, has resulted in all three of China's main oil companies having sufficient retained earnings to pay for all but the largest projects.[8] This strong financial position has been further enhanced by the absence, until 2008, of a requirement to pay dividends to the government as shareholder, as well as by some favourable tax treatment in comparison with others sectors during the years after the 1998 reform.[9] All of China's NOCs are able to take advantage of low-interest loans from state-owned policy banks. In 2009, for example, the China Development Bank provided CNPC with a five-year, low-interest loan valued at US\$30 billion.[10]

In addition to cash and loans, China's oil companies draw on a much wider armoury of instruments to gain access to reserves and to bring greater benefits to themselves. The contracts to explore and develop oil and gas fields may be explicitly or implicitly linked to the construction of oil refineries or export pipelines within the host country and to long-term agreements to export oil to China. In addition, the Chinese oil companies bring their own service and construction companies. The most complete example is CNPC's involvement in Sudan where the company has been responsible for the development of almost an entire petroleum industry.[11] Investments in Kazakhstan and Turkmenistan have also linked production, export agreements and pipelines. Not all attempts to use one project to leverage another are successful. In both Angola and Nigeria, proposals to build an oil refinery have been scrapped or have run into difficulties.[12]

Further bait that the Chinese oil companies can offer is the opportunity for the NOC from the host country to invest in refinery, petrochemical and other downstream projects in China. This has proved particularly attractive to the major oil producers in the Middle East, such as Saudi Arabia and Kuwait, which have plenty of cash and wish to integrate their business downstream and gain a foothold in what will soon be one of the world's largest oil markets.[13] The first of these was Saudi Aramco, which entered negotiations with Sinopec as early as 1993 to construct new refining capacity at Qingdao, in Shandong Province. This project only came onstream in 2008 and without the participation of Saudi Aramco who, in late 2009, were still negotiating participation with Sinopec. Saudi Aramco's first cooperative refinery project with Sinopec, in Fujian Province, was commissioned in 2009. Another Saudi company, Saudi Basic Industries Corporation (SABIC), plans to build a cracking plant in Tianjin, while the Kuwait Petroleum Corporation and the Qatar Petroleum Company also plan to build refinery and petrochemical plants. These companies also plan to be involved in the construction of oil storage facilities as well as participating in the retail of oil products.

In addition to the service and construction companies, China's shipping companies are also riding on the back of these overseas activities. Keen to take advantage of the growing quantities of oil being shipped to China from around the world, whether or not it be Chinese equity oil, the shipping companies are investing heavily in a rapid expansion of their tanker fleets. In 2007 Chinese-owned tankers carried just 20 per cent of oil arriving in the country. This is set to rise to 50 per cent in 2010 and 75 per cent by 2020; and these percentages are of ever increasing absolute quantities of oil.[14]

Although China's NOCs do indeed have oil production and oil export agreements in the same countries, it is certainly not the case that all or even most equity oil production is sent back to China nor that the oil provided under the export agreement is the same oil as that produced under the production agreement. Though detailed statistics are not published through official channels, it appears that most equity oil production to date has been sold to international markets rather than being sent back to China, for a number of reasons: the company may choose to get a better price for the oil on the open market; the crude oil may be sour and therefore less suitable for Chinese refineries; or there may be no infrastructure to take the oil to China.[15]

China's companies undertake most of their investments in partnership with one or more other companies. This is a standard practice in the industry to spread risk and capital requirements. Indeed in many countries it is a legal requirement for a foreign investor to involve the host national company. Chinese companies display four types of behaviour in their choice of operating partners, depending on local circumstances and on the technological challenges of the project. In a few examples the Chinese company is the sole investor. This tends to be the case in smaller projects and where there is no requirement to have a local partner, particularly in Africa. In many countries the host NOC is a partner either in a joint venture company or as a participant in a production sharing agreement, for example in Sudan, Russia, Algeria, Libya, Kazakhstan, Uzbekistan, Venezuela, Nigeria, Iran and Myanmar.

For projects with technological requirements or with risks beyond their capacity, Chinese companies join consortia led by IOCs or establish new partnerships with them, as this is the only way to gain access to these resources. Such cooperation forms a vital part of the corporate learning experience. The years 2009 and 2010 have seen all of China's NOCs substantially enhance the scale and scope of their activities that involve collaboration with IOCs outside China: in the large, complex oilfields of Iraq; in the tar sands of Canada; in Australian coal-bed methane basins; and in the deep-water plays of Brazil and the USA. Not all of these partnerships are one-off deals. Rather, certain companies appear to be forming long-term strategic partnerships with specific objectives, particularly in the case of gas. Examples include Shell and PetroChina, with shared interests in China, Qatar and Australia, and CNOOC and BG. Both these partnerships are directed as much at the exploitation of domestic gas resources within China as at the development of overseas gas resources and their shipment back to China.

Finally, in a few countries, the Chinese NOC has chosen as partners NOCs from other developing states. Sudan is the prime example of this. Here, Petronas of Malaysia and ONGC of India are longstanding partners of CNPC. ONGC is also partnering with CNPC in Syria and with Sinopec in Colombia and Cote D'Ivoire. Though ONGC may, in some cases, be a preferred partner, and though the governments of China and India have pledged cooperation through their NOCs, these companies often end up bidding against each other, for example in Kazakhstan and Angola.[16]

From the foregoing description it is evident that China's NOCs have expanded into the international oil and gas arena with increasing determination and speed. While concrete evidence is not available, it would appear that this haste may have been caused by a perception that there was a limited window of opportunity provided by favourable conditions, the duration of which remain uncertain. These conditions include the strong position of the companies in the Chinese domestic markets, their favourable tax and dividend treatment, the support received from the Chinese government and banks, the recent high level of crude oil prices both at home and abroad, and the current financial crisis. Further, the companies have proved very adept at influencing China's national energy policy and using these policies as levers for gaining support from the government for their overseas activities.[17]

The role of China's government

China's government is far from being a passive partner in the overseas activities of the NOCs. Indeed it was evident from the earliest days that the government had a key role to play in supporting the companies and, in some cases, creating the opportunities.[18]

The desire to build closer political and economic relations with key oil and gas producers has been high on the government's diplomatic agenda since the early 1990s. In some cases this had to start from scratch with the establishment or re-establishment of formal diplomatic relations, for example, in 1990 with both Indonesia and Saudi Arabia. Indeed, in a number of African countries China has succeeded in persuading governments of resource-rich countries to switch their recognition from Taiwan to the People's Republic.[19]

For obvious reasons, diplomatic efforts relating to energy have been focused on selected targets: those countries with the largest reserves, for example, in the Middle East; those countries with reserves and which are close to China, as is the case with Kazakhstan, Russia and Turkmenistan; those countries with reserves and which have special political relations with China, such as Iran, Venezuela and Sudan; countries that have large reserves of high-value, sweet crude oil, for example, Angola and Nigeria; and countries that lie along existing or potential oil transportation routes, particularly in South Asia, for example Myanmar.[20]

China's engagement with such countries of strategic importance is multi-faceted and highly variable, and in some cases energy may not be the most important component of the relationship. As is the case with China's NOCs, the government has a range of instruments it can and does deploy. In addition to deepening bilateral relations and holding high-level summit meetings, China may provide active political support for the host government on the international stage, for example at the UN Security Council in the cases of Sudan, Myanmar and Iran (see Chapters 8, 9 and 10). Political support extends to the supply of military weapons and training, again in Sudan, Myanmar and Iran, as well as Equatorial Guinea, Ethiopia, Eritrea, Burundi, Tanzania, and Zimbabwe (see Chapter 10). More common is the provision of packages of economic measures that may include financing for oil and gas projects, loans for other infrastructure projects, credit lines and debt write-offs for governments, support for other Chinese companies seeking to invest in or trade with the host country and the provision of labour to carry out large construction projects. Such economic engagement may amount to several billion dollars, excluding investment in the oil and gas sector. Prime examples are Sudan and Angola (see Chapter 10).

Though it may appear that such packages of deals and their articulation with the oil and gas agreements emerge from carefully considered planning processes within the Chinese government, in many cases they probably arise in a more random and reactive fashion and after the first steps have already been taken by the NOC to invest in the host country.

The first point of call for the Chinese oil company is the NDRC, which must approve any significant investment, at home or abroad. If more than one Chinese company is bidding for a project, the NDRC will decide which bid will be allowed to go forward. As a result it was rare in the past to see Chinese oil companies bidding against each other, even if more than one has shown interest in bidding.[21] It appears that this control mechanism has failed in recent years, for the NDRC was forced into issuing a directive in April 2010 requiring the NOCs to form consortia rather than bidding against each other.[22] All projects over US$200 million must gain further approval from the State Council. NDRC approval is also needed by the China EXIM Bank if loans are to be made to the project.

The Ministry of Commerce plays a key role in supporting the implementation of projects, when required, and in coordinating the package of economic and commercial measures as it develops. In the past, the Ministry of Foreign Trade and Economic Cooperation and the SETC would have taken on this role.[23] The Ministry of Commerce periodically issues a list of countries that are preferred destinations for outward investment. Nearly all the countries of significant oil and gas value to China are on this list. The coordination of diplomatic and economic priorities and measures occurs between the Ministry of Commerce and the Ministry of Foreign Affairs. In the case of Africa, for example, this takes place through the Secretariat of the China-Africa Cooperation Forum.

In addition to building bilateral relations with oil and gas producing countries, China has been engaging with regional and global multi-lateral organisations and with energy importing nations. At a regional level, energy plays a significant role in the deliberations of the Shanghai Cooperation Organisation (SCO), Association of Southeast Asian Nations (ASEAN)+3 and the recently formed Greater Mekong Sub-region Cooperation, though it is unclear what concrete impact these organisations have had on oil and gas activities to date.[24] At a global level China is engaging progressively more closely with the climate change negotiations, the IEA, the Energy Charter Secretariat and the International Energy Forum though, again, firm commitments have been avoided. China's government has also enhanced its dialogue with energy importing nations that, in some cases, such as the USA, the EU and Japan, has been long-standing.[25]

Partly in support of its energy diplomacy China has also embarked on an expansion of its naval capabilities. This expansion includes the development of a blue-water navy capable of deployment across the world's oceans and cooperation with governments in south Asia to construct ports that can receive these vessels as well as oil tankers and cargo vessels, for example in Pakistan, Bangladesh, Myanmar and Sri Lanka.[26]

Motivations for the overseas investment

Since the late 1990s when China's oil companies started going overseas in a sustained manner, much has been written and spoken about how the government has been using the companies as an instrument to enhance security of oil and gas supply. While this allegation contains a certain amount of truth, it is essential to understand that the government and the companies have possessed different sets of motives for this overseas investment. The programmes of investment have moved forward rapidly because these two sets of interests have converged to a greater or lesser extent.

This section examines the motives of the companies and the government, and then examines possible sources of future divergence between the interests of these two parties.

The Chinese oil companies

The prime movers behind this growth of overseas activity have been the companies; not just the three main NOCs, but also their subsidiary service companies, smaller oil companies and various provincial companies. China's NOCs are part of a much wider growth of overseas direct investment by Chinese corporations. Indeed, between 1978 and 1998, only about 30 per cent of the outward directed investment was related to the search for natural resources.[27]

General studies of China's outward investment have identified a number of important drivers for this investment and have examined the range of strategies employed and advantages possessed by Chinese enterprises of different types.[28] Though many Chinese companies, including the oil service and construction companies, are seeking new markets, the NOCs themselves are seeking new resources, and the proportion of overseas investment coming from China that is directed at natural resources has grown dramatically in the first decade of the twenty-first century. In the search for international growth, Chinese NOCs are greatly assisted by national government policy, by their status as state-owned enterprises, and by capital market imperfections and networks in their home country, which together provide them with political support, with easy access to finance and with a greater ability to absorb risk.

For most of the Chinese NOCs the driving forces for internationalisation have been a combination of necessity and opportunity.[29] The necessity has arisen from constraints and threats in their home ground, within China. China's onshore areas and, to a lesser extent, its offshore seas have been well explored. Since the early 1990s the NOCs have struggled to increase oil production within China, though new discoveries have allowed the output of gas to increase dramatically, as described in Chapter 2. The possession of oil and gas reserves for future production is a fundamental requirement for the long-term success of an oil company. With limited opportunity at home, the Chinese companies have been forced to go overseas in order to secure their long-term survival. As well as just surviving, the commercialisation and overseas listing of the NOCs in the late 1990s placed on them the clear obligation to seek growth in revenues, profits and value.

A second domestic threat arises from the manner in which oil and natural gas are priced. As discussed in Chapter 2, the Chinese government retains the right to control or set the prices of all energy products. Though producer prices for oil have risen along with international prices, producer prices for natural gas have not kept pace, and consumer prices for most forms of energy have been tightly controlled at a relatively low level. As a result, companies that refine crude oil have been making massive financial losses, and those supplying natural gas have had their profits constrained. With tightly controlled energy markets at home, China's oil companies have evident incentives to invest abroad in such a way that they can sell their products at international prices with no restrictions.

The opportunities for these companies are multiple. First, and most importantly, overseas expansion allows them to take the first steps towards becoming truly international corporations rather than just very large NOCs. This is the prime ambition of PetroChina, Sinopec and CNOOC. To become major international players they will require capital, assets and skills. They have the capital, they are building their asset base around the world, and they are starting to develop their technical and managerial expertise to international levels, building on many decades of domestic experience.

Within this context, overseas expansion allows these companies to expand their range of activities beyond their historical bases more rapidly than they could at home. Sinopec can gain oilfields to supply its Chinese refineries, CNPC can build its refining activities, and all three companies can expand their participation in natural gas markets.

Underpinning all these opportunities is the enhanced freedom that the NOCs have enjoyed since the radical restructuring in 1998. China's government has relaxed substantially the degree of operational and strategic control over both the listed subsidiaries and, to a lesser extent, the holding companies. This has allowed the companies to develop their own strategies for growth and performance, though they are still subject to approval by government and remain liable to be called upon to address national priorities.[30]

China's government

China's government has many reasons for the scale and scope of the support it is giving to the internationalisation of its oil and gas companies. In the 1990s and early 2000s China's government appeared to be taking what was variously called a 'strategic'[31] or 'neomercantilist'[32] approach in addressing these security of supply challenges. A belief existed in government and in its circle of advisers that security of supply could be enhanced by owning rights to oil and gas in the ground around the world, and by producing this oil and gas. The NOCs would be instruments of this policy. Such resources would be secure, the produced equity oil could be sent directly to China and this oil would be cheaper than oil bought on the open market. Given that the world's remaining oil and gas reserves appeared to be limited, it was vital for China to move quickly to gain its fair share of what was remaining.[33]

In addition to these objectives relating to security of supply, the government had other aims in its support for the overseas strategies of the oil companies. The most important of these relate to industrial and foreign policies.

Since the late 1990s the government has held an official policy to protect a small number of 'pillar' industries that remained in state hands and to promote their development into major international players. The oil industry was one of these.[34] The restructuring and partial listing of the NOCs in the late 1990s confirmed that the managers shared these ambitions. Indeed, as discussed above, the very survival of the companies depended on success abroad.

Allied to this was the desire on the part of the government and of the oil companies to promote opportunities for the oilfield service companies to win business overseas. This would not only keep a greater proportion for the oil companies' revenues in Chinese hands, but it would also provide employment for tens or hundreds of thousands of oilfield workers and managers. Further, as both oil companies and service companies expanded their businesses overseas they would provide more tax revenues and more foreign exchange to the government.[35]

Just as foreign policy can support energy policy, so energy policy can be used to support foreign policy. Indeed it has long been recognised that energy and funds to invest in energy development can be wielded in the international arena either as a carrot or as a stick. Given its status as an energy importer, China has chosen to apply energy as a diplomatic carrot. It has used energy as a starting point for building new relations, and as a catalyst to renew dormant relations and to deepen existing relations.[36] As described above, energy has been packaged together with other instruments to achieve both political and economic gains, and in some countries energy forms a critical component of China's diplomatic strategy.

Finally, China's loans to oil producing countries and the financial support given to the overseas activities of its NOCs assists the government in addressing two of its international financial objectives: to enhance the international role of the renminbi, for some of the loans are denominated in China's currency, and to diversify the portfolio of its foreign exchange investments away from the US dollar.[37]

An emerging divergence?

From this examination of the Chinese government's approach to enhancing the security of international supplies of oil and gas it is clear that there has been a high degree of convergence between the interests of the government and those of its NOCs.[38] In recent years evidence has emerged that parties within the government have been reconsidering some of the issues and concerns, and that opinions have shifted. The questions raised relate to the validity of the economic, diplomatic and military aspects of the strategy.

As has been asserted by western observers for several years, some Chinese analysts have been arguing that key elements of the strategy of securing oil reserves overseas may yield little or no benefit to the nation in terms of security of supply. In times of a major crisis in the oil markets, it is likely that neither the possession of reserves overseas and of equity oil production nor the existence of long-term supply agreements may be of any value.[39] Even if China has its own tanker fleet, this will count for little if supplies are scarce or sealanes are blocked.

Likewise, though the existence of onshore pipelines certainly does succeed in diversifying the sources and modes of oil and gas import, pipelines themselves are no more secure than sea lanes if aggressors are determined to disrupt these flows. Further, the militaristic nature of China's approach to security of supply, with its obsessive fear of a blockade, can be viewed as quite inappropriate and likely to be less effective than focusing on economic and political measures emphasising peacetime priorities.[40]

In the context of international relations, the question has been raised as to whether these overseas oil and gas activities damage rather than enhance China's international reputation.[41] This question has two facets. The first relates to the behaviour of the oil companies and the risks faced by these companies overseas.[42] Chinese companies in general, and not specifically the oil companies, have been accused in a number of countries of failing to meet the standards of behaviour expected of international companies with respect to labour conditions, safety and environment.[43] One particular charge against China's oil industry is that the companies bring their own labour force. While this practice may help ensure that projects are completed on schedule, it necessarily diminishes the opportunities for employment for the local population and slows down the transfer of skills and technology.[44]

Chinese companies are also finding that they are not immune to the resentment of foreign oil companies by the population of the host countries. In extreme cases their staff is therefore exposed to the same high security risks as others and therefore liable to kidnapping, as has occurred in Nigeria, Pakistan, Sudan and Ethiopia.[45]

In response to these challenges, China's government has introduced a number of measures to improve the standard of governance in its companies operating overseas. At the end of 2007, SASAC issued guidelines on social responsibility to all centrally-owned state enterprises.[46] Though the text does not explicitly mention overseas operations, it does urge the companies to aspire to international standards. In 2008 the National Audit Office established a new department to oversee the international operations of state-owned enterprises, as part of a wider effort to improve the scrutiny of these companies both at home and abroad.[47] The following year, the newly-created Ministry of Environmental Protection issued draft environmental guidelines for Chinese companies operating abroad, though these were still under deliberation a year later.[48]

The second facet of reputation loss relates to the behaviour of China's government as it seeks to maintain good working relations with governments of resource-rich countries that are spurned by the international community. Examples include Iran, Sudan, Syria and Myanmar. Although China's government has taken small steps to meet the concerns of the international community in some of these cases, it appears that it is unlikely to capitulate to western pressures in the near future.[49] What is less clear is the extent to which energy supply concerns, rather than wider diplomatic objectives, underpin China's strongly held position.

It is becoming increasingly clear that the 'strategic' or 'neomercantilist' approach to international oil and gas security that the Chinese government appeared to be taking in the 1990s is being tempered and may slowly be evolving in a direction that recognises the role of international markets and the value of multi-lateral cooperation. In this respect, it is likely that the degree of relatively unconditional support given by the government to its NOCs abroad may start to decline as their interests diverge.

The pull from the host countries

The success on the part of the Chinese oil companies in building such a large portfolio of assets in a short time can be attributed not just to the 'push' from China's government but also to the 'pull' from many host governments and oil companies.

The host governments

The host governments play a key role in the internationalisation of China's oil companies, for it is they, or their NOCs, who agree the deals and award the contracts. Though many host governments treat the Chinese companies in the same way as companies from other countries, a number of governments have their own specific objectives when seeking investment into their oil and gas sectors from China. These objectives range from the mainly economic to the largely political.[50]

Countries such as Iran, Sudan, Myanmar and Syria urgently require foreign investment in their energy sectors, and yet the USA and other western governments forbid or discourage their companies from investing there. As a result, these governments have no choice but to seek investment from countries that do not pursue the same political agenda, such as China, India, Russia and Malaysia. Of these, China has the largest oil companies with the greatest ambitions for internationalisation and the largest sources of finance, though Russia's Gazprom is also taking steps to become a major international gas player.

Then there are those governments that are successful at attracting investment but wish to reduce their dependence on certain outside parties. Countries such as Libya, Equatorial Guinea and Kazakhstan have clearly stated that they wish to diversify investment away from the western oil companies, and Kazakhstan and Turkmenistan want to break their historic dependence on Russia.

In Africa many countries are in great need of investment both in their petroleum sectors and also in general infrastructure to accelerate their economic development. The governments of Angola, Sudan, Nigeria and other African countries were keen to accept such assistance from China in association with the oil investments because this aid came with none of the conditions associated with aid programmes from the West and has been delivered in a very timely manner.[51]

Governments of certain petroleum-rich countries in the Middle East have a quite different set of objectives that relate to their search for security of demand and to the ambitions of their own NOCs. These governments know that Asia, rather than the West, will be their biggest customer in the future and therefore they must build better economic and political relations with governments in the region, and with China in particular. Thus they are keen to sign long-term supply agreements and are willing to allow Chinese companies to invest in their domestic petroleum sectors. In the same context, their NOCs wish to integrate downstream into the growing markets, and therefore are involved in building refineries and other projects in China, as described above.[52]

Finally, there are governments that have purely political motives, either domestic or international. The governments of Russia and Kazakhstan appear to have used Chinese oil companies in order to regain control of assets held in foreign, private hands. The loan of US$5 billion made by CNPC to Rosneft in 2005 allowed for the renationalisation of assets owned by Yukos. In the same year, CNPC's purchase of PetroKazakhstan from Canadian owners was made conditional on the sale of 33 per cent of the company to Kazakhstan's NOC, KazMunaiGas.[53] In 2009, a loan from China allowed KazMunaiGas and CNPC to jointly purchase MangistauMunaiGas from Indonesian owners.

From the perspective of foreign relations, certain governments appear to take pleasure in inviting the Chinese to invest, in order to 'thumb their nose' at the West and, particularly at the USA. Venezuela and, possibly, Canada are examples. Other governments are keen to build economic and political relations with China for the political benefits that this may bring them in the international arena, for example in the UN Security Council. Iran and Sudan both fall firmly in this category.

While these and other motivations may have lain behind the willingness and enthusiasm with which host governments have welcomed Chinese investment in their oil and gas sectors, it is already evident that such support is not unconditional and is not to be relied on indefinitely. As mentioned above, experience in Angola and Nigeria has shown that host governments may unilaterally renege on or at least review commitments to allow Chinese companies to build oil refineries and other projects. In the case of Nigeria, only after a new head-of-state was installed did the government eventually confirm its willingness to allow the China State Construction Engineering Corporation to build three oil refineries and a petrochemical complex; but 80 per cent of the funds will come from Chinese financial institutions.[54]

In other countries, the government may declare that they wish to do business with Chinese oil companies, but actual deals take years to reach conclusion. Russia is the best example of this.[55] Further, a number of countries that initially embraced China as a non-colonial power are now considering whether China's form of economic and political engagement is indeed as desirable as first imagined. This would seem to be the case in many African countries, as well as in Kazakhstan and Iran.[56]

The available evidence suggests that while many governments still welcome investment from China, the degree of convergence of interests between these host governments and the government and companies of China may not be as strong as the Chinese parties hope and, in some cases, may actually be diminishing. Given the strong political context of some of the investments, it is certain that the political support from the host governments for these investments will depend highly on the priorities and outlook of those in power. For those projects that relied on a deep political involvement of the host government, any change of government may enhance the risk faced by the project, and the more radical the change in nature of the government, the greater the risk.

Host country national oil companies

While the objectives of the NOCs belonging to the host country are usually broadly consistent with those of their government, these NOCs are likely to have a number of specific business goals. First, the NOC may be willing to use Chinese service and construction companies on account of their relatively cheap price and on account of the work ethic, which usually results in timely completion of even the toughest projects. This has certainly been the case in Africa and the Middle East.

Second, the host NOC may lack the cash to implement its investment programme and may be keen to have a cash-rich, Chinese joint venture partner or indeed to receive cash loans from China's government or NOCs. For example, in February 2009, the Chinese government agreed to lend US$25 billion to two of Russia's state oil companies, Rosneft and Transneft, in return for a guarantee of supply of 15 million tonnes per year for 20 years. That same week, the China Development Bank agreed to lend Brazil's NOC, Petrobras, US$10 billion in return for up to eight million tonnes of oil per year, as described in Chapter 6.

Finally, as mentioned above, the larger NOCs of those Middle Eastern countries that lack a large domestic market are keen to integrate vertically downstream into refining, petrochemicals and retailing in a large market such as China. This strategy mirrors, to a certain extent, that of the Chinese NOCs and may help them to develop into major, internationalised companies.

Conclusions

This rapid internationalisation of China's oil industry has been made possible by a convergence of interests between China's government, the Chinese NOCs, the host governments and the host NOCs. This convergence of interests cannot be assumed to be permanent. Indeed, slight tensions have already appeared between the Chinese government and its NOCs, and more serious differences have arisen between the Chinese NOCs and some of their overseas hosts.

Though the aggregate scale of these investments and the total overseas reserves under the control of China's NOCs are modest in relation to those of the largest IOCs companies, they continue to attract concern, fear and even hostility from OECD governments, from IOCs, from the governments of other energy importing countries, and from a wide range of political and economic analysts.

The main roots of these concerns lie in the state-ownership of China's oil companies, their close relationship with government and the strong political support they receive as a consequence, their apparent unlimited supplies of funds, which allows them to outbid commercial competitors from other countries, and the apparent willingness of China's government and NOCs to undermine western diplomacy by working with governments that the West considers to be unsavoury.

Part 2

Energy policy and China's foreign policy

7 Integration, the West and international energy policy

Introduction

The previous chapters have sought to identify the linkages between China's domestic energy needs and its increasingly ambitious international energy policy, which is focused in particular on ensuring the secure supply of oil from international markets and from equity investments. As the previous chapter highlighted, Chinese oil companies have been major drivers of this ambitious international expansion, though they have also responded to the needs and interests of the host oil-producing countries. The Chinese government has taken a leading role in seeking to guide and support this international strategy. This goes back to the 1999 announcement by the Central Committee of the Communist Party of the 'go out' (zouchuqu) strategy, offering an array of investment incentives for Chinese companies to expand overseas, which was particularly directed at encouraging these companies to secure contracts with oil and gas producing countries.[1] Government interest in the international energy sector only increased during the 2000s as prices rose and US intervention into Iraq and Afghanistan accentuated fears that China's access to global energy sources was under threat. In early 2004, Li Junru, vice-president of the CCP's Central Party School, argued that it is the global competition for energy resources, rather than Taiwan, which was now the most important factor affecting China's 'peaceful rise'.[2] Hu Jintao's reported enunciation of the so-called 'Malacca dilemma' at around the same time, which is discussed further in Chapter 9, highlighted the real anxiety in Beijing about the potential threat of a US-imposed oil embargo on China.

As a consequence of the growing strategic importance of energy, international energy policy has become an increasingly important element in China's broader foreign policy. The focus of this chapter and more generally of this second section of the book is on the implications of China's rapidly developing international energy policy for its foreign and security policy. The role that energy plays in China's broader foreign and security policy has a dual character. On the one hand, China's growing energy needs provide the government and the foreign policy establishment, as well as the military, with new strategic opportunities to be involved in parts of the world where they had previously only had a weak or limited presence. The most striking demonstration of this is in sub-Saharan Africa and in Latin America where, as Chapter 10 shows, the Chinese energy-driven expansion has radically changed China's geopolitical weight in both regions. China's influence has similarly increased in other oil-rich regions, such as the Middle East and central Asia, and China's energy tentacles extend even to western energy-rich countries such as Australia and Canada.

The other side of this dual character is that the growing salience of an energy-driven foreign policy raises significant anxieties and concerns. These can be found internally within the Chinese government with fears at how its growing oil imports increase China's international vulnerability. But these sources of anxiety are also acute for external actors who have viewed China's energy-driven foreign policy expansion with growing concern and apprehension. This has become an important element in the broader debate about how to interpret and understand China's rise as an increasingly powerful international actor. Does this relatively new and increasingly prominent energy dimension to China's rise confirm the Chinese government's claim that it is adopting a purely economic and developmental strategy that is fundamentally non-aggressive and peaceful? Or does the drive for energy provide China with a new instrument for realising its nationalistic and even aggressive ambitions?

This chapter focuses on addressing these two questions in the light of China's relations with the West, focusing mainly on the United States as China's most important western strategic partner. First, the chapter draws from the main theoretical traditions within International Relations (IR), realism and liberalism, to explain how western, and particularly American, interpretations of China's rise remain divided between those who see China as relatively benignly integrating with the West and those who see the future of China more negatively as a major potential future threat to US and western interests. It is argued that economic integration is the principal overriding objective for China's foreign policy, as liberal IR theory argues, but that this integration is crucially constrained and limited by mutual distrust between China and the West, as realist theory suggests. The chapter examines how this dynamic of integration, and obstacles to that integration, is reflected in China's international energy policy, particularly in China's energy-related interaction with the United States. The chapter concludes with providing some key elements for a more nuanced and sophisticated conceptual framework for understanding the opportunities and constraints that condition China's international energy policy and its engagement with the West.

The main conclusion of the chapter is that to understand how China's energy strategy influences foreign and security policy, we must incorporate a significant degree of unpredictability and indeterminacy that makes problematic any projection of a clear and well-defined future trajectory. Indeed, it is this inherent unpredictability and indeterminacy that has led to China adopting multiple, and not necessarily compatible, energy policies, which veer from promoting integration with, to balancing against, the West (Chapter 8), from accommodating to challenging US regional hegemony (Chapter 9) and from being perceived as a benign developmental to being perceived as a malign neo-imperialist actor in international politics (Chapter 10). It is these multiple faces of China's energy-driven foreign policy that will be the main focus of this and the following chapters of this second part of the book.

Integration and Chinese foreign policy

Realism and liberalism are very much part of the stock theoretical tradition of the academic discipline of IR. But they also provide a simple explanatory framework for understanding Sino-US relations that captures not just elite but also popular perceptions in the broader US and western debate about China's rise. A significant part of the reason for this popularity is that IR theories, and most particularly realism and liberalism, are centrally involved in seeking to understand the balance of power between the Great Powers and, since the end of the Cold War, it has been China that has generally be seen as the most significant strategic competitor to the United States.[3]

China's rise has a particularly strong fascination for realists and neo-realists. This is because a core assumption of neo-realism is that changes or shifts at the systemic level, when the existing Great Power configuration is challenged and overturned, necessarily involve instability and conflicts. For realists, the core strategic question about China's rise is whether it can be accommodated without major confrontation or war. Most realists are pessimistic about the outcome. John Mearsheimer is probably the best known neo-realist scholar who argues almost without equivocation that China's growing capabilities will lead to an 'aggressive state determined to achieve regional hegemony'.[4] Other power-based neo-realist thinkers might less confidently predict such a stark outcome but nevertheless argue that, as a general proposition, 'as its relative power increases, a rising state attempts to change the rules governing the system'.[5] Such a state might do this through deliberate intent and naked ambition, as with Hitler's Germany, or it can be a more innocent outcome of the resistance of existing powers to accommodate challenges to their hegemony or to cede or share their authority, as was arguably the case with the pre-World War I European Great Powers and Germany.

The general historical record, realists argue, shows that transitions from one hegemonic arrangement to another are rarely, if ever, achieved without significant instability and contestation and there is no reason to believe that China's rise will be an exception to this rule.[6] Moreover, it is particularly in periods of intense industrialisation and fast economic growth, which China is currently experiencing, when pressures for external expansion appear to be particularly powerful. It was in such periods of societal transformation that the imperial expansion of Britain, France, the USA, Russia/USSR and Japan was at its most intense. In part, the imperial drive was conditioned by the need to provide some external outlet for the harsh domestic pressures and societal dislocations that such fast economic development provokes. But it was also linked to the sheer necessity to obtain the natural resources, and to secure the necessary markets, for the goods being produced domestically. In this regard, the search to obtain the energy resources critical for industrialisation has, historically, a close linkage with imperial expansion, as seen in the post-Ottoman European carving up of the Middle East, the German drive during World War II for oil supplies in the Caucasus, or Japan's 'zone of co-prosperity'. Such historical patterns suggest, realists argue, that China will be strongly tempted to act in a similarly expansive manner. Moreover, the importance of a strong anti-western dimension in China's nationalist rhetoric, which sees China's historic mission to overturn the 'century of humiliation' imposed unjustly by external European powers, adds to realists' fears that China might be particularly prone to aggression when slighted or refused the respect and status to which its new-found power makes it feel entitled.[7]

Such gloomy realist-driven predictions of conflict and global insecurity are counter-balanced by more benign interpretations of China's ambitions. As Aaron Friedberg points out, most Americans, and one might also add most Europeans, are liberals and tend towards greater optimism for China's prospective integration into global economic and political structures.[8] This is based on the classic liberal view, as expressed from Adam Smith and David Ricardo onwards, that free trade and economic integration have political as well as economic benefits. The liberal perspective on China suggests that there are parallels with the European process of integration, whereby the desire to overcome the horrors and excesses of the 'cultural revolution' and other irrational Maoist projects has similarities with Europe's desire to overcome the destruction of two world wars through the building of dense economic linkages and interdependencies so as to make it increasingly irrational to use force for the resolution of political conflicts.[9] China's commitment to economic interdependence can be seen in the enormous expansion of trade with the United States, its principal strategic rival from a realist perspective, which has grown from US$1 billion in 1978 to US$95 billion in 1999 to US$230 billion in 2004 to US$366 billion in 2009. More generally, China has one of the most open economies with a current trade-to-GDP ratio of about 70 per cent as against roughly 20 per cent trade-to-GDP ratios for the United States or Japanese economies. As such, China fits firmly into Richard Rosecrance's definition of a 'trading state' rather than a traditional 'military-territorial state' and where the core strategic imperative is the conquest of markets rather than territory.[10]

Liberal theory also proposes that economic interdependence promotes socialisation of states into regional and international structures and institutions externally, and to democratisation internally.[11] Evidence can be found to suggest that China is itself conforming to this developmental trajectory. Alastair Iain Johnston has sought to show how, over time, China has increasingly eschewed its traditional realist approach to international politics and has modified its practice and behaviour so as to conform to the liberal norms underpinning the international regimes and institutions to which China has increasingly participated and been socialised.[12] For example, as against its long-standing passivity in the UN Security Council, China has taken an increasingly pro-active role, which can be seen in its contribution to the UN Millennium Summit and in its willingness to commit troops to UN peacekeeping operations.[13] In December 2001, China joined the World Trade Organization (WTO) and accepted, in principle if not always in practice, the conditions and obligations of membership. Similar advances in China's conforming with international norms is also evident in the areas of arms control and non-proliferation policy, where China has ceased to act as a persistent rogue element, most notably by becoming a signatory of the Nuclear Non-Proliferation Treaty in 1996.[14] In its regional and global policies, China has also been far more willing to engage constructively in bilateral and multilateral relations. It has developed a comprehensive strategic partnership with Russia since the mid-1990s, more limited strategic partnerships with the EU and Japan in the 2000s, and has been an active participant in multilateral regional Asian fora, such as the Asia-Pacific Economic Cooperation Forum (APEC), the ASEAN Regional Forum (ARF), ASEAN+3, and the East Asia Summit. China has also been unreservedly proud of its leadership role in the creation and increasing institutionalisation of the SCO, the 'first international organization named after a Chinese city'.[15]

Evidence of progress towards democratisation within China is less immediately evident, as the CCP continues to sustain its monopoly over political power. But there are also undoubted advances in terms of relative personal and individual freedoms as compared to the Maoist period, an emergent middle class is beginning to assert its preferences for greater autonomy, and democratic electoral processes have been initiated at the local level.[16] There are, certainly, commentators such as James Mann who argue that such liberal assumptions of a deterministic path from economic inter-dependence towards democracy represents the triumph of wishful thinking over reality.[17] There are also those who point out that the process of democratisation is itself a period of instability and unpredictability, which is more likely to lead to international conflict than a 'democratic peace'.[18] But, despite these qualifications, there is no reason as yet to presume that China has managed definitively to overturn the strong empirical evidence that correlates increased wealth with democratisation.[19]

In general, the strength of liberal international theory is that it captures the reality that integration into the global economy is the core strategic objective of China's foreign policy and that China generally seeks to join and work within the existing international system. The political roots of this come from Deng Xiaoping's decision after he came to power to reverse the revisionism and rejectionism of the Maoist period. In the post-Cold War period, the Chinese leadership drew particular lessons from the 1995–6 Taiwan crisis and the dispute over Mischief Reef in the South China Seas in 1995, when external perceptions of China's confrontational diplomacy strengthened the sense of a 'China threat'.[20] Since that time, China has sought to demonstrate, both in actions and in ideological discourse, that it prioritises economic over nationalist interests and that it consciously eschews military confrontation and expansion in its growing integration into global structures and institutions.[21] As noted above, China has increasingly engaged with multilateral regional and international institutions. But, beyond this, Beijing has also been acutely aware of promoting its image as a peaceful and constructive international actor. In this regard, it has become aware of the dangers of the 'security dilemma', whereby negative perceptions of others' intentions, even if ungrounded, can feed a dangerous spiral and the need to counter this in explaining and justifying its actions.[22]

A key element in this counter-narrative is to ensure that there is no sustained confrontation with the United States, despite the continuing tensions and mutual misunderstandings. Chinese scholars have themselves increasingly promoted liberal and constructivist theories and associated ideas of the salience of 'soft power' and of positive-sum 'win-win' scenarios.[23] On the official level, there is considerable sensitivity concerning the language and ideological concepts used to define China's foreign policy objectives. Thus, the desire for a 'multipolar world', with its connotations of deliberate counter-hegemonic balancing against the United States, has increasingly been re-defined as the search for a more multilateral and democratic international system. Similarly, the speed with which the term 'peaceful rise' grew and then was discarded in official ideological discourse illustrated sensitivity that the very concept of 'rise' could engender disquiet and negative external perceptions.[24]

There are, however, clear limits and significant constraints on China's integrationist strategy. One of the best ways to understand this is through the distinction made by Raymond Aron between heterogeneous and homogeneous systems in the historical evolution of international politics.[25] Heterogeneous systems are ones where there is more than one principle of domestic legitimacy, such as was the case with the Great Power concert of the nineteenth century, which included both liberal and monarchical authoritarian states, and the Cold War system, when liberal capitalist and communist systems co-existed. What is distinctive about the post-Cold War system, which emerged through the collapse of the Soviet Union, is the sense of the absolute ascendance of one set of values of domestic legitimacy, based on the free market and democracy. The early triumphalism over this onset of a 'homogeneous system', which heralded the 'end of history', might have been discredited for its naive enthusiasm.[26] But there still remains a strong sense that those states that resist capitalism or democratisation are on the wrong side of history, at worst deviants or rogues, or at best condemned to be part of the periphery rather than the core.[27] China fits somewhat uneasily into this bifurcated world, as it has clearly adapted to global capitalism but not to liberal democracy. Robert Cooper has captured this ambivalence by locating China in the category of 'modern' states, engaged in strenuous attempts to develop but still dedicated to outmoded principles of state sovereignty and authoritarianism, which separates it from the 'post-modern' core of the liberal democratic industrialised West.[28]

It is this sense of China being apart and separated from the 'liberal core' that places the greatest physical and ideological constraints on China's integrationist ambitions. The problem is that China's claim for inclusion in this core, and the respect and status that comes with this, is continually undermined by its rigid definitions of national sovereignty, particularly over Taiwan and Tibet, its record on human rights and the refusal of the CCP to cede power in any meaningful manner.[29] For its part, the clear subtext of the Chinese leadership's constant reiteration of the need for the democratisation of IR, for the promotion of a 'multi-coloured' world, or for the building of a 'harmonious world', is the competing claim of the legitimacy of a 'heterogeneous system', where the western political system is not the only source of domestic legitimacy. It is also implicit in China's ideological reservations towards policies of sanctions and its great sensitivity to any international legitimation of overriding the principle of non-intervention and depicting certain countries as 'pariah' states.

Overall, it is the Chinese government's determination to integrate into the global international system but so as to strengthen, rather than to undermine, its internal domestic political system, which leads to conflict with the West. Realist theory is thus correct to capture this core element of conflict and contestation but its weakness is in locating this purely in terms of power differentials. The imbalance of power between the United States and its allies and China is certainly an aggravating and complicating factor. But at its core the conflict is ideological and about competing versions of the very meaning and content of political legitimacy.

Energy security and China's foreign policy

Following the integrationist logic of China's economic and foreign policy more generally, there is much that makes it logical and rational for China to promote its energy security through integration with western norms and institutions. For a start, China is not an oil-rich, exporting state, which is able to rely on the rents of such production to provide autonomy from societal demands and, as is the case with countries like Russia, Iran or Venezuela, to promote a resource nationalism that is the basis for a revisionist anti-western foreign policy. China does not also suffer from the so-called 'resource curse,' which undermines economic development in non-energy sectors of the economy, contributes to mismanagement and corruption, and acts to consolidate unresponsive and authoritarian structures of power. [30] China's economic rise is based on a radically different strategy, similar to other resource-poor countries in east Asia, which is based on integration with the global economy and a relatively autonomous government seeking to develop the national economy in a comprehensive manner. In terms of its economic structures and energy dependence, China's interests lie logically more with other large oil-importing states, such as the United States, Japan or the EU, than with oil-producing states. From this perspective, there is a certain anomaly in the emergence of what some commentators have called the 'new oil axis', which groups China with other revisionist oil-producing states such as Russia or Iran.[31]

Both from within China and the United States, as well as in other western states, there is recognition that energy policy and energy security are potentially fruitful areas for cooperation. Senator Joseph Liebermann even argued in a speech to the Council of Foreign Affairs that Sino-US energy cooperation has the same significance for the twenty-first century as US arms control negotiations with the Soviet Union had for the twentieth century.[32] Similarly, Chinese thinking on energy security has gradually shifted towards a more cooperative stance. As argued in Chapter 2, there has been a marked switch in elite Chinese thinking away from an exclusively mercantilist supply-driven conception of energy security to one that accords greater priority to energy efficiency and demand management. At the 2006 Euro-Asian Summit in Helsinki, Premier Wen Jiabao reflected this shift by focusing attention primarily on international markets and free access to resources, noting that 'geopolitical disputes should not stand in the way of global energy supply and energy issues should not be politicized'.[33] In the United States, there is similarly evidence of a conscious attempt to reduce the degree of friction in this area, with a Department of Energy report in 2006 concluding that Chinese purchases of energy assets were not damaging to the United States and that they could actually be beneficial as they 'will enlarge the total global oil supply'.[34]

There is, in fact, a clear rationale to see Sino-US energy cooperation as a vital mechanism for managing and supporting the intense economic interdependence that exists between the two states. US military hegemony in the Middle East and Persian Gulf region, however much it accentuates China's sense of vulnerability, also serves a vital function, which some Chinese commentators are willing to recognise, of ensuring oil supply security and support for oil price stability, which are critical for China's economic growth. In addition, China's dependence on the US market and its large trade surplus, at over US$226 billion in 2009, means that China has a clear interest to ensure that international energy disputes do not contribute to protectionist pressures domestically within the US, which ultimately is a greater threat to China's national interests. This means that China always acts cautiously in its relations with countries like Iran, Venezuela and Russia, which have adopted a more strident anti-American political stance. Chinese support for these countries is carefully calibrated so that it does not upset the more important economic and strategic relationship with the US. For the US, there is a complementary interest to ensure that sufficient energy supplies reach China so that US consumers can continue to benefit from the cheap imports produced in China. More generally, it is understood in Washington that it is important to address and assuage Chinese fears that the US is planning an option of an oil embargo to weaken or undermine China, which genuinely adds to the difficulty of constructing a more trusting bilateral relationship.

There are currently multiple forums and frameworks for such a Sino-American energy engagement to be developed. These include the US-China Energy Policy Dialogue, which was formed in May 2004 and the establishment in 2008 of the ten-year Energy and Environment Cooperation Framework under the high-level US-China Strategic and Economic Dialogue. There is also the US-China Oil and Gas Industry Forum, which seeks to facilitate Chinese familiarity with western business practices, the US-China Economic Development and Reform Dialogue, and the US-China Defence Consultative Talks, which has included in-depth discussions on global energy security issues.[35] There is a similar array of formats for substantive dialogue on energy issues with the EU and Japan. In 2005 the EU and China launched a number of bilateral initiatives relating variously to climate change, clean coal, energy efficiency, renewable energy, and transport. More recent plans have created a joint project to develop and test carbon capture and storage technologies.[36]

Although the topics for discussion are varied, four principal avenues for supporting cooperative engagement can be identified. The first is the ways in which Washington and other western governments can promote and support policies that will reduce China's demand for hydrocarbons. Greater dependence of China on alternative sources of energy, such as nuclear and 'clean' coal, would help reduce the need for oil imports. Modifying western, particularly US, export control policies so as to facilitate appropriate technology transfer to China is also seen as vital. This would help in areas such as clean coal technology, improving recovery rates of coal and oil production, achieving better user efficiency, promoting the broader societal challenges of more energy-efficient urban planning and encouraging lifestyle changes to conserve energy. For the Chinese government, the challenge is to provide greater protection of intellectual property rights, as current weaknesses in this area undermine the interest of western companies to transfer best available technologies.

A second area of potential enhanced mutual cooperation is through encouraging the participation of US oil companies in joint ventures with Chinese oil companies, including upstream exploration and production. This would help to socialise both sides to their respective business practices, build human contacts and networks, and contribute to a sense of shared responsibility for providing global energy security. European, Japanese and Indian companies have already made this a significant part of their upstream strategies. For example, a good and productive relationship has developed between BP and CNPC, which led to their joint collaboration in the successful bid for the large Rumaila oilfield in Iraq in 2009.

A third area is in encouraging China to shift its interests and engagement more towards oil-consuming than oil-producing states. Promoting Chinese membership of regional and international institutions that reflect these oil-importing interests would help to socialise China into adopting a more solidaristic stance. The key institution in this regard is the IEA, though the OECD and G8 are relevant as well. The US and other western countries have been supportive of China joining the IEA and there are clearly advantages of having China being able to act collectively with other importing states in the case of a major supply crisis. The problem is that membership of the IEA requires OECD membership as well as members having a 90-day oil stockpile, while China is only belatedly building such a strategic stockpile that is aimed at providing thirty days' supply. Nevertheless, China is keen to reinforce its relations with the IEA as was seen in the joint statement between the two parties issued in October 2009, which identified key priorities, one of which included security of oil and gas supply.[37] China, though not signatory of the Energy Charter Treaty, is now an observer member and, given its increasing interest in reliable transboundary flow of oil and gas from central Asia and Russia, this should enhance China's interest in the Treaty. In Asia itself, there is also considerable potential for enhancing the institutional cooperation between China and the other large Asian consumer countries, such as India, Japan, China and South Korea, so as to help them join forces more effectively and to act collectively in relation to OPEC and other oil-exporting states. This would enhance their bargaining power, potentially helping to eliminate the price premium that Asian consumers pay for their oil from the Persian Gulf compared to their European counterparts.

The fourth broad area is in relation to the strategic, diplomatic and military dimensions of energy security. Given China's ever-growing dependence on oil from the Middle East, and its reliance on the sea-lines of communication (SLOCs) from the Middle East to China, there is a strategic rationale for the US and other engaged external countries to seek ways in which it could encourage Chinese participation in diplomatic processes that promote stability in the Middle East and in engaging China to be involved in protecting critical SLOCs. From the Chinese side, there is a similar need to provide greater transparency over the factors driving Chinese international energy expansion into countries and regions, such as Iran, Africa and Latin America, which cause concern in Washington.

The problem is that such logics for integration and greater cooperation are undermined by the mutual suspicions and distrust, conforming to realist logic, which consistently emerge over China's perceived geo-strategic ambitions in its international energy policies. Thus, despite the Department of Energy report, there has been a strong temptation among US leaders to view the sharp rise in oil prices in the 2000s as linked to China's attempts to buy oil at source rather than on the world market. In 2005, US Deputy Secretary of State Robert Zoellick made a harsh assessment that accused China of seeking to 'lock up' energy supplies, referring to a 'cauldron of anxiety' in the US and other parts of the world over Chinese intentions.[38] Chinese analysts naturally took this poorly and as an implicit confirmation that the US was seeking to contain China's rise so as to maintain its own hegemony. It was also viewed as demonstrating a transparent example of double standards, given the US record in the Middle East where it had just a fought a war in Iraq that had a clear oil and energy dimension.

The fragility of Sino-US energy cooperation, and its potential to be derailed by mutual suspicions and distrust, found its most public expression in the failed bid by CNOOC to buy the Union Oil Company of California (UNOCAL) in 2005. As news of this bid emerged, there was a storm of protest in the US media at the prospect of Beijing buying up a US energy company and gaining a stranglehold over US energy security. The House of Representatives voted overwhelmingly that allowing CNOOC to buy UNOCAL would 'threaten to impair the national security of the US'.[39] Chevron, which had put in a competing bid, also accentuated the energy security risks of a Chinese purchase of the company. Although CNOOC's bid had been substantially larger than Chevron's, it eventually pulled out due to the overwhelmingly negative public and political response. In reality, the Chinese government had been initially completely unaware of the bid by CNOOC. For its part, CNOOC had felt that the bid was relatively uncontroversial as all of UNOCAL's assets were outside the US, 70 per cent of which were in Asia, and that less than 1 per cent of US oil and gas consumption came from UNOCAL. As such, the eventual outcome left a bitter taste among Chinese analysts, undermining the belief that the US was really committed to market principles in international energy policy and that its polices were driven in practice by the mercantilist principles that it regularly denounced China for pursuing.[40]

When the sources of US distrust and suspicion over China's international energy policies are analysed, they can be broken down into three main dimensions. The first is the perception that, due to China's non-democratic and authoritarian political system, Chinese companies are driven by the political dictates of the Chinese government and that geopolitical, rather than strictly economic, objectives are pursued and supported through state support and various forms of hidden subsidies. Thus, there is a strong perception that Chinese companies do not play by the international 'rules of the game' and that this is driven by the incomplete nature of China's transformation as a market economy and as a political democracy. The second dimension is the limits, despite what it preaches to others, of US commitment to international markets for energy security. Particularly when oil prices rose substantially in the mid-2000s, the political discourse emphasised the ambition of energy independence and the need, however illogical in liberal economic terms, of eliminating US dependence on foreign sources of energy supply. The perceived political costs of dealing with the domestic sources of energy insecurity, particularly through managing and reducing energy demand, meant that it was politically easier to focus on external scapegoats – China being a convenient candidate in this respect. The third dimension reflects the prevalence among US decision-makers and public opinion of the realist-inspired perception of the threat posed by China's rise and the ways in which China's drive for energy security might contribute towards this. From this perspective, energy security potentially provides the legitimation and drive for a more confident global Chinese diplomatic and military expansion and is something to be feared as well as managed. The belief, for example, that China's energy needs are driving and justifying the establishment of naval bases in the Indian Ocean, the so-called 'string of pearls' strategy (see Chapter 9), and that this aims to reduce US power and influence, fits this more pessimistic frame of thinking.

For the Chinese, the sources of distrust and suspicion are almost the mirror images of those of the US. There is, first, the sense that the US is not actually committed to market principles in its international energy policy and, as demonstrated in its Middle Eastern policy and the invasion of Iraq in 2003, there are militaristic as well as mercantilist drivers to its policies. Second, there is the continuing concern, which is particularly captured by the notion of the 'Malacca dilemma', that the US continues to seek to preserve its capability to impose an energy blockade on China in case of a major conflict or war, such as over Taiwan. And, third, there is the fundamental underlying ideological conflict where Chinese leaders see the US as continually seeking to challenge and oppose China's rise so long as China fails to transform itself into the free market liberal democracy demanded by the US. It is China's commitment to its own developmental trajectory and to a 'heterogeneous' system of international politics that is, as argued above, the fundamental source of the constraints and limitations of China's pro-western integrationist dynamic in international energy markets.

Re-thinking China's international energy policy

The ways in which China's international energy policy is driven by a complex dynamic of integration and resistance to such integration, of trust and confidence mixed with suspicion and anxiety, suggests that a relatively complex analytical and theoretical framework is required to capture these seemingly contradictory processes. There is an inevitable degree of strategic ambiguity in China's policies, which reflect its only partial incorporation and acceptance of western norms and institutions. This complex strategic indeterminacy is not adequately captured by traditional realist and liberal accounts, however many crucial insights they provide, which reflects a general shift away from thinking that any one theoretical approach captures all of international reality.[41] In the study of Asian security, Katzenstein and Sil have promoted an agenda of 'analytical eclecticism' seeking to integrate and combine the insights of various IR theoretical traditions.[42] This is developed further by Friedberg in an influential article that draws out how diverging perspectives on China's rise can be found *within* as well as *between* differing IR theories.[43] He shows how there are realist, liberal, and constructivist 'optimist' accounts of China's rise that contrast with contending 'pessimist' realist, liberal and constructivist interpretations. He argues that a dynamic theoretical synthesis can potentially be constructed through bringing these various theoretically diverse 'optimist' and 'pessimist' accounts together in differing ways.

In seeking to develop such a more sophisticated analytical framework for conceptualising China's international energy strategy, it is critical to include four key elements. The first is the inclusion of domestic policy and politics that is often ignored or marginalised in IR theories. The weakness of rationalist theoretical accounts is that they tend to assume that China is an autonomous and unitary rational actor. The reality of Chinese policy-making is, as the earlier chapters demonstrated, far divorced from this. Rather than a monolithic and autonomous actor, which acts independently from the society over which it rules, the Chinese government is constrained in its energy policy by powerful societal and structural legacies. Energy policy cannot be divorced, as argued in Chapter 3, from ideological frameworks and commitments that have defined the social and political trajectory of communist rule of modern China. These include the role of powerful mobilising and legitimating ideas such as self-reliance, asserting mastery over nature, and the ideological commitment to social equity. China's energy policy framework is also similarly constrained by decisions made in the past, which limit the potential scope and freedom of action for decisions in the present or the future. Such path-dependencies, to use the language of 'new institutionalism', include such factors as the long-standing priority given to coal for ensuring domestic energy needs, the development of transport infrastructures that favour the use of cars, and the widespread commitment given to pursuing economic growth, which makes it difficult, for example, to shift to an environmental agenda.[44]

China's energy policy-making system is also far removed from the ideal of the rational actor model, with its emphasis on hierarchical centralised control. In contrast, there is a multiplicity of differing interest groups and actors, a highly fragmented policy-making structure, and a government that continually struggles to impose a degree of order and unity. Policies are often formulated in haphazard and unpredictable ways, where the rhetoric of decisive action often disguises limited prospects for implementation, and where narrow interest groups can 'capture' policy for their own particular purposes. This domestic energy system is an integral part of a broader domestic political system where the weakness or absence of transparent or accountable systems means that policy decisions frequently emerge unpredictably and where the implementation of policy is similarly haphazard. It is this element of unpredictability and lack of transparency that is critically important when incorporating the Chinese domestic energy policy system into a broader international context and to understanding the strategic ambiguities in China's international energy policy.

The second crucial element is the importance of perceptions and how perceptions form inter-subjective ideas, values and identities that are critical for understanding international politics. This builds upon constructivist theory that accords explanatory significance to how ideas and perceptions influence and structure international reality.[45] In terms of China's international energy policy, an illustration of this dynamic inter-systemic and mutually constitutive effect can be seen in how external perceptions of China's domestic energy policy – the extent to which, for example, Chinese oil companies are viewed as genuinely independent of government or the extent to which the government is seen to be genuinely committed to shifting policies towards energy efficiency – influences how China's engagement with the international energy system is perceived. Similarly, whether China is perceived to be acting in a market-friendly or neo-mercantilist way ultimately feeds into perceptions of the benign or potentially malign nature of China's rise. From the Chinese perspective, it is the ways in which these western perceptions of China's energy policies are themselves judged to be fair and legitimate that influence, in turn, the extent to which Chinese policymakers perceive western actions as supporting or undermining China's legitimate energy security interests and its rights as a global actor. It is how these perceptions mutually constitute inter-subjective understandings that are a critical element in understanding China's incorporation into the international energy and international political systems.

This leads to a third aspect that is how to incorporate systematically these more dynamic and interactive effects that are often not captured by more traditional theories. Systems theory and particularly the concept of positive feedback can help here.[46] Positive feedback mechanisms are those where change in one direction sets in motion reinforcing pressures that produce further change in the same direction. Some positive feedback processes can be of a stabilising nature, setting in place and consolidating pacifying and integrative dynamics. For instance, in the China case, increasingly market-driven policies adopted at the domestic energy system level, which focus on making Chinese oil companies more independent and where energy efficiency becomes the dominant policy concern, can have a beneficial impact on perceptions of China's global energy policies, which in turn build confidence in China's integration into the international political system. However, there are also potentially positive feedback dynamics that stimulate conflict, where negative perceptions on one side engender negative responses on the other side and where this can spiral out of control without the deliberate intention of either side. In IR, this is classically captured in the so-called 'security dilemma', where insecurity can be produced even when both sides have relatively benign peaceful intentions.[47] The potential for damaging spirals between the domestic, international energy, and international political systems, is a genuine possibility. As discussed above, the crisis surrounding CNOOC's failure to take control of UNOCAL illustrates the possibility of how international energy issues can influence mutual perceptions and have a potentially damaging longer-term impact on China-US relations. Fortunately, Chinese and US leaders are generally reflexively self-aware of the potential damage of allowing such spirals to escalate and the need to take counter-measures that forestall such spiralling dynamics. But such self-reflexive restraint is not a foregone conclusion.

The final dimension is one that highlights the strong element of contingency and unpredictability of all systems. It is that exogenous impacts can be highly significant and have immediate and unexpected effects. For China, the Taiwan issue is the most significant immediate source of exogenous shock. If there did emerge a conflict over Taiwan, which brought the US and China into confrontation, this would raise critical energy security challenges for China. In practice, US-Chinese relations are regularly interspersed by such generally unexpected exogenous shocks – such as the bombing of the Chinese embassy in Belgrade in 1999, the EP-3 plane issue in 2001, the repression of Tibetan uprising in 2008 – which have had more generalised impacts on broader bilateral relations. One dimension of this is the potential international impacts of a domestic economic and political crisis within China. If China is, as Shirk argues, a 'fragile power', the consequences of such domestic unrest could be highly unpredictable.

Conclusion

The principal conclusion from this chapter is that China's relations with the West in its international energy policy cannot be thought simply in terms of a realist or liberal theoretical framework. China's expansion of its international energy commitments is neither uniquely threatening nor a confirmation that China is inexorably being integrated into western norms, practices and institutions. The reality is a more dynamic and strategically ambiguous context where the Chinese have adopted multiple strategies and approaches so as to maximize the flexibility and resilience of its international energy policy. This reflects the fact that there is much unpredictability and indeterminacy in China's policy-making that is in part a consequence of domestic constraints but is also due to an external international context that is far from secure or predictable.

The chapter has not denied or challenged that peaceful integration into global economic and political structures is the core ambition of China in its international politics. This ambition has made it logical for China to seek to integrate and coordinate its policies and strategies in the energy domain with the large western energy-consuming countries. But the chapter has also demonstrated the limits and constraints to such integration. In part, as realist theories argue, it is how China is perceived to threaten existing balances of power that limits the dynamic of integration. But, a greater constraint, it is argued, is an essentially ideological dispute over the meaning of international society, where a western commitment to a 'homogeneous' system of liberal democratic capitalist states conflicts with Chinese resolve to maintain its own distinctive non-democratic political system within a broadly 'heterogeneous' international political system. This, in turn, limits the potential for China of integration and unconditional cooperation with the US and the West over its international energy policy. It is this that provides the context for serious consideration of alternative energy-driven strategic engagements to compliment the western-centric integrationist dynamic. Inevitably, however, consideration and policy implementation of these alternative strategies potentially compromise relations with the West and can have a significant damaging effect on those relations.

The following three chapters examine the alternative strategies in three different contexts. In the next chapter, this context is the increasingly important energy relations between China, Russia and the energy-rich states of central Asia. The question here is whether the clear economic logic of developing and enhancing energy ties between China and Russia and central Asia is also helping to cement a more ideological relationship that challenges and provides a 'balance' against the West. Chapter 9 examines whether China's increasing energy-driven expansion into the Middle East and other parts of south and east China is aimed at challenging, or is in fact acquiescing in, traditional US hegemony in these regions. In Chapter 10, the context shifts to Africa and Latin America where the speed and extent of China's energy-driven engagement have been major new geopolitical developments in both regions and which have raised questions as to whether this is aiming to supplant or challenge western power and, if so, on what terms. The next chapter, however, assesses the considerable post-Cold War improvement in Sino-Russian relations and the extent to which energy is helping to consolidate their mutual relations.

8 The revisionist alternative

Energy and the Sino-Russian axis

Introduction

If China's ambition to integrate into the global international system is likely, as the previous chapter suggests, to be significantly constrained by conflicting approaches and continuing tensions with the West, to what extent will China seek to challenge and confront this order? According to classical realist thought, it is only natural that China as a rising power will seek ways to balance against the dominant global powers and that it will look for similarly disaffected allies to construct a countervailing anti-hegemonic alliance. Even if 'hard balancing', which involves establishing a full military alliance, is currently impractical due to the unchallengeable military superiority of the United States, a strategy of 'soft balancing' can still be pursued that implies diplomatic, political and military steps that seek to hinder and undermine, if not directly overturn, US global hegemony.[1]

In the global balance of power, a number of the most powerful and uninhibited revisionist and anti-western states are energy-rich states, such as Russia, Iran, Venezuela, Myanmar and Sudan, and it is also with these states that China has developed increasingly close energy-driven relations. This raises the question of the extent to which China's international energy strategy, and the clear ambition to gain access to the world's principal sources of oil and gas, is contributing to the consolidation of an anti-western political order.[2] Is there evidence of an emergent anti-western energy nexus, bringing China with its rapidly growing demand for energy into an increasingly closer embrace with those energy-rich states whose opposition to the United States and the West is well entrenched?[3]

Of all the potential energy-related bilateral relationships, it is the prospect of a deeper and more consolidated partnership between China and Russia that is the greatest potential threat to western dominance. A full-bloodied alliance between these two countries would marry territorial depth, encompassing much of the Eurasian continent, a large combined population, a significant military capacity, including nuclear weapons, and a fast growing economic capability with a substantial share of the world's natural resources.

Whether such an alliance is actually being constructed and whether it is seeking directly to challenge the West is contested, not only among western but also Russian and Chinese analysts. Those who see a growing synergy between Russia and China emphasise the remarkable improvement in bilateral relations since the end of the Cold War, the increased 'normative' convergence on global governance issues, such as defending the principle of non-intervention and state immunity against western-supported human rights and democracy promotion, and the increasing number of bilateral initiatives that have an openly anti-western or anti-US intent.[4] In the period 2004–05 alone, these initiatives included the demand for the US to vacate its military bases in central Asia, the first ever joint military exercise between the two countries called 'Peace Mission 2005', and an implicitly anti-western joint declaration between the Russian and Chinese leaders, Vladimir Putin and Hu Jintao, on an 'international order for the 21st century'. Energy links are seen to be the material and economic glue of the relationship, providing Russia with a lucrative new market and China with a reliable source for its energy needs that is less vulnerable to US pressure than supplies from the Middle East and elsewhere.

For other analysts, such a strategic convergence is more rhetorical than substantive. It only obscures the multiple conflicts of interests between the two states and the pragmatic reality that the most important economic and political relations for both these countries remain with the West. Bobo Lo argues that the Sino-Russian relationship is best characterised as an 'axis of convenience' rather than as a substantive partnership and that it falls far short of a genuine attempt to construct a countervailing balance to western hegemony.[5] He highlights in particular the considerable difficulties and disappointments in the bilateral energy relationship where much-vaunted joint projects, such as the building of gas and oil pipelines between the two countries, have failed to materialise or have been heavily delayed and China has been forced to look elsewhere, such as in central Asia or as far away as West Africa to ensure its oil and gas supplies. It is here that Lo notes that the 'gulf between image and reality is greatest'.[6]

This chapter argues that neither of these contrasting views on the emerging Sino-Russian relationship captures the full reality. As against the more alarmist convergence view, one cannot ignore the continuing tensions and conflicts between the two countries and the fact that neither country wishes radically to re-orient relations to the West, which ultimately remains their political and strategic priority. Neither country, singly or combined, has the capacity or the interest to engage in serious 'hard balancing'. In the energy field, early expectations and hopes that Russia would emerge as China's most important energy partner have simply failed to materialise.

But this does not mean that their relationship is, as the sceptics suggest, purely tactical or just hard-headed pragmatism. Since the end of the Cold War, both countries have seen clear mutual benefits in enhancing relations, which include not only a normative and political but also a more strictly geo-economic dimension. This is evident in the energy relationship that, after the many disappointments during the 1990s and early 2000s, has subsequently improved and become more substantial in the late 2000s. The gap between 'image and reality' has therefore been diminishing. But understanding the significance of the energy relationship needs also to take into account not only the bilateral but also the more global geopolitical energy-related dimensions. For China, Russia provides critical support for Beijing's global energy ambitions in various parts of the world, such as in central Asia where China benefits from Russian acquiescence to its economic presence in the region, or in countries like Iran where Russian support provides some degree of political cover for Chinese oil companies and the Chinese government to resist western pressures to disinvest. From the Chinese energy perspective, this provides a belt of oil and energy resources from Siberia through central Asia to Iran, which benefit from not being directly under US hegemonic control and thus can be relied upon in the advent of any Sino-US conflict limiting oil supplies from the Middle East. It is these fruits of the broader warming of China's relations with Russia, which involves a growing convergence in strategic outlook, which should also be taken into account when assessing the Sino-Russia energy relationship.

Context of the Sino-Russian rapprochement

It is this broader post-Cold War Sino-Russian rapprochement that needs therefore to be contextualised. One common perception is that this warming of relations has primarily been driven by the antagonism shared by the Russian and Chinese leaderships to the unilateralism of the George W. Bush presidency (2000–08) and the associated ambitious transformative agenda of democracy promotion and military intervention.[7] If this is the case, one might then expect that as President Obama has promoted a more cautious multilateralist agenda towards Russia through the 'strategic re-set' policy, much of the driving force for the bilateral warming will dissipate and that the multiple underlying tensions and conflicts between Russia and China, which in the past almost led to outright war, will probably re-surface.[8]

While there is a certain validity to this view and bilateral relations did become notably warmer in the context of a common perceived threat posed by the US in the mid-2000s, it overlooks the more substantive and durable roots of the improvement in relations. In reality, the dynamic and impulse towards reconciliation has historical roots in the 'new thinking' Mikhail Gorbachev promoted in the late 1980s, and many of the factors in the drive to overcome the most debilitating effects of the historical legacies of Sino-Russian distrust cannot simply be understood as a function of US global and regional policies but have their own specific rationales and have been pursued for the broader perceived benefits that they confer on both countries. As such, this indicates that the improvement in relations can be expected to have a greater durability and longevity than the shifting patterns of the global balance of power might suggest.

This more extensive and determined political and diplomatic process is evident in attempts by the political leaderships in both countries to overcome the tensions and conflicts in three core areas. First, in settling the historical legacies of war, imperialism and the resulting border disputes and irredentist claims. Second, in overcoming the fear within both countries that the other country might 'defect' to the West opportunistically and without warning. And, third, in the need to come to terms with the distrust habitually engendered by the lack of transparency and the opacity of decision-making characteristic of the policy-making processes in both countries.

The memory of the perceived injustices, past imperial annexations and perceptions of hostility and distrust are not just historical but continuing and live issues in both Russia and China. The Russian historical narrative of centuries of suffering under the 'Mongol yoke' continues to pervade popular perceptions, which leads to a barely disguised quasi-racist views of the Chinese as the 'yellow peril' who can never be completely trusted.[9] For their part, the Chinese have not forgotten that Tsarist Russia was one of the European imperialist powers imposing 'unequal treaties' in the nineteenth century and annexing large tracts of historic Chinese territory and that the Soviet Union subsequently acted in a similarly aggressive and 'imperialist' manner.[10] At the height of the Sino-Soviet split, Mao claimed that Russia had taken over the 'area east of Baikal, Vladivostok, Khabarovsk, Khamkatka' and noted that 'we have not yet presented our account for this list'.[11] Russians living in Russian Far East, who number only 5 million as against the 110 million Chinese across the border in north-eastern China, continue to hold highly xenophobic and exaggerated fears of Chinese immigration and insist that China has never really relinquished its longer-term goal of reclaiming large tracts of Russian territory.[12] For the Chinese, the perception that Russia continues to act in an high-minded manner and cannot be fully trusted is reflected in their irritation that Moscow refuses to provide the most advanced military technology which it is however willing to sell to its traditionally closer ally of India.

But, despite these historical legacies of distrust, the pragmatic reality is that significant steps have been made to settle the core issues that contributed to the freezing of relations from the late 1950s onwards. As early as July 1986, Gorbachev in a speech in Vladivostok proposed the creation of a 'zone of peace' in the region surrounding the much disputed Sino-Russian border and offered the first major concession by a Soviet leader, proposing that the border be in the middle (thalweg) of the Amur and not on the Chinese side of the river. The momentum for further progress was maintained during the Yeltsin administrations in the 1990s that resulted in the formal upgrading of the bilateral relationship to a 'strategic partnership of equality, mutual confidence and mutual coordination for the 21st century' and the conclusion of series of territorial agreements that led to most of the key border issues being resolved. In 2004, Putin was finally able to override the recalcitrance of the governors of the Russian Far East, who had held up the implementation of these Yeltsin-era agreements, and brought a final settlement to the remaining border issues.[13] In addition, during the Putin period, not only were political and diplomatic relations enhanced but bilateral trade increased substantially. Trade rose from a pitiful US$380 million in 1989 to US$8 billion in 2000 and to about US$48 billion in 2007, though it should be noted that this still represents only a small fraction of Russia's trade with the EU (US$204 billion) and China's trade with the United States (US$356 billion) or Japan (US$302 billion). The Russian arms trade with China represents a significant proportion of bilateral trade with US$8 billion of arms being sold up to 2000 and US$27 billion from 2000 onwards.

The second source of distrust and tension is the potential vulnerability of the bilateral relationship to sharp shifts from either country towards an enhanced strategic relationship with the West. The classic historical instance of this was the dramatic Sino-US rapprochement in the early 1970s, when the US and China's mutual interests converged in seeking to balance against and undermine Soviet global ambitions. The fear of such *realpolitik* shifts in alliance partners remains an ongoing concern into the post-Cold War period. With the collapse of the Soviet Union, it was the Chinese leadership that feared that Russia would definitively seek to move to the 'civilized, democratic side of the barrier' as Andrei Kozyrev the pro-western Russian foreign minister stated in 1993, and that Russia's destiny was with the democratic West rather than with the authoritarian East.[14] The replacement of Kozyrev by Yevgeny Primakov in 1996 assuaged Chinese concerns to a certain extent and bilateral relations were consolidated. But again Chinese fears were raised by the initial pro-western shift in Putin's response to the post-9/11 'war on terror', when he supported the US request for military bases in central Asia and did not directly challenge the US unilateral abrogation of the 1972 Anti-Ballistic Missile (ABM) Treaty.[15]

But despite these recurrent fears of succumbing or submitting to the West, the dynamic in bilateral relations, particularly with the increased centralisation of power in Russia during Putin's presidency, has promoted a growing strategic convergence over a number of core issues relating to political governance and approaches to international politics. One of the key sources of this convergence is that both countries are large multinational societies with restive minorities who threaten the integrity of the state, whether in the north Caucasus for Russia or in Tibet and Xinjiang for China. This provides the basis for a common perception of western promoted policies – such as NATO enlargement, the promotion of 'coloured revolutions' in the former Soviet space, and humanitarian interventions into Kosovo or Iraq or elsewhere – as representing threats both to their own political integrity and to the traditional principles of state sovereignty and non-intervention, which both Russia and China see as critical to international stability.[16] The Russian-promoted concept of 'sovereign democracy' has close parallels with Chinese political concepts, such as the idea of a 'harmonious society'. These doctrines converge in asserting that the distinctive national paths of development will preclude the dominant liberal paradigm of democratisation and will involve a much greater role for the state to determine the developmental trajectory. The model that both countries are effectively promoting is that of the east Asian 'developmental state', which relies on political authoritarianism, state-directed long-term economic development, and state mobilisation of resources within the basic framework of a market economy.[17] It is this underlying convergence of the political, economic and social systems in Russia and China that suggests that their strategic cooperation is likely to endure, even if US and western policy were to move significantly away from the unilateralist approach of the Bush Administration.

There is, though, one final area of underlying distrust between Russia and China that is a consequence of the very nature of their increasingly similar political and economic systems. This is the lack of transparency and the unpredictability of policy-making that is characteristic of both countries. The problems that this creates for the effective articulation and implementation of China's energy policy have already been extensively covered in Chapter 4. In terms of Sino-Russian energy cooperation, the market distortion in the low domestic price for gas in China has, for example, been a substantial obstacle to the development of a gas pipeline from Russia to China. But it was the chaotic situation in Russia during the 1990s and the effective lack of any consistent energy strategy during this period, which was a more significant deterrent to bilateral energy cooperation. This policy paralysis in Russia continued into the early 2000s but has subsequently significantly stabilised with the re-assertion of state control over private companies and over the energy sector as a whole. It is in this context, where both China and Russia view their respective energy sectors as 'pillar' industries, with ultimate control residing in the state, which has helped to facilitate, if far from ensure, state-to-state energy cooperation.

Sino-Russian energy cooperation

The story of Sino-Russian energy cooperation since the early 1990s amply reflects this trajectory of early optimism and expectation to disappointment and mutual distrust and then to a more pragmatic and realistic accommodation. The early period of hopeful expectation was driven by what appeared to be a real convergence of economic and political interests as China shifted in 1993 from being an oil-exporting to an oil-importing nation, and began to consider the need for gas imports, and Russia saw the opportunity with the end of the Cold War to open potentially highly lucrative new markets in Asia to balance its existing dependence on energy exports to Europe.[18] For China, the Russian option was particularly attractive, at least in economic efficiency terms. Compared to the other alternatives of pipelines being developed to bring oil and gas from west China (Xinjiang) and central Asia to the principal markets in eastern China, with the vast distances that would need to be covered and the uncertainty over the volume of available reserves, the oil and gas in neighbouring Russia was assured to be plentiful and was relatively much closer to Chinese markets. Moreover, in the context of the improvement in the broader bilateral Sino-Russian relationship in the mid-1990s, which was more advanced on the political than the economic front, the development of this energy linkage appeared to have a clear political and economic rationale.[19]

It was in the period 1993–4 that the first substantive proposals for oil and gas pipelines emerged in the post-Soviet era. The main actor on the Russian side who became the strongest advocate for the oil pipeline was the company Yukos that, as a result of privatisation, had emerged as one the leaders in oil production and processing in Russia. Yukos was also one of the first companies to formulate a corporate strategy for the East of the country, seeking to develop the resources of Eastern Siberia and to export them to Asia-Pacific markets. In 1999, Yukos bought Tomskneft and gained the rights to exploit one of the largest deposits in Eastern Siberia and, at the same time, started trial deliveries of oil from Western Siberia through Eastern Siberia and then on to China by rail.[20] In September 2001, Yukos's persistence was rewarded when Russia and China signed a general agreement to carry out the engineering design for an oil pipeline that would be delivered from Angarsk to Daqing at a total length of 2,400 km and with total projected annual throughput of 30 million tonnes. In March 2003, Yukos and CNPC concluded an agreement to proceed with construction. The Yukos plan had a number of advantages. The oil resource base was well prepared, a feasibility study had been completed and the relatively direct routing of the pipeline kept the length and costs of the pipeline low. From the Chinese perspective, the pipeline would provide a substantial quantity of crude oil imports within a relatively short time frame and would supply this oil into an already important oil producing region that had significant oil refining capacity.[21]

The idea of a gas pipeline, which would take gas from the Kovytka field near Irkutsk to China, was first broached in 1994, then confirmed by an inter-governmental agreement in 1997, and led in 1999 to Rusia Petroleum and CNPC, later joined by the Korean Gas Corporation (KOGAS) in 2000, to agree to a feasibility study for the proposed gas pipeline. British Petroleum, through its joint venture with TNK, bought in late 1997 a 10 per cent share of Sidanko, the main shareholder of Rusia Petroleum, with the specific objective of gaining access to Rusia Petroleum's energy exports to China. The main discussion as this stage was the preferred route for the proposed gas pipeline, whether this would go to South Korea directly from China or would also transit Mongolia or North Korea. The final feasibility study in 2003 recommended avoiding transit through either Mongolia or North Korea, which would involve a route through China to South Korea with the pipeline under the Yellow Sea. The inclusion of South Korea as a destination for the gas was made as the major perceived commercial risk was the ability and willingness of customers in China to pay a price for the gas that was acceptable to the Russian suppliers.[22] Overall, the project was planned to deliver 4 billion cubic metres per year to local markets in Eastern Siberia, 20 billion cubic metres per year to China and 10 billion cubic metres per year to South Korea.

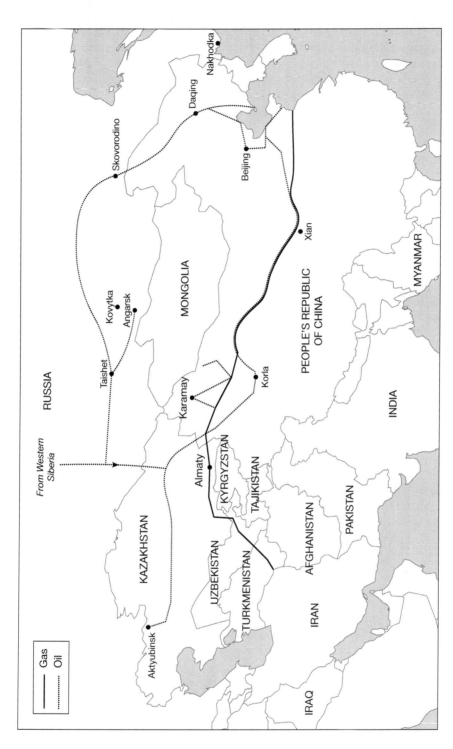

Map 8.1 Map of Asia showing the main pipeline routes from Russia and central Asia to China.

The various plans and preparations for oil and gas pipelines, which had appeared to build up a considerable momentum by the early 2000s, were all to suffer swift and seemingly radical reverses. The main catalyst for this was the forcible reassertion of Russian state control on the oil and gas sector, through the direct personal intervention of the new President, Vladimir Putin, which led to a radical restructuring and renationalisation of the industry.[23] The new national framework was set out in the 'Energy Strategy' of 2003, which explicitly sought to increase state control over oil and gas companies, primarily through control over the export networks but also through demanding greater consideration of the domestic energy needs of the country.

This had a direct impact on both Yukos, the company behind the proposed Angarsk to Daqing oil pipeline, and TNK-BP, which by 2004 had assumed control of the Kovytka gas project.[24] Yukos was forcibly dismantled, its CEO Mikhail Khodorkhovsky imprisoned, and the assets of the company were redistributed to the benefit of the large vertically-integrated and state-owned company Rosneft, whose CEO is Igor Sechin, one of Putin's closest political allies. Transneft, the state-controlled operator of the oil pipeline network in Russia, proposed that the oil pipeline should now transport oil from Eastern Siberia to the Pacific coast instead of to China and that it would run to the north rather than to the south of Lake Baikal.[25] The Kovytka gas project suffered a similar fate with the state monopoly, Gazprom, taking strategic control of the development of gas resources in Eastern Siberia and decisions on the possible export of gas to the markets of China and other countries in the Asia-Pacific region. Gazprom's priorities were very different from those of TNK-BP. Its key export markets are in Europe and its investment priorities are to ensure continued supply to those markets, such as the building of the Nordstream gas pipeline and the development of the Yamal gas fields. Gazprom is also, as a state-controlled company, more constrained by its obligation to ensure there are adequate gas supplies for the domestic Russian market. As a consequence, Gazprom proposed that the gas pipeline from Kovytka should be constructed towards the west, rather than towards the east and Asian export markets, so as to create a unified system of gas supply in Russia. A barely veiled underlying strategic objective of denying TNK-BP its Chinese export plans was to wrest control over the Kovytka field from TNK-BP, which has been a source of continuing conflict between Gazprom and TNK-BP, thus further holding up serious consideration of developing a gas export potential.[26] In 2007, TNK-BP agreed to sell the field to Gazprom for about US$1 billion. The deal was never finalised and so, in June 2010, TNK-BP decided to push its subsidiary and Kovytka's license holder, Rusia Petroleum, into bankruptcy.[27]

For China, the cumulative effects of all these rapid and unexpected reversals to earlier seemingly mutually agreed and politically supported plans was naturally one of disappointment and frustration. Apart from the questionable nature of some of the reasons put forward for these reversals, such as the threat of ecological damage to any pipeline going to the region south of Lake

Baikal, there was also a perception in Beijing of malign geopolitical manoeuvring. The decision announced by Russia in 2004 to favour the oil pipeline route to the Pacific port of Nakhodka, completely bypassing China, coincided with energetic Japanese diplomatic and commercial activity, which included the offer of a US$5 billion investment in the construction of the pipeline and a further US$7.5 billion to explore reserves in Eastern Siberia.[28] For many Chinese commentators, this Russian change in position appeared strongly linked to the Japanese intervention.[29] The further implicit rationalisation for this Russian preference – that it avoided a Chinese monopoly over the supplies provided by the pipeline, and that the Nakhodka option meant that the oil would be available to the whole Asia-Pacific region – added to the sense of Russia continuing to perceive China as more of an economic threat than opportunity.[30] The suspension of the plans for the Kovytka gas pipeline added a further level of frustration as it provided additional evidence that bilateral and seemingly assured agreements between the two countries were highly vulnerable to the internal struggle for power within the Russian energy sector. A final humiliation in these series of setbacks was the enforced withdrawal of CNPC in 2002 from the auction to gain a 75 per cent stake in the Russian oil company Slavneft, which was the result of strong opposition in the Russian state Duma and a public statement by Russian government representatives that the participation of a Chinese NOC in the privatisation of a Russian state company was undesirable.[31]

It was, at least in part, as a consequence of these series of disappointments with Russia that the Chinese government shifted its priorities towards developing oil and gas pipelines from western China and from central Asia. By 2010, this has resulted in a massive and very expensive network of pipelines that extend all the way from eastern Kazakhstan and Turkmenistan via Xinjiang and then to the key markets in eastern China (as described below). But it is important to emphasise that this remarkable exercise of political will over immediate economic efficiency was not just driven by a disillusionment with the Russian energy relationship. The decision in Spring 2000 to focus on Xinjiang and to build a West-to-East gas pipeline from the Tarim Basin to Shanghai was a flagship project of the so-called Develop the West programme that was a core strategic priority of the Chinese leadership. The manifold concerns expressed by many Chinese analysts over the economic viability and efficiency of the project were simply overridden by a high-level political decision, which had the personal imprimatur of the Chinese leadership, including the support of Jiang Zemin and Zhu Rongji.[32] This political priority was driven by the general perceived strategic need to extend China's prosperity from the east to the west so as to reduce economic inequalities and ensure domestic stability. But it also addressed the more specific concern of ensuring Xinjiang's integrity, given its ethnically central Asian Uighur majority population who, it was feared, had secessionist ambitions and could be tempted to seek to follow their central Asian brethren in demanding independence.[33] For the Chinese leadership, obsessed as they are by the need to maintain the political integrity of the country, the key to ensuring Xinjiang's further integration into the Chinese economic and political system was through the development of its energy resources and building interdependencies between China and the rest of central Asia. It was a logical consequence of this decision to build an East-to-West pipeline that the dynamic for oil and gas pipelines with the central Asian states should also gain a high political priority and assume a greater economic viability.

This strategic orientation towards western China and central Asia, which is as much driven by internal political priorities as by disillusionment with Russia, has also not precluded the subsequent development of enhanced and mutually beneficial energy relations between China and Russia. The reasons for this are linked to geopolitical considerations with a deterioration of Russian relations with Japan due to unresolved territorial issues contributing to Moscow re-focusing its attentions towards China and promising again to provide a branch pipeline to reach China. But there were also more strictly commercial factors. The most significant of these is the realisation by Russian NOCs that they need substantial foreign investment if they are going to be able to develop their assets and ensure future exports and that Chinese oil companies have access to billions of dollars for investment purposes. This economic convergence of interests has facilitated a more durable and solid energy relationship, particularly in relation to oil. In 2005, CNPC lent US$6 billion to Rosneft so that the Russian company could afford to purchase Yukos's most valuable subsidiary, Yugansneftegaz, in exchange for the future delivery of 50 million tonnes of oil between 2005 and 2010. As a consequence of this, deliveries of crude oil from Russia to China increased from 500,000 tonnes in 1999 to 11–15 million tonnes per year over the period 2005–08, which is close to the capacity possible to deliver without a dedicated oil pipeline.[34] In October 2008, China agreed to provide Rosneft with an additional loan of US$15 billion and Transneft with US$10 billion so as to ensure that the much-delayed oil pipeline to China would be completed and that shipments would reach 15 million tonnes by 2011.[35]

Since 2006, both Sinopec and CNPC have also succeeded in establishing their first joint ventures in Russia with Rosneft and thus have overcome the earlier failure to gain a stake in Sibneft. These include a joint venture oil production company, Udmurtneft, a joint development of the Veninsky block on the Sakhalin shelf, and a refining and marketing joint venture in north-east China. A number of future opportunities are being actively explored.

However, the one area where progress has not been substantially advanced is over gas cooperation where constant bilateral discussions have failed to reach any conclusive agreement. Russia's overall strategic plan for gas in the East certainly includes exports to China but the reality is that strategic priorities remain in ensuring an adequate domestic supply, in Gazprom's determination to gain strategic control over the gas fields of Eastern Siberia and its focus on Yamal and Sakhalin rather than on constructing export capacity for China. And the fact is that China's requirement for gas up to 2020 is probably already satisfied through growing domestic supplies, LNG imports, and pipeline imports from central Asia. Administrative and regulatory disputes over price and market share continue to complicate relations. As a consequence, it is likely that Russia will decide to postpone development of further gas deposits in Eastern Siberia until after 2020 given the prospective absence of sufficient Chinese demand.[36]

The Sino-Russian energy relationship in a broader global context

The overall lesson to be drawn from the bilateral energy relationship is that it illustrates both the constraints and opportunities in the development of this critical geo-economic dimension of their relationship. Undoubtedly, a significant opportunity was missed to develop a Russian-Chinese transborder energy infrastructure in the late 1990s and early 2000s, which led China to diversify supplies to other neighbouring resource-rich countries, most notably to central Asia. But this was not solely due to policy paralysis in Russia and Chinese disappointment at what appeared to be Russia reneging on earlier promises, but was also a consequence of the strategic decision by the top Chinese leadership to Develop the West and give priority to developing an energy network to Xinjiang and beyond to central Asia. Moreover, despite these setbacks, bilateral Sino-Russian energy relations revived significantly from the mid-2000s onwards, which included the construction of an oil pipeline, large-scale Chinese investments in the Russian energy sector, and increased levels of cooperation between Russia and Chinese oil companies.

It would be a mistake, though, to limit the Sino-Russian energy relationship to its strictly bilateral dimension. There is an important, and often neglected, regional and geopolitical dimension that is critical for understanding the broader context of China's energy-driven relationship with Russia. This is the common interest in China and in Russia to ensure that their common strategic hinterland in central Asia does not fall under US hegemony. For China, this is particularly important in the energy sphere as the region from Russia to central Asia and Iran possesses ample supplies of oil and gas that can be transported directly to China without passing through territory or seas controlled by the US, which is the case for shipments from the Middle East or elsewhere. It is, therefore, a critical interest for China that Russia supports, or at least acquiesces in, its regional and international energy policies, most notably in central Asia, and that it provides political and diplomatic support where Chinese international energy interests might conflict with western policies, most notably in Iran.

In central Asia, it is China's diplomatic convergence with Russia in seeking to limit and constrain western penetration into the region that has brought clear benefits. Chinese oil companies have increased their involvement in the central Asian energy sector without generating the anxieties and counter-measures that might have been expected from Moscow. This contrasts with

Moscow's vigorous attempts to limit western engagement into the Caspian region, which has been likened to a new 'Great Game' and has involved a whole host of complex economic and political manoeuvrings by Moscow.[37] Although Moscow ultimately could not stop the construction of the Baku-Tbilisi-Ceyhan oil pipeline, it has been waging a long-term battle to prevent the building of the EU-promoted Nabucco gas pipeline through the proposed construction of an alternative South Stream pipeline.[38]

As Russia's diplomatic energies have been concentrated on limiting western influence, China's economic interests have quietly but inexorably risen. The first significant investment in the region was in Kazakhstan in 1997 when CNPC/PetroChina out-bid Texaco and Amoco to buy a 60 per cent equity share of the company Aktobemunaygaz, gaining control of two substantial fields in the Aktyubinsk region.[39] This deal, along with a purchase of an oilfield at Uzen, involved investing US$4.3 billion over twenty years. There was also an agreement to build a 2,800km cross-border pipeline from Kazakhstan to China. However, concerns about whether there were sufficient reserves at the fields in Aktyubinsk and Uzen, along with the fall in the price of oil in the late 1990s, led to an abandonment of these projects, much to the displeasure of the Kazakh authorities. But China returned with vigour to Kazakhstan in 2003 when CNPC purchased a further 25.4 per cent in Aktobemunaygaz, giving it a 85.4 per cent share of the company. In May 2004, agreement was finalised for the construction of the oil pipeline from the west of Kazakhstan (Atyrau) to China's western border in Xinjiang, which was built in three stages and completed in 2009 with an annual capacity of 20 million tonnes, which represents roughly 5 per cent of China's overall oil demand. In 2005, CNPC made a number of further investments, including the takeover of the Canadian oil company PetroKazakhstan for US$4.2 billion in October 2005. The little known Hong Kong-based company, CITIC, paid US$1.9 billion to purchase JSC Karazhanbasmunai, which was the sole owner of rights to the Karazhanbas oilfield in western Kazakstan.[40] Overall, equity oil production reached 15 million tonnes by 2009, representing about one quarter of China's foreign oil production. After Sudan, Kazakhstan is the most significant country for Chinese foreign investment in the oil/gas sector.

The speed and the scale of China's engagement and investment in oil production in Kazakhstan is impressive, But it is probable that it will be Caspian gas, rather than oil, which will ultimately play a more significant role in China's overall energy mix. In 2007, China signed a twenty-year sale and purchase agreement with Turkmenistan to import 30 bcm per year and then followed this by reaching deals with Turkmenistan, Uzbekistan and Kazakhstan to construct the necessary 2,000 km pipeline. In 2008, the Turkmen government confirmed that it would seek to provide 40 billion cubic metres per year, part of the gas being sourced from a field being developed by CNPC on the right bank of the Amu Darya river in southeast Turkmenistan. If this output is secured, Turkmenistan should theoretically be able to fill a large part of China's projected future needs, which are estimated to be

200 billion cubic metres per year by 2020, with 140 billion cubic metres being produced domestically and about 20 billion cubic metres from existing and planned LNG terminals.[41] Overall, the decisiveness and speed in developing this gas pipeline with distant Turkmenistan is a remarkable development – in the 1990s, the idea of such a pipeline was generally thought to be a 'pipe dream' due to the costs and distances involved.[42] A further surprising feature is that there has seemed to be little concern over the security implications of a pipeline that would have to pass through both Uzbekistan and Kazakhstan, neither of which are known for their internal stability. This contrasts with the almost excessive anxiety that Beijing demonstrated in the 1990s about the possibility of any gas pipeline from Russia needing to transit through Mongolia, which is hardly a country representing a significant geo-strategic threat to China.

The further surprising feature is that this significant penetration of China, and the expansion of its direct security interests into a region that is traditionally seen in Moscow as its exclusive 'sphere of influence', has not engendered the degree of Russian obstruction and opposition that might have been expected. The negative economic impact on Russia has been significant, as China's engagement has enhanced the bargaining power of the central Asian states, which has resulted in Russia having to pay substantially higher prices for the gas that it receives from the region.[43] Russian analysts have also not been afraid to highlight, in often quite dramatic terms, the longer-term strategic threat represented by China's growing presence in central Asia.[44] Russian companies have, at times, sought to pre-empt or block Chinese deals being finalised, such as the opposition of Lukoil to the CNPC purchase of PetroKazakhstan in 2005. The Russian government has also exerted considerable political and diplomatic efforts to develop multilateral bodies, such as the Collective Security Treaty Organisation, which specifically exclude China and seek to sustain the privileged politico-military relations between Russia and the states of central Asia.[45]

What then explains Russia's reticence towards China's burgeoning economic presence? In part, it is a common interest to ensure that the central Asian region remains stable and that US influence does not extend into the region that would have a negative impact for both Russia and China. In part, it is a recognition of China's economic might and Russia's relative weakness and that Moscow cannot simply prohibit the central Asian states from gaining access to the dynamic markets of China and the Asia-Pacific region. Even if the central Asian states themselves have historic suspicions of China, the prospect of diversifying away from their almost total dependence on Russia has naturally been attractive. Chinese companies also have a simple competitive advantage compared to their Russian counterparts with access to substantial funds for investment as well as a proven capacity to implement large-scale projects swiftly and efficiently.[46]

But another critical factor is that China has expertly, and with considerable diplomatic dexterity, utilised the growing political, economic and normative convergence with Russia to ensure a relatively benign Russian response to its activities in central Asia. China has been very careful to not directly challenge Russia's political and military dominance in the region and its self-image as a 'Great Power'. The Chinese government has consistently sought to demonstrate that its strategic interests in the region are convergent with those of Russia, most notably in seeking to limit western penetration, to crack down on Islamist and secessionist forces, and to support existing authoritarian regimes from pressures for democratisation. China and Russia, for instance, provided unequivocal backing to President Karimov in Uzbekistan after his brutal repression of an uprising in Andizhan in 2005.[47] China has also sought to dampen the potential competitive dynamic with Russia by multilateralising the relationship through the SCO, which is an organisation that has developed from a loose association focused on demarcating borders in the late 1990s to a considerably more institutionalised body that aims to establish regional confidence-building measures and combat what Chinese policymakers call the 'three evils' of terrorism, religious extremism and secessionism.[48]

It is this strategic rapprochement with Russia that has facilitated China's extensive energy-driven economic engagement in the region. China's multi-lateral initiative is not without its tensions. Russia seeks to make the SCO a more politico-military anti-western institution that extends to other large regional actors, such as Iran and India, which is not something that China supports. For its part, Beijing places its focus on economic issues, promoting the idea of a free trade area to which Russia and the central Asian states are opposed.[49] But, despite these tensions, the SCO does genuinely offer a framework for managing competition and where China's much beloved goal of creating 'win-win' situations can be realised. For instance, the development of two oil pipelines to China from Eastern Siberia and from Kazakhstan permits both Russia and Kazakhstan to utilise either pipeline to deliver oil to Chinese markets. Chinese oil companies have also actively sought to develop joint cooperative ventures with Russian oil companies in central Asia. The Chinese apparent lack of overt concern about the gas pipeline traversing Uzbekistan and Kazakhstan is also probably linked to this sense of the benefits of developing interdependencies within the region. Even the Russian idea of an SCO 'Energy Club' has been favourably received in Beijing, even if there are clearly reservations about multilateralising Chinese energy investments in central Asia.[50]

Just south of the central Asia states, Iran provides an additional key case of China benefiting from its diplomatic and political relations with Russia. For China, Iran is a critical energy market (as discussed further in the next chapter) but where, compared to central Asia, Chinese companies face significantly greater challenges from the West to limit or reduce their investments and economic engagement. In this context, the strategic benefits of Sino-Russian diplomatic cooperation over Iran is not just that both countries adopt a common political position, which strengthens China's own diplomatic stance, but that Russia takes, and is generally perceived in the West to take, at least until recently, the leading role in resisting western ambitions to impose stricter economic sanctions over Iran's nuclear ambitions. China, as the other key permanent member of the UN Security Council with reservations to the imposition of sanctions, is generally perceived to be in the diplomatic background. This is part of a general pattern where Russia, rather than China, is seen by external actors as more openly willing to challenge US hegemony and defend revisionist anti-western states such as Iran, while China is viewed as being more passive, more willing to adopt a balanced position, and where its overriding foreign policy objective is seen to avoid as far as possible confrontation or direct challenges to the US.

But these external perceptions of an assertive and belligerent Russia and a cautious and potentially accommodating China do not reflect the material and economic interests of both countries in Iran, as have become increasingly evident in 2010 and the renewed attempts to impose stricter sanctions on Iran. Certainly, Russia views its close relationship with Iran as a valuable 'strategic card', which can be a useful bargaining chip with the West and as something that enhances its international status. But in economic terms, Iran is a relatively minor partner, considerably less important than neighbouring Turkey, and even areas where Russian companies have been traditionally heavily engaged, such as arms and nuclear power, have suffered significant declines.[51] Although Russia and Iran have considerably improved relations since the end of the Cold War due to a convergence of interests over many regional issues, most notably concerning central Asia and Afghanistan, this has not erased historic memories of distrust and suspicion and has not been sufficient to resolve some critical bilateral conflicts, such as the demarcation of the Caspian Sea. Russia also views Iranian nuclear proliferation as a serious international threat, not least because Russian territory would itself be vulnerable, and Russian toleration of Iran's stance has become much more strained once it became evident in 2002 that Iran was deliberately lying about its ambitions.

China, in contrast to Russia, does not have the historical burden of an imperialist legacy with Iran. There is also much about China and Iran's respective pasts that forges a sense of common identity; the fact that they are both ancient and proud civilisations; the ways in which both countries view imperialism as having retarded their progress as nations; their strong commitment to national sovereignty and their opposition to infringements in the internal affairs of states; and a common commitment to a multipolar world and against 'hegemonic bullying'.[52] As a consequence, there is much sympathy within China to Iran's resolve to resist US pressures and considerably less anxiety about the prospects of a nuclear-armed Iran, though China formally is strongly committed to the Nuclear Non-Proliferation Treaty.

Economically, China is also significantly more engaged in Iran than Russia. In the early 2000s, China replaced Germany as the major trading partner for Iran. In 2009, China imported around 20 million tonnes of oil, which is slightly more than a quarter of China's oil imports from the Middle East.[53] The Islamic Republic has consistently been one of China's three leading suppliers of crude oil along with Saudi Arabia and Angola. However, the particular advantage for China of Iran, at least as compared with other Arab Gulf states, is that foreign oil companies have the possibility to access upstream resources directly. Given the Chinese leadership's obsession about the vulnerability of seaborne routes, which are vulnerable to US interdiction, Iran also offers the alluring prospect of oil and gas potentially routed to China through pipelines running across central Asia rather than by sea.[54]

In terms of direct investments, Chinese oil companies made fairly cautious forays in the early 2000s, agreeing to relatively small-scale service contracts and concluding MOUs rather than committing themselves to investment contracts, probably due to fears of being subjected to secondary sanctions under US law.[55] But this restraint has been significantly reduced since 2007 as a series of large-scale Chinese investments have been concluded. These include Sinopec concluding a US$2 billion contract for the development of the Yadavaran oilfield, which was followed by CNPC signing a US$1.76 billion contract in January 2009 to develop the North Azadegan oilfield. CNOOC in 2008 signed an upstream contract to develop the North Pars gas field, which was followed by CNPC concluding in June 2009 an agreement with the Iranian government to replace Total in the contract to develop Phase II of the South Pars gas field.[56] All of these substantial signed contracts demonstrate the seriousness with which Chinese companies are seeking to enter Iran's upstream market and their willingness, supported by their government, to take the risk of alienating the US and having secondary sanctions imposed upon them. It also illustrates the much greater economic stake that China has in Iran than Russia and the benefits that China gains from Russia's support and its leadership in resisting western pressures to impose stricter sanctions on Iran, which could potentially affect the export of Iran's energy resources.

Conclusion

This global energy-related geo-economic dimension of the Sino-Russian relationship provides a broader context for assessing the opportunities offered by China's post-Cold War rapprochement with Russia. As this chapter argues, there are benefits that China gains in its international energy strategy by the political and diplomatic support offered by Russia. The case of Iran can also be extended to other areas or countries, such as Venezuela where Russia similarly plays the harder geopolitical part (the 'bad cop') through such acts as strengthening defence links with the anti-US President Hugo Chavez, while China is more reticent and seeks not to upset the US. This does not mean that China would necessarily change its stance if it lacked Russian support, but the costs to China and its relations with the West would be greater. An example of where China has definitely faced a much tougher struggle to defend its energy-related interest, and where it notably lacked Russia's protective cover, is in Sudan. As Chapter 10 describes, China was much more vulnerable to international criticism due to the perception that it was the main external actor in Sudan and there was no Russia to whom such criticism might be diverted or at least shared.

The overall conclusion is not, though, that Russia and China have now combined forces to promote a global anti-western front in a classical realist balancing fashion. For both countries, the West is still a more critical partner than either China and Russia is to each other. Their mutual relations are driven more by pragmatism than ideology. In addition, bilateral energy relations since the collapse of the Soviet Union have generally been disappointing and highlighting, as Lo argues, the gap 'between rhetoric and reality' of their new-found fraternal relations. Nevertheless, due recognition should be given to the growing convergence of political and economic interests, particularly since the mid-2000s, which has not only aided a revival in bilateral Sino-Russian energy relations but has also had a broader global dimension that is often ignored. From the Chinese perspective on its international energy needs, Russia is the key country to ensure that the vital energy resources of the former Soviet Union, and potentially also from Iran, can be securely supplied to Chinese markets even in the context of a severe deterioration in Sino-US relations. Russia and central Asia provide China with not just military but also a vital energy strategic depth as oil and gas can potentially be transported by pipelines rather than having to pass vulnerable sea-lines of communication. However, such security is not the case for the region where the largest part of China's imports will continue to need to come from – the Middle East – and which is the focus of the next chapter.

9 Hegemony, oil and Asian regional politics

Introduction

The concept of hegemony within IR can be understood in different ways. It can be viewed as a relatively neutral description of the preponderance of power in the international system, which can be as much a source of stability and prosperity as of conflict and instability. Some influential theories of IR argue that it is precisely when one power has unrivalled hegemony that there exist the most propitious conditions for international economic and political progress.[1] An alternative view of hegemony sees the concept in a more emotive and negative light, as the concrete expression of the desire and ambition of the more powerful to exert control over the weaker and less powerful. It is this concept of hegemony that is most common in the Chinese understanding of the term and reflects the long historical memories of how strong external powers have been seen to interfere in China's internal affairs and imposed, for example, a series of unequal treaties in the so-called 'century of humiliation' (1842–1949).[2] In the post-Cold War period, the key questions for Chinese analysts have been the longevity of the period of US hegemony, whether or not a multipolar system is emerging to replace US unipolarity, and the practical ability of China to avoid the negative, controlling aspects of contemporary US hegemony, which is generally viewed as constraining and limiting China's autonomy and development.[3]

From the Chinese energy security perspective, the key advantage of the strategic relationship with Russia is that, as argued in the previous chapter, it provides a certain degree of protection from US hegemony and the threat of the imposition of US control over Chinese energy imports. Oil and potentially gas coming from Russia flow directly into China through pipelines or by railway and do not pass through territory that is directly threatened by US forces. Good relations with Russia also provide China with the opportunity to develop the energy resources of central Asia and for these to be transported directly to China. In broader global energy politics, Russia provides China with a degree of diplomatic cover and its energy interests are protected in states that are viewed as 'pariahs' or 'rogues' in Washington, such as Iran or Venezuela. It is these various and multifaceted ways in which Russia contributes to China's international energy security policies that has provided, as argued in the previous chapter, a strong impetus for China to seek to overturn the long-standing historical enmities with Russia and develop a more substantive and durable bilateral relationship.

Such Russian partnership does not, though, extend to China's south-eastern and south-western dimensions in its foreign policy. It is here that the perceived threat from US hegemony is at its most intense. The most critical unresolved national sovereignty and border issues are located in this broad region – most notably Taiwan, but also Tibet, and the South and East China Seas. Over all these issues, the US presence and its strategic capabilities act as a constraint and an irritant to Chinese national objectives. US regional hegemony is further consolidated through a network of criss-crossing bilateral alliances and by the cooption of the other major regional powers, most significantly Japan and India, into an implicit anti-Chinese containment or hedging strategy. The resultant Chinese sense of insecurity is only magnified by the growing need for energy imports. The unpalatable but unavoidable reality, from the perspective of the Chinese leadership, is that a fast-growing proportion of China's critical energy supplies have to traverse a large expanse of the world that is under the strategic hegemonic domination of the United States. Even the most optimistic of China's foreign policy elites realise that this represents a major potential security threat that needs to be addressed.

It is not, though, an easy issue to resolve. In part, this is because there are different but interlinked dimensions to China's Asian energy insecurity. These can be thought of in terms of three geographical circles that constitute three distinctive energy security dilemmas for China. The first circle is that of the Middle East where the majority of the world's reserves are to be found and where China's dependence on imported oil is greatest but where the US hegemony is most pervasive and unchallenged. The dilemma that faces China in the Middle East, which might be called the 'Persian Gulf dilemma', is that even if the government and the Chinese companies succeed in diversifying supplies to obtain an increasing proportion of the country's energy needs from other parts of the world, the fact of China's growing import dependence, and the size and magnitude of Persian Gulf reserves, means that China will inevitably become more, rather than less, dependent on Middle Eastern energy supplies. Indeed this will increasingly become the case for most oil and gas importing countries. How to ensure the security of these critical supplies from a region where US hegemony is likely to be unchallenged for the foreseeable future is at the heart of this dilemma.

The second circle is that of the Indian Ocean and Southeast Asia, which incorporates the principal SLOCs for not only China's energy imports but also for much of its international trade. The strategic dilemma this poses has been popularly called the 'Malacca dilemma', referring to the narrow Straits of Malacca, which connect the Pacific and the Indian Oceans and where most shipping has to go to reach the Chinese mainland, and which symbolises the

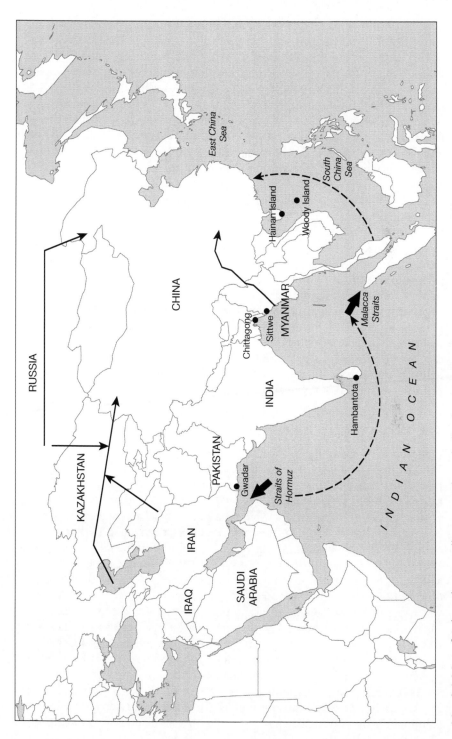

Map 9.1 Map of Asia and surrounding seas, schematically showing oil and gas transport routes to China.

Explanation: solid lines – pipelines; dashed lines – sea-lines; heavy dots – 'String of Pearls'; heavy arrows – choke points

general sense of vulnerability that China feels towards this strategic maritime chokepoint.

The third circle is that closest to the Chinese homeland and it is where unresolved sovereignty issues intersect with potential oil or gas exploration and development. This is most notably the case in the cases of the South China and East China Seas. This dilemma might be called the 'sovereignty dilemma' where the critical question is whether the introduction of an energy dimension to the sovereignty dispute serves to exacerbate the conflict or, alternatively, whether it can be used creatively to promote joint cooperation and thus foster the trust that is required ultimately to resolve these sovereignty disputes.

The overarching challenge for China from these three separate but interconnected dilemmas is that the manner in which China seeks to resolve them will have a determining effect on how others perceive its rise and its own emergence as a hegemonic power. As Chapter 7 highlights, positive feedback plays a critical role in determining prospects for future conflict or cooperation. The more that China seeks to relieve its energy insecurities through cooperation and consensual diplomacy, the more that China's growing power and hegemony will be perceived in a benign and positive manner; the more that policies are driven by the ambition to control and exclude, the more that this power and hegemony will be resented and perceived negatively. And it is crucially in this broader geo-strategic Asian region that the balance of power between the United States and China, the existing and the challenging hegemon, is most crucially being played out.

The 'Persian Gulf dilemma'

In the early 1990s, China's oil imports overwhelmingly came from the Asia-Pacific region and only a small percentage from the Middle East. By the mid-1990s, when China started to be a net-importing country, this ratio changed to being almost equally divided between Asia-Pacific and the Middle East. By the late 2000s, imports from Asia-Pacific had been reduced to a mere 2–3 per cent, while supplies from the Middle East remained fairly constant at between 45–55 per cent of imports. It was also only the very determined efforts by the Chinese government to diversify oil supplies away from the Middle East, which involved increasing significantly supplies from Eurasia (as described in Chapter 8) and from Africa (as described in Chapter 10), which ensured that the overall proportion of China's oil imports from the Middle East remained relatively constant and did not increase significantly. But, it is going to be increasingly difficult for China to reduce its dependence on the Middle East since the region holds almost 60 per cent of the world's proven conventional oil reserves and about 40 per cent of the world's proven natural gas reserves. The Middle East's share of internationally traded oil and gas, which is currently relatively low, is also set to increase significantly in the future.[4] This is primarily due to the fact that an increasing number of oil and gas exporters around the world will become net importers as a result of declining reserves and rising domestic demand.[5] As a consequence, China is set to become ever increasingly economically dependent on the complex political and geo-strategic turbulence of the Middle East. It is this that is at the heart of China's 'Persian Gulf dilemma'.

The challenge for China is that it needs to strengthen its economic position in a region where historically it has rarely played a major or influential role. Beijing lacks the knowledge and the historically forged links and connections that the western external powers enjoy. During the Cold War, China did try to play a role in the Middle East through being more radical and revolutionary than the Soviet Union and supporting some of the more extreme rejectionist Arab groups.[6] But this essentially rhetorical strategy failed to break through the regional dominance of the US and the USSR and even this brief radical moment fizzled out with the pragmatic modernisation agenda promoted by Deng Xiaoping in the late 1970s. During the 1980s, China found a new niche as an arms exporter to the region, most notably to Iran and Iraq, benefiting from the partial international embargo imposed on both countries during the Iran-Iraq war.[7] In 1984 as much as 78 per cent of China's total exports to the Middle East were arms sales. But even in this period, China's average share of arms sales was only around 7–8 per cent of the total sales to the region and the trade was still dominated by the traditional suppliers – the United States, the USSR, the UK and France.[8] During the 1990s, this niche for Chinese economic penetration essentially disappeared as the end of the Cold War resulted in a reassertion of western domination of the regional arms market.

In this post-Cold War context, with the retreat of the Soviet Union from the Middle East and the US emerging unchallenged, China has appeared to submit, if without enthusiasm, to the reality of US hegemony. In 1997, the Chinese government responded to consistent US pressure on the Iranian proliferation issue by providing a written pledge to refrain from any new nuclear cooperation with Iran, which was then followed by an agreement to cease ballistic missile assistance.[9] These concessions fitted more broadly with China's incorporation into the global non-proliferation regime during the 1990s. China's opposition to the two Gulf wars, those of 1990–91 and 2003, was muted and carefully calibrated so as to ensure that longer-term relations with the US and the West were not materially harmed in the process.[10] A similarly cautious approach has been taken towards UN-mandated sanctions against Iraq and Iran. This deliberately non-confrontational approach, allied with policies that have sought to show China acting as a regional 'responsible stakeholder', such as the decision to contribute troops to the peacekeeping operation in Lebanon in 2006, shows that the Chinese government continuously seeks to avoid directly challenging US power and influence in the region.

But this does not mean that China has been inactive in the region. China has a number of strategic advantages that it has promoted so as to enhance its economic and political influence in the region. The first of these is that China does not, as compared to the major western countries, suffer from a historical legacy of colonial domination and failure. This along with the much-proclaimed Chinese policy of 'non-intervention' in the internal affairs of other states is attractive for Middle Eastern states, particularly in the aftermath of the Bush administrations' policies of unilateral military intervention and regime change, which generated considerable resentment in the Arab and Muslim world. It was particularly in the period of the Iraq war that provided the opening for China significantly to enhance its relations with Saudi Arabia, as well as other Arab countries.[11] Arab states, disillusioned with the perceived failure of the EU and Russia to constrain the US, have increasingly come to see China as a potentially more effective balance to the US.[12]

As an economic actor in the energy field, China also has a number of advantages. First, Chinese companies are generally willing to operate in energy-rich US-designated 'pariah' or 'rogue' states and are more willing to resist US pressure to cease or limit activities than other western or pro-western companies. The Chinese government has also generally supported their companies in challenging, within limits, western-imposed sanctions and policies. Second, the Chinese domestic market exerts its own power and influence as China, along with the rest of Asia-Pacific, is an increasingly important destination for Persian Gulf oil and gas. China offers a large potential market for Middle East states to engage in downstream activities, to sell their refined products and chemicals and generally to diversify their economies away from raw commodity exports. China has been active in offering opportunities for Middle Eastern investment in its domestic market and thereby enhance mutual energy security through economic and energy interdependence. A further source of economic advantage is the access of Chinese oil companies to large amounts of state capital and finance, which has become even more valuable in the aftermath of the global credit crunch in 2008–9. With such ready and easily available resources, Chinese oil companies have often been willing to invest in the Middle East at a considerably higher level of economic and political risk than IOCs.

The principal targets of China's energy-directed diplomatic and economic engagement are those oil-producing countries in the Middle East with the largest reserves of oil and gas. The two countries with the largest reserves are Iran and Saudi Arabia and it is to these countries that China has expended considerable diplomatic and political energy. As was set out in the previous chapter, Iran is important for China since it is not only one of the largest exporters of oil to China but is also one of the few countries in the Middle East where it is possible for outside companies to invest in upstream oil sector through the so-called 'buy-back' system.[13] The reason for this relative degree of openness in Iran is the chronic under-investment in the energy sector due to international economic sanctions. This economic opening for Chinese companies and for the government comes, though, with a considerable political risk – the threat of being deemed to have broken the sanctions regime that is at the heart of the US politico-military strategy towards Iran. As noted in the previous chapter, up until 2007 Chinese oil companies only engaged cautiously in Iran, reflecting a mix of fear of political instability and of being the target of US sanctions. But that caution appeared to diminish during 2007, linked in part to the US National Intelligence Assessment report that stated that Iran was currently not engaged in nuclear weapons production and which thereby reduced the prospect of a US-Iranian military confrontation. Subsequent to this, a series of large-scale Chinese investments were concluded, which greatly increased China's economic engagement in Iran – there was the Sinopec US$2 billion contract for the Yadavaran oilfield in 2007, the CNOOC upstream contract for the North Pars gas field in 2009, and in 2010 CNPC taking over Total's role in Phase II of the South Pars gas field. It was notable that in the Security Council negotiations in the first half of 2010, it was China rather than Russia that stood out as the country most resistant to any tightening of the regime and sought to 'water down' any eventual UN resolution.[14] In the post-Cold War record of negotiations over Iranian sanctions, this was the first time that China moved clearly out of the protective diplomatic cover provided by Russia to assert its own economic interests towards Iran at the UN Security Council.

China's relations with Saudi Arabia are of a similar intensity and strategic importance as Iran. But the nature and form of these relations are very different. The main reason for this is that Saudi Arabia has very tight restrictions on inward investment to its oil sector and its NOC, Saudi Aramco, has a high degree of competence and thus has little need to engage Chinese NOCs. There is thus little opportunity for China to be involved in upstream activity within the kingdom. In 2004, Sinopec did win a contract for an exploration and production project for non-associated gas in the Rub al-Khali but this was widely viewed as a political rather than an economic decision by the Chinese oil company.[15] Where there has, though, been a productive economic-driven synergy between the two countries is, in exchange for Saudi oil supplies, China has permitted access for Saudi companies to the domestic downstream sector and, in particular, the refining and petrochemicals market. This is critical for Saudi Arabia's ambition to become a global economic power through the development and export of its chemicals and other energy-based products.[16] Some analysts have suggested that 'dollar for dollar, the Saudis make more from their petrochemical business in China than any place else'.[17] But the Saudi experience in China is far from unproblematic. The negotiations that started in 1993 for Saudi Aramco to construct new refining capacity in Qingdao, Shandong Province, led to an agreement in 2005 and only came on stream in 2008. Middle East oil companies regularly complain that China's domestic pricing policy for oil products undermines the commercial viability of their refinery projects within China.[18] Despite these continuing problems, Saudi Aramco was commissioned in 2009 to develop a second refinery project with Sinopec, in Fujian province, and another Saudi company, SABIC, plans to build a cracking plant in Tianjian.

In relation to the second tier of oil and gas producing states – Iraq, Kuwait, the United Arab Emirates and Qatar (with its large gas reserves) – it is only in Iraq that Chinese oil companies have an opportunity, as in Iran, to invest upstream. China's relations with Kuwait, the UAE and Qatar are similar to those with Saudi Arabia and are predominantly economic in nature. But, in Iraq, the Chinese government and oil companies have been very active and have been determined to seize the opportunity of developing a significant economic role and presence within the country. The challenge in Iraq is different from that in Iran – Iraq does not suffer from external sanctions and the dangers of China upsetting the US are less pronounced. But, Iraq's internal situation is considerably more unstable than Iran's, with chronic insecurity and enormous legal, economic and political uncertainties, which means that only the bravest, and many would say the most foolhardy, would be willing to invest.

However, Chinese NOCs see themselves as having a once-in-a-lifetime opportunity to penetrate a key oil-producing Middle East market and that their more cavalier attitude to risk, allied with greater access to capital, gives them a short-term strategic advantage over the IOCs. This economic ambition is supported by the Chinese government, which views Iraq as a major political and strategic opportunity for China to enhance its presence and influence in the Middle East. After an ice-breaking agreement concluded in 2007 to develop the al-Ahdab field, an agreement initially made under Saddam Hussein, three large-scale deals have been concluded in 2009–10, which highlight the depth and seriousness of China's energy-related economic ambitions. CNPC and BP jointly won a bid to develop the giant South Rumaila field in southern Iraq; Sinopec launched a friendly bid for the Swiss company, Addax, which has been producing oilfields in the Kurdish region of Iraq; and CNPC, Total and Petronas won a deal to develop the Halfaya oilfield. By March 2010, some estimates suggested that Chinese companies had access to 18 per cent of Iraq's reserves and was thus the largest external actor in the Iraqi oil market.[19]

In all these countries, with the partial exception of Iran, most of the economic and political engagement of China is not directed against the West. Indeed, what is more evident is a high degree of pragmatism with, for example, the recent deals in Iraq involving joint collaboration between the Chinese oil companies, western IOCs and the local NOC. Only in Iran is there an explicitly internationally contentious and politicised dimension and, even here, the Chinese government has been keen to ensure that its energy-related ambitions in Iran do not materially undermine the broader Sino-US relationship. China is thus not seeking directly to challenge US hegemony in the Middle East nor realistically sees itself as capable of developing an alternative hegemonic order. But China still has a clear political resolve and set of objectives in the region. It is determined to increase its influence in the region and to use its growing economic needs and penetration as the principal vehicle for increasing its influence. It is courting the states of the Middle East, most notably those with the largest oil and gas reserves, to diversify their relations, to direct their attention increasingly to China and the Asia-Pacific region, and to reduce over time their dependence and political subordination to the US. By so doing,

China sees itself as not just increasing its energy security but also as building the foundations for a substantive political role in the future that would diminish its vulnerability to US hegemonic control.

The 'Malacca dilemma'

Moving eastwards from the Persian Gulf region into the Indian Ocean and beyond to the Chinese mainland, the principal dilemma facing Beijing is not the issue of access to oil and gas reserves, which would help seriously to diminish China's energy security needs. The Asia-Pacific region is notable for having less than 4 per cent of the world's proven oil reserves and for having few options to increase or even maintain current levels of production.[20] Of the major Asia-Pacific oil importers, China is in fact relatively well-endowed when compared to Japan and South Korea who are almost completely dependent on oil imports from the Middle East. Of the oil producers of the region, only Brunei, Malaysia, Papua New Guinea and Vietnam remain net exporters.

Historically, China did obtain much of its oil imports from Southeast Asia, most notably from Indonesia and Malaysia, but these have now been dwarfed by the imports coming from the Middle East, Africa and Eurasia. Chinese oil companies invested significantly in the energy sectors in a number of the countries of the region, such as CNOOC, which is the largest offshore producer in Indonesia, but their attention has similarly shifted to more ambitious projects in other regions, which have larger reserves.[21] There are certainly greater opportunities for expanding gas as against oil production in the Asia-Pacific and much of the energy hopes for the future rest on developing these reserves. China is seeking to increase natural gas consumption as part of its energy diversification strategy but gas represents a considerably less significant energy security concern as there is no shortage of potential suppliers – from domestic production, from pipelines coming from central Asia or from Russia (see Chapter 8), as well as LNG supplies from the Middle East. Gas is also, to some extent, an energy source of 'choice' as it can relatively easily be substituted by other energy sources, such as coal. Since 2009 China has seen an upsurge in interest in exploring for and exploiting potentially large resources of unconventional gas in the form of tight gas, shale gas and coal-bed methane. Should these efforts be successful, the country's dependence on external supplies could be dramatically reduced.

It is thus oil and the difficulty of diversifying supplies away from geopolitically insecure regions, the 'Persian Gulf dilemma', which is the fundamental energy security problem for China. Although Southeast Asia does not help directly to alleviate this, the region is critical because it acts as the principal route of transportation of Chinese oil imports not only from the Middle East but also from Africa and even further afield from Latin America. The 'Malacca dilemma', which was reportedly enunciated by President Hu Jintao at a CCP meeting in November 2003, expresses this perceived threat of the insecurity of supply as oil is transported from west to east Asia.[22] The particular significance of the Malacca Straits is that it is the shortest direct route to China, approximately 2,000 km less than the next fastest route through the Sunda Strait, and that China is dependent on the Malacca Straits for over 80 per cent of its oil imports. China is not alone in this strategic dependence as over 90 per cent of Japan's oil imports and 100 per cent of South Korea's imports also come through these Straits.[23] But the key difference between China and these countries is that China is the only one that is not allied with the United States and it is the US that ultimately asserts naval dominance over the region. For China, the threat that the US could, along with its allies, impose an embargo on Chinese oil imports through the Straits, in the context, for example, of a Sino-US conflict over Taiwan, appears a real, tangible and even existential threat. [24]

The strategic dilemma for China is made more complicated in that this is not just a bilateral Sino-US issue. The 'Malacca dilemma' involves other significant Asian regional actors who have their own sources of conflict, and potentially antagonistic relations, with China. These include Japan, which, as noted above, is also highly dependent on the security of sea lanes and has a substantial political and military presence in the region, despite the post-World War II restrictions on its military activities and capacities. It also critically involves India, which has a larger and more capable navy than China and which increasingly sees itself as a guarantor of sea lanes not only in the Indian Ocean but also beyond into Southeast Asia. And in Southeast Asia itself, the ASEAN regional institution provides a strategic capacity for the smaller states of Southeast Asia to act as a unified actor so as to increase their bargaining power towards China.[25] This interaction also includes the tensions and competing claims for the sovereignty of the South China Sea. Chinese policy-making towards the 'Malacca dilemma' has, therefore, to take into account a complex multi-dimensional strategic environment.

Given these complexities, the persistence of unresolved disputes, and the high stakes involved, it is not difficult to present dark and threatening scenarios for future conflicts. Michael Klare, the influential US analyst, has consistently claimed that military conflict is a real threat as a consequence of China's quest for oil and gas resources and its competition with other Asian oil consumers.[26] Similarly, Robert Kaplan has argued in a lead article in *Foreign Affairs* that the Indian Ocean will be 'where the global struggles will lay out in the twenty-first century' and that these sea lanes are 'as strategically important as the Fulda gap' during the Cold War period.[27] Even some more hawkish Chinese analysts have highlighted the potential threat of China fighting a war over oil.[28]

But these more alarmist scenarios often make assumptions that are left unchallenged and ignore factors and developments that might promote cooperation rather than conflict. For example, the assumption of a US blockade of China is in fact more problematic than normally presented. Despite its undoubted naval supremacy, it is practically impossible for the US to impose a naval blockade of China's oil imports that would also not affect the supply of oil to its key regional allies, such as Japan and South Korea. China could also relatively easily circumvent the embargo through using alternative sea routes or through the transhipment of oil via third parties.[29] Another often unquestioned assumption is that China is implacably hostile to the US presence in the region. While it is certainly the case that the Chinese leadership does perceive a real threat of US military encirclement, there is also a pragmatic recognition that US hegemony does help to control the escalation of threats from regional allies, such as Taiwan, and that China's energy security would suffer, at least in the short to medium term, from a precipitate loss of US naval and military control of the oceanic sea lanes.

China has also increasingly come to realise that its own strategies and policies towards seeking to resolve the 'Malacca dilemma' can themselves contribute to forging more cooperative rather than conflictual outcomes. Over the last two decades, China's regional strategy has evolved to include three major strands that have shown greater sensitivity to this. The first and most innovative of these strands is one of proactively projecting reassurance, an ambitious 'charm offensive', utilising the instruments of 'soft' rather than 'hard' power.[30] One of the lessons of Chinese policies in the 1990s was that a forceful militarised strategy was ultimately counterproductive, and that actions like the military interventions into the South China Seas and the strategic escalation over the Taiwan Straits in 1995–6 only reinforced external perceptions of Chinese hegemonic threat. In a change of policy set out in 1997 in the New Security Concept, China shifted to embracing multilateral and regional regimes and institutions, such as ASEAN, emphasising economic interdependence, looking for 'win-win' solutions, and being willing to consider joint energy cooperation, whether through joint bids or joint exploration and development. The second strand is that of strategic avoidance or, more concretely, a policy of diversification, looking in particular at ways in which the vulnerability to US-controlled sea lanes can be minimized through finding alternative routes to transport oil imports. It is only the third strand that directly seeks to increase China's power capabilities and its strategic presence, most notably through developing an enhanced naval capacity. Nevertheless, China's hope is that this enhancement of its power capabilities will be viewed, due in part to the efforts made in developing the first two strands, as a natural consequence of China's rise as a power and not as a source of hegemonic threat.

Clearly, these three strands are in a certain tension with each other and are not necessarily easily reconcilable. These difficulties can be seen in China's complex and evolving relations with India, which is increasingly emerging as the principal regional competitor with China. At the heart of the relationship is a significant legacy of distrust and suspicion, where India has not forgotten or forgiven the Chinese invasion and military defeat in 1962 and the Chinese have not forgotten that the Indian nuclear tests in 1998 were publicly announced to counter the 'China threat'. There remain also important and unresolved border disputes between the two countries, the last remaining land territorial disputes of China with its neighbours. Both countries can be thought to subscribe to what Alastair Iain Johnston has called the doctrine of 'hyper-sovereignty', which is a highly rigid and inflexible definition of territorial sovereignty.[31] Bilateral relations are also complicated by the fact that both countries have large populations and a proud historical and cultural past and both are rising fast in their global presence and power. Although there is much that draws them together and makes them complement each other, as is captured in the 'two pagodas of hardware and software' in Prime Minister Wen Jiabao's image, there is also much room for strategic competition.[32] This is certainly the case in the area of energy security as both countries are fast growing importers of oil, both are highly dependent on supplies from the Persian Gulf, and both have NOCs with ambitious international strategies. For China, the particular source of perceived vulnerability is that India has a much stronger and more capable navy, controlling much of the Indian Ocean, and that India has the strategic advantage of not itself facing a 'Malacca dilemma'. Indeed, India has tended to accentuate China's own 'Malacca dilemma' by, for example, expressing its ambition for extending its naval hegemonic reach into Southeast Asia, most notably from its base on the Andaman islands, which lie just west of the Malacca Straits.

China has utilised all three strands of its energy security strategy in its attempts to improve its relations with India while defending and promoting its energy-related interests. The cooperative first strand developed through the mutual recognition that it increasingly made sense for Chinese and Indian oil companies, who were often effectively out-bidding each other and contributing to a significant increase in costs, to work together and coordinate their bids. The cost of this was particularly evident in Angola in 2004 when ONGC believed that it had been successful in its US$800 million bid for a 50 per cent stake in an oilfield previously owned by Shell but then was outbid by a US$2 billion offer from China's Sinopec. To seek to counter this competitive out-bidding, a memorandum of understanding for energy cooperation was signed between India and China in January 2006 with the two countries agreeing to pool their investments and technology. CNPC and ONGC are not new to the experience of working together, as they have been joint equity partners in Sudan since 1997. But the new agreement did precipitate more extensive joint acquisition of assets in Peru, Syria, Colombia and also in the Yadavaran oilfield in Iran.[33]

But there are certain practical limits to how much governments can direct the decision-making of relatively autonomous, if ultimately state-controlled, companies. When it has not been seen to be in their interest, Chinese oil companies have not refrained from continuing to outbid Indian companies. At the same time as the Sino-Indian negotiations were taking place during 2005, CNPC acted unilaterally to sign a deal with Myanmar for a gas pipeline to China, which undercut the long-negotiated Myanmar–Bangladesh–India pipeline. Even in the joint acquisitions made with Chinese and Indian involvement, it is generally the case that the Chinese company takes the leadership role and the greater share, as with the Yadavaran oilfield where Sinopec has a 51 per cent and ONGC a 29 per cent stake. This entrenches a perception that India is continually taking a 'back seat' in relation to China.[34]

The challenge for both countries over complex issues like this is to separate the economic from the political and to avoid the politicisation of what might be relatively innocent economic competition. This is evident, for example, in the gas pipeline decision. In the Indian popular press and among many Indian politicians, the decision was viewed in zero-sum terms as a loss for India and as a strategic gain for China and part of its strategic ambition to build an alliance with the 'pariah' regime in Myanmar at India's expense.[35] However, this ignores the fact that negotiations over the pipeline to India via Bangladesh had been stalled by the Indian refusal to accede to Bangladeshi demands for its role as a transit country and it was this paralysis in the process that had provided the opportunity for China to push its alternative route.[36] From the perspective of the Burmese region, there is a also a good economic and political rationale to seek to avoid dependence on a transit country, as the historical lesson is that transit countries, for example Ukraine for Russia, can be significant sources of conflict.[37] The Chinese government offered not only a direct route for the proposed gas pipeline but aimed to build a parallel oil pipeline as part of its aim to diversify its oil import routes from the Middle East.

The fact that China offered a good economic rationale for its pipeline route does not mean that Myanmar is submitting to a form of Chinese hegemonic control. In fact, it has sought to benefit from the strategic competition between India and China so as to increase its own autonomy and freedom from the hegemonic ambitions of both countries. The Burmese military, despite the support that they have received from Beijing, is conscious of the strong anti-Chinese sentiments within the country and seeks to balance India and China precisely so as to avoid becoming a satellite of China. The decision to offer the gas and oil pipelines to China was not, therefore, part of a decision to 'bandwagon' with China rather than to 'balance' with India, though the regime undoubtedly benefits from the diplomatic cover that China provides at the UN Security Council.

The construction of the oil and gas pipelines through Myanmar is part of the second strand of China's energy security dilemma, that of diversification. The pipelines are one of the alternatives being pursued by China in its overarching objective to develop energy transportation routes, which would reduce the threat of maritime intervention, whether from India or from the United States. Another alternative considered has been the building of a canal through southern Thailand at the Isthmus of Kra so as to bypass the Malacca Straits. This has, though, failed to appeal to the Thai government, one element of which being fears that this could foster a greater degree of self-identity and desire for secession in the predominantly Muslim south. Another option that is being actively pursued is the development of a comprehensive

5,500 km trans-Asian railway network that would link China to many ASEAN countries and create an efficient means to transport energy as well as other goods.[38] This is an ambitious plan that will require considerable investment and political cooperation, not least over the different rail gauges used in the different countries. A further and even more ambitious diversification initiative has been to promote the prospect of an oil pipeline from the Pakistani port of Gawdar in Balochistan through the North-west Territories and into Xinjiang.[39] The particular strategic advantage of this option for China is that the port is close to the Strait of Hormuz and thus avoids not only the Malacca Straits but also the Indian Ocean. However, this alternative has also proved difficult to develop, not least due to the endemic insecurity within Pakistan and the counter-insurgency campaign in its tribal areas.

The third strand of China's strategy is more direct and potentially provocative, particularly for India and the US, and is the clearly stated ambition to develop a fully fledged blue-water navy by 2050.[40] Although this is a perfectly legitimate ambition for a fast-rising power such as China, it clearly has implications for the US and Indian navies. This has become even more so with the evidence in 2009 that the Chinese government has committed itself to developing and building an aircraft carrier, with the ultimate aim of building six carrier groups.[41] The need to promote energy security has also become a major factor in the rationale and justification offered by the People's Liberation Army (PLA) Navy (PLAN) for its ambitious expansion. But it should be kept in mind that the Chinese navy is still many years away from being close to competing with either their US or Indian counterparts. India, for example, has three times as many combat vessels and five times as many personnel. Nevertheless, considerable progress has been made over the last decade with the PLAN becoming increasingly more confident, taking part, for example, in anti-piracy patrols off Somalia in 2009; initiating a first visit to the Persian Gulf a year later; and an unprecedented large-scale deployment of Chinese warships into the South China Sea in the early part of 2010 as a demonstration of intent over a dispute with Vietnam over fishing rights, which was followed by a further unprecedented deployment into the East China Sea.[42]

Particularly in relation to India, the strategic dilemma for China is to persuade the other to accept a practical separation between this inevitably more provocative strand, given its challenge to the existing *status quo*, and the second diversification strand. From the perspective of policymakers in Delhi, this is not always seen to be as convincing as the efforts of China to consolidate relations with Myanmar and Pakistan through energy-related investments, so as to reduce its energy insecurity, also appearing to consolidate China's presence and influence in the region as part of a broader strategy of building a hegemonic counter-balance to India. This perception of a deliberate Chinese strategic expansion has been popularised as a 'string of pearls' strategy, where Chinese investments from Hainan island, to Woody Island in the South China Seas, to the ports of Kyaukphu in Myanmar, Chittagong in Bangladesh, Hambantota in Sri Lanka are seen as part of a deliberate longer-term ambition to displace US and Indian power.[43] This sense within India of Chinese encirclement, whether justified or not, has only accentuated the fears and distrust from within India to China's growing presence in the region.

As can be seen in the specific case of Sino-Indian relations, it is extremely difficult for China to successfully combine a policy of reassurance with those of diversification and enhanced military strategic reach. It is difficult to avoid perceptions overtaking reality. An example of this is how a presumed Chinese military presence on the Myanmar-controlled Coco Islands became a fixed item as one of the 'pearls' in the 'string of pearls' strategy. It was only in 2005 that the Chinese could finally convince their sceptical Indian counterparts that they had never had a military base on these islands.[44] The credibility of such perceptions of threat are, though, connected as much as to domestic politics and to local disputes in bilateral relations as to actual developments in their respective foreign and military policy. In the Sino-Indian case, the sovereignty question and the continuing territorial disputes continue to cloud broader bilateral relations. In 2009–10 it was the hardening of the Chinese position over Arunachel Pradesh and China's dissatisfaction at India's stance towards the Dalai Lama, which contributed more to the worsening of bilateral relations than energy-related or military disputes. It is how the sovereignty issue affects energy and resource-related issues that becomes even more important as one moves to the third circle of China's Asian energy security strategy – to the South and East China Seas.

The 'sovereignty dilemma'

It is in this final third circle of China's Asian energy security engagement, the seas closest to the Chinese mainland, that the question of access to energy resources becomes inextricably inter-linked with national sovereignty issues, most notably Chinese expansive territorial claims over the South and East China Seas, which led to violent conflict in the past and which remain strongly contested by other claimants.[45] The key question, or 'sovereignty dilemma', which the potential energy reserves in these two seas raises is whether this relatively new dimension to the conflict has contributed to accentuating and aggravating these territorial disputes and thus intensified regional suspicions of China's hegemonic ambition. Or, alternatively, whether these potential energy reserves have, in contrast, provided a means for the parties to seek cooperative and collaborative solutions, most notably through joint development of the potential reserves, which might ultimately help to resolve these territorial disputes and thus improve China's relations with its immediate southern neighbours. A third possibility is that there is, in fact, little substantive connection between the energy resources in these seas and the prospects for a resolution of the territorial disputes and the improvement in bilateral relations of the claimant countries and it is a mistake to see them as intimately connected.

There are elements of truth in all three of these alternatives. The prospect of large oil and gas discoveries in these neighbouring seas has undoubtedly raised the stakes over most of the key territorial disputes. The fact that oil and gas fields tend to cross over and fail to respect national maritime borders, and that it is difficult for oil companies to develop fields when there are competing sovereign claims, gives such maritime territorial dispute a direct economic consequence they might not have otherwise had. In the South China Sea, some Chinese sources have suggested that this could be a 'new Persian Gulf' and have given estimates of the potential oil resources that are far higher than other non-Chinese estimates.[46] Although more knowledgeable Chinese energy experts are sceptical about such inflated exaggerations, these predictions of energy riches have certainly fed the popular perception that oil and gas reserves are at the heart of the territorial disputes in the South China Sea and have strengthened the nationalist sense of China's right to defend its claims. As such, energy has certainly made these territorial disputes more salient and has given them an additional prominence. This can be further illustrated in the East China Sea. It was only with Japanese objections in 2004 that Chinese offshore gas exploration had come too close to the 'median' border, as claimed by Japan, which re-ignited the long-standing Sino-Japanese territorial dispute over the competing claims over the 'median line' and over the Diaoyu/Senkaku islands.[47]

But the fact that these energy resources, however substantial they may be, will remain unexploited unless the territorial disputes are resolved or, at the very least, put to one side suggests that they could generate more cooperative behaviour. Indeed, it has been precisely China's offer to pursue joint development and to 'shelve' the territorial dispute – Deng Xiaoping's original recommendation in 1978 over the Diaoyu/Senkaku islands – which led to four years of negotiations between Japan and China and which resulted in 2008 in a landmark 'principled consensus', which provided a common understanding of the first steps towards joint development in the East China Sea.[48] This agreement contributed to a certain relaxation of tensions between the two countries, though tension resurfaced over interpretations of what the 'principled consensus' actually covered.[49] Similarly, in the South China Sea, China has incorporated the offer of joint energy development as an integral part of its strategy of reassurance towards Southeast Asia. In 2004, China agreed to joint seismic investigations of underwater resources with the Philippines in the South China Sea, and Vietnam joined this research project in 2005. These developments follow on from a series of Chinese commitments that have sought to reassure Southeast Asian countries of its intentions, which include the 2002 ASEAN Declaration on the Conduct of Parties in the South China Sea aimed at preventing the escalation of ongoing maritime disputes over the Spratley islands and the 2003 signing of the Treaty of Amity and Cooperation (TAC) between China and ASEAN.[50] Overall, as John Lee suggests, 'China is branding itself an Asian partner sensitive to the priorities and problems of Asian nation-states and employs a language that sells in the region'.[51]

The 'charm offensive' does, though, have its limits. The Chinese have never suggested that the 'shelving' of the territorial disputes and the promotion of joint development means that their sovereign claims have become less strong or that such joint development would lead to a longer-term prospect of territorial compromise. The commitment to the doctrine of hyper-sovereignty, as noted above, makes this an unlikely prospect unless there is a prior normative shift in China's conception of national sovereignty. The countries of Southeast Asia might have been 'charmed' to a certain extent by China's reassurance strategy but they still remain sceptical and rely on the US to provide an ultimate balance and protection against China.[52] They are also increasingly worried that their traditional approach towards China is being threatened by the growing asymmetry in military power with the expansion of the PLAN.[53] And Japan is conscious, as with Chinese policy towards Taiwan, that periods of rapprochement and improvement in relations can easily be undermined by a subsequent rise of nationalist sentiment within China. Sovereignty is, in this sense, a more core national interest than energy supplies and it is this rather than energy that ultimately drives China's relations with neighbours with whom it has border disputes, including India. And it is the unpredictability of the sovereign territorial disputes, and the prospect that they could at any point flare up, with the threat of conflict percolating through and affecting the broader international energy security engagement of China. This prospect that sovereignty-related incidents might escalate into a broader energy security crisis is most notably the case with Taiwan but could also potentially extend to conflicts with the US and its allies in the South and East China Seas.[54]

Conclusion

Asia, from the Persian Gulf through the Indian Ocean to the South China Sea and on to the Chinese mainland, is at the geographical heart of China's global energy security problem. The core of this is that China's major source of supply in the Middle East is constantly threatened by the assertion of US hegemonic power in the region and that, furthermore, the United States, and its regional allies, assert hegemonic control over the transportation routes from the Strait of Hormuz all the way to China. As this chapter has demonstrated, this presents China with three inter-related strategic dilemmas; the dilemma of access to the oil and gas supplies in the Middle East, the 'Persian Gulf dilemma'; the dilemma of ensuring secure sea-lines of communication, the 'Malacca dilemma'; and the dilemma of asserting its territorial claims in maritime regions where oil and gas reserves are thought to be present, the 'sovereignty dilemma'.

In seeking to resolve these three inter-connected dilemmas, there is clear evidence that China is promoting policies that seek to reassure, to promote its policies in a peaceful and non-belligerent light, and that emphasise China's ambition of 'peaceful development'. Thus, in the Middle East, China has maintained a low-key political presence, has rarely challenged the US and has generally submitted to US pressure when it has been exerted. There is little indication that China is seeking, or sees it as realistic to challenge US regional hegemony. In the Indian Ocean, one can see a similarly circumspect posture towards the US along with attempts to forge a more collaborative and cooperative energy relationship with India. Even in the South and East China Seas, where China's regional power is most developed, there is evidence of Chinese behaviour shifting towards a more credible commitment to joint development in pursuit of the region's oil and gas reserves.

But there are also policies and postures that appear considerably less reassuring to its southern neighbours and other external actors. In the Middle East, China is increasingly becoming more assertive about its energy interests in Iran and less willing to submit to US pressure. In the Indian Ocean region, the growth in bilateral relations of China with most of India's neighbours, including ones with which New Delhi has had historically poor relations, such as Pakistan, engenders fears among Indian analysts, which are not assuaged by the claim that they are being developed for energy security reasons. In the South and East China Seas, the Chinese interest and promotion of joint development of the energy resources has led to no perceptible softening of China's territorial claims. The impressive growth of the PLAN, the clear stated commitment to a blue-water navy, and the central role that energy security plays in driving this expansion, adds to the sense of regional unease and a fear that the outward signs of reassurance may mask an inward drive towards domination and hegemony.

As China's power grows over time, this will inevitably lead to challenges to the unchecked regional Asian hegemony that the US has enjoyed, at least for the two decades since the end of the Cold War. Energy is one of the most powerful forces leading China to challenge the existing regional hegemonic status quo. Whether this shift in the balance of power between the US and China over this region will lead to conflict or cooperation is yet to be determined. In general, as noted above, there are signs of both reassurance and increased threat perception. But one additional and unpredictable factor is how a core national sovereignty issue, such as over Taiwan or the South China Sea, could create a spark that could lead to increased tensions and possible conflict further afield.

10 The neo-imperialist temptation
Africa and Latin America

Introduction

One of the most dramatic developments of the 2000s has been the emergence of China as a major external actor in sub-Saharan Africa and in Latin America. China's presence in both regions is, though, not new. There are trading links going back to the sixteenth and seventeenth centuries and Chinese officials are keen, for example, to highlight the adventures of the fifteenth-century Admiral Zheng, whose voyages reached the east coast of Africa. During the Cold War, Beijing supported revolutionary anti-imperialist movements in both Latin America and Africa, providing substantial aid to the newly independent states in Africa with over 800 projects financed and supported by China during the period 1950–80.[1] But these historic ties pale in comparison to the almost exponential growth of China's engagement with both regions during the 2000s. This is best illustrated by looking at the rapid expansion of bilateral trade. In Africa, trade with China grew from US$6.5 billion in 1999 to US$73.3 billion in 2007 and reached US$106.8bn in 2008 before dropping in 2009 due to the global recession. A very similar trajectory is evident in Latin America. In 2000, bilateral trade was at US$12.6 billion and rose to US$50.5 billion in 2005 and reached a record of US$111.5 billion in 2008. These trade figures demonstrate how China's engagement and presence in Africa and Latin America is now of a different intensity and magnitude than in earlier periods.

This is a shift not just of regional but of global significance. In the aftermath of the Cold War and the withdrawal of the Soviet Union, Africa and Latin America lost much of their strategic significance. An influential article published in 1990s and entitled 'Why Europe matters and the Third World does not' captured, if in exaggerated form, the post-Cold War strategic diminution of the Global South and particularly of sub-Saharan Africa and Latin America.[2] Both regions became strongly dependent on the West, their economies stagnated due to high levels of debt and historically low prices for commodities, and the Washington Consensus, with its strict neo-liberal economic prescriptions, was the dominant and seemingly unchallengeable ideology. The rise of China as a major new actor in both regions by the mid-2000s is the most striking indication of how the region has regained a degree of strategic significance and autonomy. As Gonzalo Paz highlights '2004 was the year when China jumped with energy into a geopolitical and geo-economic space considered until recently as the American backyard: Latin America'.[3] The shock of the reinvigorated return of China to Africa has been seen in even more dramatic terms in Africa where commentators have variously depicted a new geo-strategic 'scramble for Africa' and where the western monopoly of power, whether exercised through the US or the EU, is being seen to be seriously challenged for the first time since the collapse of the Soviet Union.[4]

China's global search for oil, and its determination to diversify its energy supplies, has certainly played a key and leading role in the expanding presence of Chinese companies, government officials and private Chinese citizens in both regions. But it is far from the sole factor driving this surge. In Africa, there have been massive infrastructure-for-resources deals over non-fossil minerals, such as the proposed US$9 billion loan to the Democratic Republic of Congo for access to its supplies of copper and minerals.[5] China has invested in various large hydropower projects across the continent and there is a vigorous trade in manufactured goods, textiles, timber and agricultural products. In fact, the largest Chinese acquisition so far in Africa is not energy-related – the US$5.5 billion paid for a 20 per cent stake in South Africa's Standard Bank.[6] Nevertheless, oil is certainly the single most important economic driver for China's engagement with Africa, with the World Bank, for example, estimating that in 2006 oil represented over 80 per cent of China's imports from Africa.[7] China's most important trading partners are also all oil-producing states, with the notable exception of mineral-rich South Africa. In Latin America, oil does certainly play a less prominent role, in part due to the very long distances to Chinese markets, and it is other commodities that are more significant drivers, such as soybeans from Argentina and Brazil and copper from Chile. But oil still plays an important role, most notably with Venezuela but also with other countries, like Brazil, Ecuador, Colombia and Peru.

This energy-driven dimension of China's external engagement does, therefore, provide a prism through which to seek to understand and interpret the evolving nature of China's foreign policy towards these regions. In the previous chapter on China's Asian strategy, the analytical framework was one of hegemony – asking to what extent was China accommodating itself to the existing hegemonic order, dominated by the US, or seeking to challenge and replace it. A similar framework is certainly also appropriate for Africa and Latin America. But there is also an alternative conceptual approach, which draws from structuralist and dependency theory and which asks whether China is following a neo-imperialist trajectory, where its drive for securing raw materials in exchange for manufactured goods only accentuates and consolidates the structure of North–South economic dependency and inequality. This is a theoretical approach that has much resonance in both Latin America and

Africa and underlies much of the local anxieties about China's rapid expansion in the region.[8] For example, Thabo Mbeki, South Africa's president, warned that

> the potential danger . . . was of the emergence of an unequal relationship similar to that which existed in the past between African colonies and the colonial powers. China cannot just come here and dig for raw materials and then go away and sell us manufactured goods.[9]

Former president of Brazil, Fernando Cardoso, originally one of the leading exponents of dependency theory, has similarly raised alarms about unequal exchange between China and Latin America exacerbating, rather than resolving, Latin America's developmental problems. One of the variants of theories of imperialism also highlights how companies, rather than governments, historically drove states, such as from Europe in the late nineteenth century, towards imperial commitments in Africa.[10] This has some contemporary resonance with contemporary Chinese commercial activity in Africa and how this created political problems and challenges for the Chinese government.

This chapter examines whether or not there is a validity in conceptualising China's powerful new interest in Africa and Latin America in neo-imperialist terms. The first section addresses this question directly, examining the most common arguments put forward for and against. The reality, however, is not easy to categorise and a more complex and differentiated picture is required. One of the key weaknesses of a neo-imperialist model for understanding China's interaction is that it tends to assume that Africa and Latin America are strategic vacuums where external powers dictate the politics of the regions. But the reality is that the power and influence of external powers is much more circumscribed and that there now exists relatively powerful autonomous states in both regions with whom China, like other external powers, has to engage. The complexities and variation of such relations is then illustrated by four country examples – Sudan, Venezuela, Angola and Nigeria – which bring out the successes and failures, the stresses and strains, of China's energy-driven engagement in Africa and Latin America.

A new neo-imperialist expansion?

There are two extremes in the broader debate about whether or not China is reproducing a neo-imperial drive into Africa and Latin America. At one end of the spectrum, there is the official Chinese view that stresses the fact that China is itself a developing country, the largest country of the developing world, and that its engagement with Africa and Latin America is one of equality and South–South interaction and has no hidden imperialist agenda. Unlike the West, Chinese officials argue that they are not seeking to impose a particular economic model but to help the countries of these regions find a path towards prosperity that draws from China's own experiences as a developing country. For example, the support given towards infrastructure development and the development of a low-cost and competitive export-led manufacturing industry reflects China's own experience of economic development, following the Asian 'flying geese' model.[11] Beijing has a fondness for the business school jargon of a 'win-win' scenario where Chinese economic interests in Africa and Latin America are presented as enhancing rather than undermining the regions' economic development. The overarching theme is one of solidarity and equality with reminders that it was 'Western powers, not China, [who] colonized Africa and looted resources there in history'.[12]

This message of mutual interest, respect and equality has generally found a sympathetic reception in much of Africa and Latin America. The emphasis on trade rather than aid, the importance given to infrastructure development, the absence of political and economic conditionalities on aid, and the assertion of the principle of non-intervention have represented a refreshing break and shift in discourse and practice for many in Africa and Latin America. For example, Paul Kagame, Rwanda's president, has argued that, in contrast to western countries who have just 'exploited Africa's resources', China 'brings Africa what it needs; investment and money for governments and companies. China invests in infrastructure, builds streets'.[13] The Zambian economist, Dambisa Moyo, who caused a significant stir with her book attacking western aid, likewise argues that China offers a counter-example to the western engagement through adopting a 'wider, more sophisticated and business-like role'.[14] In Latin America, the emergence of China as a major external actor has coincided with the shift to the left in many countries of the region with a revival of strong anti-Americanism, indigenous populism, and economic nationalism.[15] Hugo Chavez of Venezuela has been the principal regional leader who has sought to bring about a 'Bolivarian revolution' and who represents one of the most significant ideological challenges to the United States since Fidel Castro came to power in 1959. He has made much of his ideological embrace with China and his desire to shift Venezuela's economic and political orientation from the US to China, most notably in terms of oil flows. Other left-leaning populist leaders in Latin America, such as Evo Morales of Bolivia, Lula da Silva of Brazil, and Raul Castro of Cuba have similarly warmly welcomed China's entry into the region.

At the other end of the spectrum of the debate, China's engagement with both Africa and Latin America is viewed in a much more critical light with a strong neo-imperialist flavouring. For some, mainly among more hawkish policy-makers in the United States, China's move into these regions is far from strategically innocent and there is an underlying ambition to reduce the traditional influence of the US in Latin America and in Africa.[16] For civil society groups, the main threat is China's upholding of the principle of non-intervention, which is seen to promote an unquestioning support for authoritarian regimes and to turn a blind eye to human rights abuses.[17] An international campaign that highlighted China's role in support of the Sudanese regime and its 'genocidal' repression of the rebellion in the Darfur region came close to instigating a boycott of the 2008 Olympic games in Beijing.[18] On a more commercial level, there are fears that China is pursuing a form of economic mercantilism where the government is strategically supporting its state-owned companies to gain physical control of the resources of Africa and Latin America and has thereby locked out western companies. There is a litany of more local economic complaints that consolidate the sense of a neo-imperialist imposition, ranging from accusations of a systematic preference for Chinese over local labour and materials, acceptance of bribery, lack of respect for the environment, dumping of poor quality products, and low pay and poor employment practices. In Zambia, popular discontent with Chinese investment entered into the electoral process in 2006 as the opposition candidate, Michael Sata, condemned foreign investors and their exploitation of the local workforce, which included poor working conditions and a fatal explosion at the Chambishi copper mine in 2005 which resulted in over fifty deaths.[19]

These two poles of the debate over China's re-emergence in Africa and Latin America – the benign developmental and the malign 'resource grab' versions – have elements of truth in both of them. But they also need to be significantly qualified if the more complex reality of China's engagement with both regions is to be fully understood. A first important qualification is that it is essential to remember that China is a late entrant to both regions and suffers from the key disadvantage of late-comers – most of the best deals and agreements have already been concluded. American and European companies have had many decades, if not centuries, of experience of working in both regions and have made extensive and large-scale investments in both regions. This is reflected in the fact that China's accumulated foreign direct investment in both regions remains very small in comparison to the US and to European countries, with the OECD estimating, for example, that in 2008 China still only accounted for about 1 per cent of total Foreign Direct Investment (FDI) stock in Africa.[20] This strategic disadvantage is evident in the oil sector where western multinationals like ExxonMobil, Shell and BP dominate, for instance, oil extraction in the Gulf of Guinea; and companies like Chevron, Petrobas and Repsol-YPF are so well-entrenched in Latin America that they have little to fear from the Chinese NOCs. The IOCs have the additional advantage of the technological knowledge to be engaged in the more profitable deep-water drilling and which is currently beyond the capacities of the Chinese NOCs, though they are gradually gaining experience in this area. Without such a comparative technological edge, Chinese NOCs are additionally vulnerable to being excluded by local African or Latin American NOCs who themselves have ambitions for international expansion, such as Petrobas of Brazil.[21]

The consequence of this is, as in the Middle East, Chinese companies have to play to their own specific strategic strengths. The first of these is the willingness to work with 'pariah states' that have, for one reason or another, had sanctions imposed upon them by the West and where western IOCs have disinvested. This was a main factor, for example, behind the entry of China into Sudan in the mid-1990s after the Islamist government in Khartoum came into conflict with the West over claims of sponsorship of international terrorism and human rights abuses. CNPC conducted preliminary geological surveys in 1993 one year after Chevron, who had discovered the oil in 1978, sold its concessions at a loss.[22] Chinese NOCs have also benefited in Latin America from the economic nationalist policies of leaders like Hugo Chavez and gained entry into the Venezuelan oil sector, which had previously been dominated by IOCs. A second comparative strength is financial and the relatively easy access to capital that the Chinese NOCs enjoy and a recognition among Chinese officials that one of the almost inevitable consequences of 'late entrants' is that they may have to pay over the odds for entry into critical markets. There is much criticism of Chinese deals in the energy sector that they have tended to 'over-bid' and are willing to invest without concern for commercial profitability. This criticism has diminished to a certain extent as oil prices continued to rise through the 2000s and remained relatively high even during the global economic recession. But, overall, Chinese NOCs are not the dominant, all-powerful actors, which is sometimes how they are portrayed, and more often than not have to accept the deals that the IOCs have decided to walk away from.[23]

Another often ignored dimension of the overall strategic picture is that China is not the only ambitious Asian country that is seeking to enter these regional energy markets. In the previous chapter, the ambitions of Indian oil companies were highlighted, and how this has led to a mix of conflict and cooperation with China. But it is not only India that has been an important Asian player but other countries like Japan, South Korea and Malaysia. In Sudan, the political pressure has almost exclusively been exerted on China for its energy investments in the country but, in reality, CNPC is not the only investor, with Malaysia's Petronas and India's ONGC being other significant partners.[24] In Nigeria, China has been competing vigorously with Japan, South Korea and Russia for access to oil and gas fields and it is the companies of other countries, such as Gazprom's US$2.5 billion gas deal, which have been often more successful. China is also often accused of supporting its energy ambitions through arms sales but again this tends to ignore the broader context in which China is a relatively small player in the international arms market. For example, in both Sudan and Venezuela it is Russian arms companies that have concluded considerably larger arms deals.[25] Overall, China's presence and engagement does tend to receive most attention, not least due to the fact that China has the largest funds and makes the boldest moves, but this should not obscure the fact that there is a crowded buyer's market, particularly from Asia, for Africa and Latin America's energy riches.[26]

A third common misapprehension is that China's energy strategies towards Africa and Latin America are part of a unified and coherent strategy directed from Beijing by the Chinese government. The reality is very different and, as has been described in detail in Chapter 4, China's energy policy-making framework is fragmented, lacks overall political control and gives considerable power and influence to the NOCs.[27] As with the flag-following-trade model of imperialism, it is often more accurate to say that it is the Chinese NOCs, with their distinctive commercial interests at the forefront, who have driven China's expansion into Africa and Latin America and where the Chinese government has had belatedly to follow to develop the broader economic and political relationship. Part of the problem for the Chinese government has been that the Chinese companies have often simply exported domestic practices, such as a disregard for environmental protection, corruption and a lack of engagement with affected local communities, which have generated strong local and international criticisms and resentments.[28] Another problem, of which the government has been increasingly aware, is that the interests of the companies and the government do not necessarily coincide, as highlighted in Chapter 6. This has, for example, been particularly the case in Sudan where there has emerged a growing realisation in Beijing that CNPC's engagements in the country have been more driven by profits and the need to secure reserves rather than an altruistic concern for China's energy security. In 2008, Zhu Feng, a leading Chinese scholar, went so far as it say that state-owned companies, with their powerful interests, had 'hijacked China's foreign policy in Sudan'.[29]

The fact, though, that such open criticism has been permitted within China indicates that policy is developing and that policy learning is taking place. Although the dysfunctionality in the structures and processes of Chinese policy-making will not be overcome without major and contentious internal reforms, policies are still being refined and developed as knowledge and understanding of conditions in Africa and Latin America have grown and as China has had to interact with the broader international community. There has been, as the statement above indicates, a growing realisation that a mercantilist approach to energy security has its limitations and that equity oil controlled by Chinese NOCs does not mean, and should not necessarily mean, that all that oil will flow to China rather than be sold in international markets. The Chinese government has also increasingly realised that its ideological commitment to non-interference (with the exception of the issue of recognition of Taiwan) is not always compatible with support for international efforts to ensure stability within Africa and Latin America. The involvement of China in UN peacekeeping, such as in Haiti and in many African operations, along with the decision to support international naval operations to counter piracy off the coast of Somalia, highlights the growing commitment of China to assuming responsibility for international efforts to promote peace and stability.[30] Chinese NOCs have also been involved in a degree of policy learning with companies like CNPC developing their own corporate and social responsibility strategies.[31]

This leads to the final important qualification to the neo-imperialist imagery of a China indiscriminately grabbing the resources of Africa and Latin America. This is that the age of imperialism has ended and sub-Saharan Africa and Latin America do not represent strategic vacuums where external powers have a free rein to impose their preferences, as was the case in the nineteenth century. The independent states of Africa and Latin America are, with the exception of clearly failed states such as Somalia, powerful autonomous actors in their own right, even if they have often failed to provide the developmental outcomes that their citizens would have hoped for. China's expansion into Africa and Latin America, which has been itself driven by growing demand for resources from within China, has in practice strengthened rather than weakened the autonomy of the states of these regions. In particular, it has provided the local states with an enhanced bargaining power as they are able to play off the competing external powers, the IOCs and the NOCs. Given their acute sensitivities to colonial imposition, African and Latin American states have no desire to fall within a Chinese imperium but seek rather to utilise the Chinese engagement to diversify their external dependencies so as to strengthen their relative autonomy. Chinese companies are, in fact, as vulnerable as western companies to fall victim to the political manipulations, the rise of resource nationalism, and the disregard of international legal norms that has marked the policies of the local empowered resource-rich states as the economic value of their resources have grown during the 2000s.

The importance of local national politics highlights also that there are limits to what one can say in general terms about China's energy-related relations with Africa and Latin America. There is, in practice, no simple homogenous China-Africa or China-Latin America policy. China's energy-driven diplomacy is variegated and differentiated according to the particular conditions and situations within each of the states of Africa and Latin America. It is thus important to examine these policies in their specific national context. The rest of the chapter will, therefore, explore in more detail the evolution of China's policies towards the four countries that represent the most important targets for China's international strategy – Sudan, Venezuela, Angola and Nigeria. The selection of these four countries also illustrates well the complexity of the dynamics and evolution of China's energy-driven engagement with Africa and Latin America.

Sudan: dealing with a 'pariah' state

Sudan is a clear example where China has been able to enter into a lucrative oil market due to the withdrawal of western oil companies as a consequence of an increasingly politically risky environment. Chevron and Total had been the main companies operating in the country in the 1970s and 1980s and it was Chevron that discovered oil in 1978, though it then moved out of southern Sudan due to the onset of the civil war in the mid-1980s and then sold its concessions fully in 1992.[32] Total similarly suspended operations due to the war in 1985 but has nevertheless retained its rights through an annual payment of US$1 million to the Sudanese government.[33] The resurgence of the long-standing North–South civil war was certainly a major factor behind the increased political risk within Sudan but the coming to power of the National Islamic Front in 1991 added to this considerably. Under its leader, Omar al-Bashir, the new government was committed to a radical Islamisation of the country and a more repressive imposition of a Northern domination over the South. The safe haven provided by the government to radical Islamists, most notably to Osama bin Laden, led in 1993 to the country being designated by the US State Department as a sponsor of state terrorism. Sudan's regional and international isolation increased as Egypt, its large and influential neighbour, claimed that Sudanese security services had attempted to assassinate the Egyptian president in 1995. UN sanctions were imposed on the country in 1996, followed a year later by more stringent US sanctions and in 1998 the US launched a missile attack on a pharmaceutical factory in Khartoum that was believed to be supporting terrorist activities. Sudan was, in this sense, at the very early front-line of the 'war on terrorism'.[34]

It was in this context where Sudan was becoming internationally isolated as a 'pariah' state that there emerged the opportunity for China to gain access to an open oil market that was, unlike in other parts of Africa, not already effectively monopolised by western companies. The Sudanese government also had little option but to rely on China since it desperately needed oil revenues to wage its war against the South. China's commitment to the principle of 'non-interference' meant that it was willing, unlike western countries, to separate economic engagement from the broader political context.[35] The entry of CNPC into Sudan in the mid-1990s was one of the first and most significant of its international economic engagements and involved taking a 40 per cent stake in 1997 in the Greater Nile Petroleum Operating Company (GNPOC) consortium, which operates the most productive oil blocks in the country. In 2000 CNPC acquired a 41 per cent stake in the Petrodar consortium, which operates a further two blocks in the Melut basin of the Upper Nile. The CNPC stake in the Sudanese oil market has continued to be augmented with the awards of further blocks in 2005 and 2007. In the ten years following the initial agreement in 1997, China has invested up to US$15 billion in various package deals, whereby access to oil has been exchanged for infrastructure investment and arms sales.[36] For China, Sudan has become the most important source of equity oil apart from Kazakhstan. It provides about 10 million tonnes per year of crude oil to China and is the sixth largest source of imported oil.

From the Chinese perspective, the Sudanese oil-driven engagement appears as a significant success story. In a complex and politically risky environment, China has helped Sudan to shift from being an oil-importing country in the mid-1990s to a major oil-exporting country in the mid-2000s with annual production at around 24 million tonnes, 5 per cent of Africa's total output. It has thereby greatly strengthened the economic power and capacity of the Sudanese government and considerably enhanced prospects for broader economic development within the country. China has also been involved in an integrated manner in Sudan's oil sector through exploration, production, processing and the exporting of the oil. CNPC was involved in the completion of the oil pipeline from Heglig to Port Sudan, which permitted Sudan to export oil for the first time in 1999. CNPC also provided the oil infrastructure from the Upper Melut basin and built a further 1,400 km oil pipeline that became operational in 2006. CNPC was involved in a joint venture with the Ministry of Energy for building the oil refinery in Khartoum. China can, therefore, legitimately claim that it has been the driving force in transforming the fortunes of Sudan and providing the essential infrastructure for it to become a major oil-exporting country.

For its part, China has benefited from the consistency and relative reliability of the Sudanese government. Unlike its experiences in other oil-producing countries, like Kazakhstan and Venezuela, there has been no major renegotiation of contracts and the Sudanese government has generally maintained its side of the bargain. This does not mean that Sudan has willingly become part of a Chinese imperium, as it has also ensured that other Asian companies, most notably Malaysia's Petronas and India's ONGC, have had significant stakes in GNOPC consortium. The fact that Total has been able to retain its oil exploration rights over all these years of sanctions and political isolation indicates that western companies would undoubtedly have been welcomed back if the political situation were more hospitable.[37] But, despite the contingent nature of the relationship and that Khartoum is very much the driving force in the relationship, Sino-Sudanese relations do have an intensity and breadth that is unparalleled in the rest of sub-Saharan Africa and which extend not just to oil but also other types of business, such as telecommunications, textiles, arms and agriculture.

It is the very intensity of these relations, and the fact that China is so closely associated with the Sudanese government, that has also exposed China to the broader political risks of being associated with 'pariah' states. Unlike in Iran, China cannot rely on Russia to take the leading role in resisting western pressure and limiting the economic effects of the imposition of international sanctions. China has become too closely tied to the Sudanese regime for this to be possible, even though in practice the Russian government is the largest arms supplier to Sudan. The implications of this became evident with the deterioration of the political situation in Darfur from 2004 onwards, when the Sudanese government become increasingly blamed for the brutal repression of the revolt through the so-called Janjaweed militias. As the death toll mounted, and international dismay grew, the Chinese stance was initially intransigent, stating that this was solely an internal matter for the Sudanese government. In the UN Security Council, China ensured that the resolutions in relation to the Darfur issue were significantly watered down through the threat of the use of its veto.[38] The fact that China was the most significant source of small arms during this period added to the sense of an implicit underlying support for the government's actions in Darfur.[39]

China's rigidly non-interventionist stance only began to shift when Darfur became a centre of international attention with claims that the repression had turned into an act of genocide and various celebrities, such as Mia Farrow and George Clooney, targetting China for facilitating the Sudanese government's actions.[40] Human rights activists made this a central issue in the period leading up to the 2008 Beijing Olympics, threatening to mobilise a boycott of the 'genocide games'. It was at this point that there was a shift in China's stance. In 2006, President Hu Jintao urged the Sudanese government to accept a UN peacekeeping force and in February 2007, the Chinese ambassador to the UN, Wang Guangya, let slip that 'usually China doesn't send messages, but this time [it] did'.[41] In May 2007, Liu Guijin was appointed as a special envoy to Darfur and he was centrally involved in seeking to gain Sudan's support for a hybrid UN-African Union peacekeeping force that was authorised by UNSCR 1769 in July 2007 during China's term as chair of the Security Council. China then provided 315 military engineers as a contribution to the peacekeeping force. All of this was warmly received in western capitals and the US special representative to Darfur, Andrew Natsios, noted that 'China in my view has been very cooperative. The level of coordination and cooperation has been improving each month'.[42]

In the end, China came through this period managing to limit the damage both to its privileged relationship with the Sudanese government and to its role as a 'responsible stakeholder' in international affairs. But there were repercussions and the affair did generate a significant internal debate.[43] The more hawkish line was that China was being deliberately and unfairly victimised, which again demonstrated western hypocrisy given the support by the US and other western countries for the equally repressive government of oil-rich Equatorial Guinea.[44] From this perspective, China was a useful scapegoat for the West to deflect populist pressure to intervene militarily in the situation in Darfur. However, the more progressive line was that the Darfur crisis illustrated how Sudan's oil assets were simply not valuable enough for the political costs that they brought. This includes a human dimension since Chinese civilians in Sudan have increasingly been targeted by Darfuri rebels. For example, in October 2008, nine CNPC employees were captured by Darfuri rebels and four of them were subsequently brutally murdered. Chinese NOCs were criticised for exaggerating the strategic value of their involvement in Sudan, particularly when much of the equity oil produced has frequently been sold on international markets. This was taken to be a case of commercial 'hijacking' of China's foreign policy, which has only contributed to negative local and international images of China as a resource-grabbing and neo-imperialist actor in contrast to the more positive developmental image that the government is seeking to promote.

Venezuela: dealing with a populist nationalist state

As in Sudan, the first incursion of Chinese oil companies into Venezuela was in 1997 when CNPC obtained production rights in the Caracoles and Intercampo fields. But unlike the CNPC agreements in Sudan in the same period, this was a small-scale investment yielding an estimated 1.25 million tonnes per year by 2005, giving CNPC 1 per cent of Venezuela's oil production.[45] The real expansion of China's interest and engagement in Venezuela was, as in the rest of the Latin America, in the mid-2000s when the drive to secure raw materials gained a truly global dimension. Venezuela was a natural target since its oil reserves are second only to those of Saudi Arabia once its substantial heavy oil reserves are included. By the mid-2000s, the political conditions for providing access to the Venezuelan oil market was also propitious with President Chavez making clear his ambition to shift oil supplies away from the US to Asia. More explicitly, he set a goal of expanding oil supplies to China from four million tonnes in 2007 to 50 million tonnes by 2012. Chavez has also encouraged Chinese investment in the domestic oil market where IOCs have suffered from nationalisation of the oil industry and where they have had to accept new regulations with the Venezuelan NOC, Petróleos de Venezuela S.A. (PDVSA), maintaining the majority share.[46] Chavez has not disguised his ambition to seek non-western oil companies, not only from China but also Russia, Malaysia and Iran, to invest in the country.

The political context has, therefore, some similarities with that of Sudan in that China has enjoyed a strategic opportunity to enter the Venezuelan market due to the partial withdrawal of the IOCs. But there are also critical differences. The first is that Venezuela under Chavez does not constitute a 'pariah state' and has, compared to Sudan, no association with international terrorism or with brutal large-scale internal repression. Chavez is a traditional Latin American populist nationalist with a well-honed anti-elitist and anti-American ideology that certainly irritates the US but is insufficient to warrant the imposition of sanctions. The dangers of China receiving the type of international opprobrium that it received over Sudan is therefore limited. But this is balanced by the fact that Venezuela, compared to Sudan, is much closer and of far greater strategic interest to the United States. This has potentially serious consequences for Sino-US relations, particularly if China is perceived in Washington to be developing Venezuela as a major strategic ally. When Chavez first threatened the US with halting oil shipments in 2004, this caused such concern that Senator Richard Lugar requested a report on the potential effects for the US of such a disruption.[47] The potential for Sino-US suspicion over Latin America is increased by the strong anti-American rhetoric of Chavez who frequently extols China as an example of how to 'be a world power without being an empire'.[48] Another difference, more economic in nature, between Venezuela and Sudan is that the Chinese have sound reasons to doubt whether Chavez will be as reliable and as trustworthy as al-Bashir of Sudan in ensuring that its energy-related economic agreements and investments will be safeguarded. Chinese oil companies have already suffered from Chavez's populist and often arbitrary economic decisions as he insisted on the renegotiation of existing Chinese contracts, as with all companies in the country, and claimed back from CNPC in 2005 US$101 million in alleged back-taxes.[49]

These various political sensitivities and economic considerations mean that China's undoubted enthusiasm for entering the Venezuelan oil market is tempered with a considerable degree of caution. China has certainly embraced the prospect of enhanced relations with Venezuela and has not distanced itself from the country due to any excessive deference to the United States. Its growing strategic interest is demonstrated by the offers of more favourable and larger loans in exchange for oil supplies; in 2007, a joint investment fund of US$6 billion was established, which was then increased in US$12 billion in 2009. A year later in April 2010, there was an agreement for a US$20 billion loan with a repayment period of ten years. At the same time as the new loan was agreed, CNPC agreed to set up a joint company with PDVSA to develop the Orinoco belt's Junin-4 block with total investment projected to be around US$16 billion.[50] China has also welcomed the opportunity to increase oil supplies from Venezuela, which is seen to contribute to its general strategy of energy diversification.

But China has also been keen to emphasise that these loans and agreements are nothing out of the ordinary and follow an economic rather than a political or ideological agenda. Brazil, Argentina and other Latin American countries have also been the targets of China's economic expansion with, for example, Brazil receiving a US$10 billion loan in 2009 in exchange for guaranteed oil supplies and which the Brazilian government will use to help fund the development of its ambitious plans for extraction of oil from its offshore sub-salt region.[51] China has also been careful to ensure that it distances itself from some of the more inflammatory anti-American rhetoric emanating from Caracas. This contrasts with Russia and Iran, the other countries that Chavez has sought to construct a multipolar world, who have been much more open in promoting enhanced relations with Venezuela as a direct challenge to US hegemony. The US$3 billion Russian arms deal with Venezuela is actually far more of a strategic challenge to the US than China's more cautious engagement.[52] Chinese diplomats have also been keen to counter Chavez's claims that Venezuela is diverting oil supplies from the US to China, noting that the 'the natural markets for Venezuelan oil are North and South America' and that there are real economic obstacles significantly to increase oil supplies to China, such as the lack of refineries in China that can handle heavy Venezuelan crude and the very long distances involved.[53] To meet the ambition of supplying 50 million tonnes per year by 2012, Venezuelan production would need to expand significantly and this is far from happening due to chronic economic mismanagement. In 2009, Venezuela reported oil sales to China of 19 million tonnes but Chinese data indicated less than 10 million tonnes.[54]

Chinese companies have similarly exercised considerable caution with the numerous and outwardly very attractive projects offered by the Venezuelan government. In the Orinoco River Belt Junin-4 agreement of 2010, all that was actually agreed was one more non-binding Memorandum of Agreement and this was after two years of negotiations. There is still a long path before a concrete agreement is finalised. In practice, there is a considerable distaste in China for the populist economic policies common in Latin America and which have, for instance, disrupted the supply of soybeans from Argentina. In the case of Venezuela, the demand for Chinese economic and political engagement is driven primarily from the Venezuelan government, while the Chinese government and Chinese companies are more reticent. There is little strategic interest in facilitating Chavez's anti-imperialist and anti-American ambitions. Nevertheless, the expansion of China's economic presence within Venezuela reflects a real and genuine shift in the geo-strategic orientation of Latin America where the trans-pacific linkages, with China at its centre, are beginning to challenge and in places supplant the traditional transcontinental and transatlantic orientation of Latin American countries.

Angola and Nigeria: gaining access to the Gulf of Guinea

The Gulf of Guinea possesses the most substantial oil reserves in sub-Saharan Africa and the full energy riches of the region only become accessible in the late 1990s with the technological advances that allowed drilling in the ultra-deep waters of the Gulf. The reserves are estimated to be around 60 billion barrels, which represents about 5 per cent of global reserves, and 80 per cent of these are to be found in Nigeria and in Angola. It is thus natural that China should target these two countries in its ambitions for expanding and diversifying global supply. These countries are also attractive as they are generally open to foreign equity investment. But this is also balanced, from the Chinese perspective, by a competitive economic and political environment as neither Nigeria or Angola are isolated 'pariah' states, such as Sudan, or hold to a Venezuelan-style anti-Americanism and economic resource nationalism. Western IOCs have a long history of being engaged in these countries and have reasonably well-entrenched and protected interests. In Nigeria, these include Shell, ExxonMobil and Total; in Angola, Gulf (which was subsequently taken over by Chevron) has remained the main operator in the oil-rich Cabinda enclave and its position was not threatened even at the height of the Soviet-backed socialist reforms of the post-independence Popular Movement for the Liberation of Angola (MPLA) government. The space available for China to enter into these oil markets has been, therefore, potentially significantly more restricted than in Sudan and Venezuela.

Without such an initially politically favourable environment, China has had to rely on its comparative advantages in the economic sphere. And the main instrument that it has utilised to secure its interests has been large-scale billion dollar oil-for-infrastructure deals where concessional loans are offered in exchange for guaranteed oil supplies. Such deals have been most visible, and controversial, in the development of the Sino-Angolan energy relationship to the extent that that this type of loan has been labelled in the World Bank as 'Angola mode'.[55] In Angola, the initial breakthrough came in 2004 with a pledge of a US$2.4 billion oil-backed loan for rebuilding the country's devastated infrastructure, which was raised to US$4.5 billion by the end of the year. This provided the context for Angola becoming one of the four largest exporters of crude oil to China and, in March 2010, Angola even temporarily supplanted Saudi Arabia as China's top supplier, shipping over one million barrels per day for a short period.[56] The deal also opened the way for Sinopec to gain equity partnership of the productive BP-operated deep-water oil Block 18 through a joint venture with the Angolan NOC, which was called Sonangol Sinopec International (SSI). SSI was subsequently awarded three other blocks (15, 17 and 18) in the 2006 round and in 2009 CNOOC and Sinopec purchased 20 per cent participating interest in Block 32 for US$1.3 billion. In support of these oil supplies and Chinese NOC equity investments, China has kick-started some 120 projects with loans of up to US$15 billion by 2009. This in turn has generated a very vibrant trade between Angola and China, which has extended to many different business areas and which has grown from US$1.8 billion in 2000 to US$25.3 billion in 2008.

The expansion of China's economic engagement with Angola has generated controversy. The 2004 Sinopec award of Block 18 involved the out-bidding of an Indian offer that included a less generous infrastructure deal, and China has generally crowded out investment from other Asian countries, such as India, Japan and South Korea.[57] These large-scale oil-for-infrastructure deals have also been seen to undermine IMF leverage over Angola's oil revenue transparency and management issues. In practice, though, it is unfair to blame China for the Angola's government's reluctance to follow the IMF and other lending facilities provided by western donors, and the greater transparency required, as rising oil revenues during the 2000s have been a more significant factor. In addition, the Angolan Ministry of Finance has increasingly disclosed details over oil revenue and production, and the 2006 licensing was quite transparent over such issues as signature bonuses and commitments to social projects.[58] It is also a mistake to see China as imposing its energy needs on a submissive Angolan government when it is really the reverse – it is the Angolan government, with President Dos Santos at the helm for over thirty years, which has been the driving force and has engaged with China for the clear economic benefits involved. The comparative strength of China is that it has been able to offer the most generous and speedy terms for resolving the chronic infrastructure problems of the country after two decades of civil war.[59] As these immediate infrastructure challenges have been met, the Angolan government has been increasingly ambivalent about the oil-for-infrastructure deals and have been seeking other partners, including returning to western investors, and has increasingly demanded China offer non-oil backed loans.[60]

The importance of recognising the autonomy and agency of the oil-rich African states for the successful engagement of China's expansive energy-related interests is illustrated by China's experience in Nigeria. In the Nigerian case, the oil-for-infrastructure formula has been a fairly comprehensive failure in comparison to that of Angola. Up until 2005, Chinese oil companies had demonstrated very little interest in the Nigerian oil market, due in part to the perception that this was a reserve of the IOCs and in part to the perceived high level of political risk, with the ongoing instability and conflict in the oil-producing Niger Delta.[61] It was only with the express initiative of President Olusegun Obasanjo in 2005 that this changed. He actively sought Asian players, not just China but also India and South Korea, to acquire oil blocks in return for their commitment to invest in downstream and infrastructure projects. Obasanjo also offered the Asian partners preferential terms, including the so-called Right of First Refusal. As a result of this, in the 2006 licensing round, CNPC was offered four blocks in exchange for its commitment to invest US$2 billion in the Kaduna refinery project in Lagos. In the 2007 round, CNOOC was offered a further four blocks in return for a US$2.5 billion China Eximbank loan for the Lagos-Kano railway upgrade and the construction of a hydropower project at Mambilla. When these deals were first announced, local and international media took this to represent a massive shift to the east in Nigeria's oil industry. In reality, none of these grand promises of infrastructure have materialised and Chinese NOCs failed to obtain rights to the blocks that they had been offered.

The main reason for this was not lack of will on the Chinese side but the endemic irregularities, corruption and instability in Nigeria's domestic politics. In May 2007, Obasanjo left office and the new President Umaru Yar'Adua began to revise or cancel many of the earlier decisions, arguing that the whole Right of First Refusal system was flawed due to lack of transparency and to the corruption involved in the whole process. As one authoritative report notes, the 'projects were vague and lacking in technical or financial detail . . . [and] in retrospect, this was an ill-thought-out, half-baked and ad hoc exercise dressed up in fine words'.[62] In practice, the reality is that China and other Asian oil companies have not been able to make any serious dent on the dominance of the international oil majors within Nigeria. The only safe acquisitions made by Chinese companies have been through private sales, such as the US$7.2 billion acquisitions of Addax by Sinopec in June 2009, which includes 3.25 million tonnes per year pumped in Nigeria. In 2006, CNOOC also paid US$2.3 billion for the rights to lucrative block in the Akpo field.

This difficult 'baptism by fire' for Chinese oil companies in Nigeria has not dampened their enthusiasm to seek possible entries into the Nigerian oil market. In September 2009, it emerged that Nigerian officials were discussing a proposal from CNOOC to acquire stakes in twenty-three prime oil blocks where Shell, Total, Chevron and ExxonMobil currently operate and which would, if successful, secure one-sixth of Nigeria's 36 billion barrels of oil reserve. The price of the deal was reported to be between US$30 billion and US$50 billion.[63] In May 2010, this was followed up by an agreement to spend up to US$23 billion to build three oil refineries and other petroleum infrastructure.[64] These proposals and agreements certainly represent a determination and resolve to seize opportunities at a time when China has deep pockets and when others suffer from the global credit crunch. These deals might ultimately herald the breakthrough that China has been seeking in Nigeria. However, earlier precedents suggest that caution needs to be exercised and that there is much work to be done to overcome the entrenched interests of Nigerian elites and their long-term connections with the western IOCs.

Conclusion

The Nigerian case study places a particular light on the issue of whether China's ambitious expansion into Africa and Latin America has an imperialist or neo-imperialist character. It illustrates that the Chinese presence and influence in Africa is small, even marginal, in comparison to the well-entrenched economic interests and long-standing investments of US and European companies, and that this is particularly the case in the energy sector. Generally in Africa and Latin America, Chinese oil companies are late-comers and suffer the disadvantages of most of the best deals having been concluded before their arrival. It is also a mistake to isolate China and Chinese oil companies as the only significant newcomer to the global energy markets – in reality, Chinese NOCs are themselves competing, and sometimes also cooperating, with ambitious oil companies from other emerging countries, such as Petrobas from Brazil, ONGC from India and Gazprom from Russia. The Nigerian case also clearly illustrates the post-imperial nature of the contemporary international relations and how political autonomy and decision-making lies predominantly with the post-colonial African states. Rather than a Chinese imposition of power and economic interest on a supine Nigerian state, the more accurate picture is of Nigerian elites manipulating the interests of Chinese oil companies to their own advantage. More generally, the reality is that the increased involvement of China in both Africa and Latin America has increased the strategic autonomy of the states of the region, allowing them to play off external powers to their own benefit. In this sense, China can be viewed, and is in practice viewed by many in the two regions, as a liberator and a beneficial force that has strengthened the independence as well as the economic prospects of the two regions.

But the rapid large-scale presence of China in Africa and Latin America is also undoubtedly one of the prominent manifestations of China's coming of age as a global power. Even if the excited talk of a new 'scramble for Africa' or a new challenge to the Monroe Doctrine might be exaggerated, China has certainly changed the geopolitical dynamics of both regions and has provided, at the very least, an alternative to the traditional western dominance. It is also evident in both regions that China has, particularly since the global economic crisis of 2008, become more confident, more assertive and more ambitious in its economic engagement. It has the outward look of a Great Power and the attempts to depict itself as a non-assertive developing country are increasingly less convincing. With this more prominent and assertive presence comes responsibility – responsibility not just to ensure that its economic engagement brings real and lasting development but also responsibility to ensure, with other interested external powers, that regional stability is promoted, such as the resolution and containment of local armed conflicts. No longer is it possible for China to argue that economics can be completely separated from politics and that its much acclaimed promotion of the principle of non-intervention means ignoring mass abuse of human rights or fundamental challenges to international law, such as non-compliance with UN Security Council resolutions.

With responsibility also comes almost inevitably resentment. China's economic expansion into Africa and Latin America is itself the result of the relative developmental success of China as against the countries of Africa and Latin America. China's economic miracle contrasts with the stagnation and much weaker economic growth in these two regions, which is itself a cause of some degree of resentment. But this is exacerbated by the structure of the trade being undertaken where Africa and Latin America are mainly exporting primary commodities, oil being but the most important of these, while China primarily exports processed and manufactured goods. This is widely seen in these regions as a structurally unequal form of economic exchange, representing the classic patterns of neo-imperialism. More localised disputes over the seeming preference for Chinese over local labour in the contracts undertaken by Chinese companies, or the lack of concern for environmental protection, only adds to a popular sense of merely following the old pattern of using both continents as 'resource grabs' without concern for the broader development prospects. This is, as noted above, not a universal view and is counter-balanced by much enthusiasm and support for China's presence and the belief that it genuinely offers new prospects for economic development. But what is certainly the case is that the assertion that China's engagement in Africa and Latin America represents a new form of neo-imperialist imposition is something that would not have made sense or had a popular resonance at the beginning of 2000 but certainly does a decade later in 2010.

11 Conclusions

In this book we have sought to provide an account of the international strategic ramifications of China's international energy strategies, primarily as they relate to oil. This analysis has drawn both on a detailed understanding of the context of energy policy-making and implementation in China and on the application of IR theories to the interpretation of the country's international engagement.

The domestic context of China's energy policy

China's energy policy will continue to be driven by the need to support economic growth in order to maintain the legitimacy of the ruling Communist Party. Energy demand will continue to rise for the foreseeable future and security of energy supply will remain the most important priority in national energy policy. In this context, self-reliance is likely to continue as the preferred approach of the government. Such a strategy is clearly no longer viable for oil, at least until such time as alternative transport fuels are widely available at acceptable prices. Thus the country's requirement for oil imports is set to rise for many years. The future growth of imports of gas and coal is less certain, and will depend, in part, on the degree of success in constraining the overall rate of increase in demand for energy, in exploiting domestic unconventional gas, and in developing nuclear and renewable energy sources.

As in any industrialised and industrialising country, the development trajectory of China's energy sector and energy policies is highly path-dependent. Constraints include the nature of the domestic energy resources and of the energy infrastructure, the intimate links between energy and almost all other national policies, the way in which government works, and the long-held beliefs, values and norms of society. This path-dependency provides for a certain degree of predictability in the development of China's energy sector over the next ten to twenty years, in the absence of any major domestic political or economic crisis. Despite the public rhetoric, we see few grounds for believing that the government will be successful in undertaking a dramatic shift in the way the domestic energy sector is managed, though clearly the efforts expended today, if sustained, will lead to incremental change.

On the other hand, the short-term trajectory of China's energy sector, and thus of the requirement for energy imports, is very difficult to predict. The main reason for this is that the government and its state-owned companies have the capacity to act very quickly in the domestic energy arena, stimulating the economy and thus energy demand, building new energy-intensive plants, constructing new power stations, or, alternatively, reversing such decisions. Further, many policy decisions fail to be implemented fully, or even to any extent at all, and policy implementation can create substantial, unexpected side effects. This unpredictability is further enhanced by the long-standing lack of transparency in policy decision-making in China. Their inability to foresee short-term changes causes major problems for players in international energy markets, for a small adjustment in China's domestic energy balance can have a major impact on the balance of supply and demand for internationally-traded energy, such is the scale of the country's total energy consumption.

The internationalisation of China's energy policy

China's ever increasing requirement for oil imports has provided the rationale for the internationalisation of its NOCs and for the progressive development of its energy diplomacy. Over the last twenty years, tens of billions of dollars have been invested in more than fifty countries in order to exploit oil and gas reserves and to transport some of this production back to China. As sources of overseas oil supply have multiplied, so energy has been used to support diplomatic initiatives just as diplomacy has been applied to address energy objectives. Many overseas ventures involve not only China's government and its NOCs, but also the state-owned banks and the construction and service companies. This gives the impression of 'China Incorporated' arriving in the host country as part of a highly coordinated national strategy. Rarely is this the case. Rather, China's government, its individual ministries, the NOCs and the other companies all have their own motivations and priorities, and may act with only a modest degree of coordination. Indeed, it is the companies that usually take the first step, and the government is left to catch up and, on occasions, to sort out the diplomatic debris.

Likewise, the host governments and NOCs have their own motivations for welcoming Chinese inward investment. The initial surge of Chinese investment will be aided by a high degree of convergence between the interests of the Chinese and those of their hosts that extends beyond the narrow scope of the oil industry. But experience has shown that such convergence may be short-lived once the host government has secured its short-term interests or if the government changes.

The international drive to ensure reliable supplies of oil imports and the ambitious international investment strategy of the Chinese NOCs has had a significant impact on China's foreign policy and how the rest of the world views China. Oil has provided Chinese foreign policy with new strategic opportunities that were not available earlier. For example, without the drive to secure oil imports, China's presence and influence in sub-Saharan Africa and Latin America would not be as strategically important as it has become. But this increased energy-related international power projection has also raised concerns and alarm. This can be seen in the most important bilateral relationship that China has – with the United States. While US policy-makers see China's growing energy needs as having the potential to promote and stimulate cooperation, such as over energy efficiency and through promoting international regimes that support the interests of the oil-importing countries, fears and anxieties lie close to the surface. This was most clearly evident in the 2005 UNOCAL affair when CNOOC's bid for control of the company was essentially vetoed by the US Congress on national security grounds. For its part, China remains fearful that the United States might use its military power to limit supplies of oil to China in the context of a major bilateral dispute or crisis.

Given this ambiguous strategic context, the Chinese government and Chinese oil companies have deliberately maintained a flexible strategy that seeks to hedge against such potential risks and threats. But such a hedging strategy tends also to lead to potentially negative unintended consequences. Thus, China's energy needs have contributed to the process of overcoming the historic distrust of Russia and developing an increasingly close relationship that helps to secure oil supplies not only from Russia but also from central Asia. However, this rapprochement can also appear as an intentional anti-western balancing strategy where Beijing is supporting the more openly revisionist diplomatic stance of Russia, and which includes support for other anti-western states such as Iran and Venezuela. Similarly, China's growing concern to ensure that it has stable supplies of oil from the Middle East and from other parts of the world that rely on the vital sea-lanes in the Indian and Pacific Oceans has led to fears that it might be seeking a more assertive regional hegemonic strategy. The intermittent but growing tensions and conflict over the South and East China Seas, and between China and India, highlight the dangers here. In more distant Latin America and Africa, there is less sense of China posing a geopolitical threat but the growing economic presence and power of China, which is driven in significant part by its energy needs, does inevitably promote an image among some observers of China as engaged in a 'resource grab' that has neo-imperialist overtones.

The rise of state capitalism: China leading the way?

This book does not, though, claim that any of these alternative approaches will necessarily emerge dominant. Indeed, we remain convinced that the core objective for the Chinese government is integration in the global economic and political system and that the aim is to do this without directly challenging the US or western interests. However, we also argue that China wants to integrate on its own terms, which includes the continuation of its domestic authoritarian political system with the state playing a central guiding and controlling role in economic development. Given the tensions this continues to generate with the West, China seeks to enhance relations with a wide array of energy suppliers who are generally sympathetic to its strategic ambitions and political philosophy.

In this regard, China is not alone in taking an approach to energy policy that is more state-centric than market-led. The governments of many major oil producing states have long played a leading if not a dominant role in the oil industry at home, and some of their NOCs are progressively internationalising, though usually at a slower pace than China. Examples include the NOCs of Malaysia, Brazil, India, Saudi Arabia, Kuwait and Russia.

This phenomenon is not restricted to the oil and gas sector. Rather, the early years of the twenty-first century have seen a steady shift in global political and economic culture from one in which liberal market capitalism was the dominant ideology to one in which the role of the state is growing. The reasons for this change are varied. They include the actual or perceived failure of elements of the liberal market approach, especially in energy and finance, as well as the shift in the balance of economic power towards countries that preferred a state-centred approach to economic governance. We can now be said to be in a global regime in which state capitalism is the dominant mode of economic governance.

In this respect, the winds of change are blowing in China's favour and China has not been slow to take advantage. Not only its oil companies, but also its mining companies and its sovereign wealth funds have been building their presence around the world, deriving their strength from cheap and plentiful domestic capital and from strong government support. Though other countries may try to emulate China, few are likely to be able to harness national resources to such great effect.

As China's requirement for oil imports grows and as its NOCs gain in competence and confidence, these strategies will progressively enhance the country's role in international oil markets and in the wider diplomatic arena. As we have described in this book, the international political and economic ramifications will be varied and complex, as is the case for other facets of China's rise. We have entered a new world, with a different prevailing economic ideology and with new geometries of political and economic power; and China is a key player in this new game. How it plays the game will depend as much on events and trends at home, as on its experience overseas. This new international regime will not last forever, but we should expect it to persist for a decade or more.

Notes

1 Introduction: China, oil and global politics

1 P. Andrews-Speed, X. Liao and R. Dannreuther, *The Strategic Implications of China's Energy Needs*, London: International Institute for Strategic Studies, Adelphi Paper no. 346, 2002.
2 A.L. Friedberg, 'The future of US-China relations: is conflict inevitable?', *International Security*, 30 (2), 2005, 7–45.

2 China's energy challenges and policy priorities

1 J.P. Dorian, *Minerals, Energy, and Economic Development in China*, Oxford: Clarendon Press, 1994.
2 V. Smil, 'Energy development in China. The need for a coherent policy', *Energy Policy*, 9, 1981, 113–26; S. Nakajima, 'China's energy problems: present and future', *The Developing Economies*, 20, 1982, 472–98.
3 National Bureau of Statistics, *China Statistical Yearbook 2006*, Beijing: China Statistics Press, 2006.
4 B. Naughton, *The Chinese Economy. Transitions and Growth*, Cambridge, Mass: MIT Press, 2007, p. 155; B. Bosworth and S. Collins, 'Accounting for growth: comparing China and India', *National Bureau of Economic Research, Working Paper* 12943, Cambridge, Mass., 2007; National Bureau of Statistics, *China Statistical Yearbook 2006*.
5 Naughton, *The Chinese Economy*; B. Chiu and M.K. Lewis, *Reforming China's State-Owned Enterprises and Banks*, Cheltenham: Edward Elgar, 2006.
6 P. Andrews-Speed, *Energy Policy and Regulation in the People's Republic of China*, The Hague: Kluwer Law, 2004.
7 J.E. Sinton and D.G. Fridley, 'What goes up: recent trends in China's energy consumption', *Energy Policy*, 28, 2000, 671–87.
8 J.E. Sinton, 'Accuracy and reliability of China's energy statistics', *China Economic Review*, 12, 2001, 373–83.
9 G.C.K. Leung, 'China's oil use, 1990–2008', *Energy Policy*, 38, 2010, 932–44.
10 L. Hang and M. Tu, 'The impacts of energy prices on energy intensity', *Energy Policy*, 35, 2007, 2978–88.
11 H. Liao, L. Fan and Y.M. Wei, 'What induced China's energy intensity to fluctuate: 1997–2006', *Energy Policy*, 35, 2007, 4640–49; J.E. Sinton, M.D. Levine and Q. Wang, 'Energy efficiency in China: accomplishments and challenges', *Energy Policy*, 26, 1988, 813–29; K. Fisher-Vanden, G.H. Jefferson, H. Liu, Q. Tao, 'What is driving China's decline in energy intensity?', *Resource and Energy Economics*, 26, 2004, 77–97; C. Ma and D. I. Stern, 'China's changing energy intensity trend: a decomposition analysis', *Energy Economics*, 30, 2008, 1037–53; P. Sheehan

and F. Sun, *Energy Use in China: Interpreting Changing Trends and Future Directions*, Centre for Strategic Economic Studies, Climate Change Working Paper no.13, Victoria University, Melbourne, 2007.

12 D. H. Rosen and T. Houser, *China Energy: A Guide for the Perplexed*, Washington DC: Peterson Institute for International Economics, 2007; Liao, Fan and Wei, 'What induced China's energy intensity to fluctuate'; J. Lin, N. Zhou, M. Levine and D. Fridley, 'Taking out 1 billion tons of CO_2: the magic of China's 11th Five-Year Plan', *Energy Policy*, 36, 2008, 954–79; P. Steenhof, 'Decomposition of electricity demand in China's industrial sector', *Energy Economics*, 28, 2006, 370–84; Z. Hu, D. Moskovitz and J. Zhao, *Demand-Side Management in China's Restructured Power Industry*, ESMAP Report 314/5, Washington DC: World Bank, 2005.

13 J. Lin, 'Energy conservation investment: a comparison between China and the USA', *Energy Policy*, 35, 2007, 916–24; Sinton, Levine and Wangi, 'Energy efficiency in China'; Sheehan and Sun, *Energy Use in China*.

14 Naughton, *The Chinese Economy*, pp. 140–57.

15 M. Liu and L. Zhu, 'A study on coordinated growth among industry structure adjustment, energy supply and consumption in China', *Energy of China*, 28 (1), 2006, 11–14 (in Chinese); Ma and Stern, 'China's changing energy intensity trend'; Lin, Zhou, Levine and Fridley, 'Taking out 1 billion tons of CO_2'; Rosen and Houser, *China Energy;* Liao, Fan and Wei, 'What induced China's energy intensity to fluctuate'.

16 Hang and Tu, 'The impacts of energy prices on energy intensity'.

17 Liao, Fan and Wei, 'What induced China's energy intensity to fluctuate'.

18 Rosen and Houser, *China Energy*.

19 H. Yang and M. Zhang, 'Analysis of impact of energy-intensive products export on China's energy', *Energy of China* 29 (1), 2007, 27–9 (in Chinese).

20 Lin, Zhou, Levine and Fridley, 'Taking out 1 billion tons of CO_2'; Ma and Stern, 'China's changing energy intensity trend'.

21 Lin, 'Energy conservation investment'.

22 Z.Y. Han, Y. Fan, J.L. Jiao, J.S. Yan and Y.M. Wei, 'Energy structure, marginal efficiency and substitution rate', *Energy*, 32, 2007, 935–42.

23 M. Shealy and J.P. Dorian, *Growing Chinese Energy Demand. Is the World in Denial?*, Washington DC: Center for Strategic and International Studies, 2007.

24 See, for example, W.P. Nel and C.J. Cooper, 'A critical review of IEA's oil demand forecast for China', *Energy Policy*, 36, 2008, 1096–106.

25 National Development and Reform Commission, *China's Medium and Long Term Energy Conservation Plan*, Beijing: NDRC, 2004.

26 U.S. Energy Information Administration, *International Energy Outlook 2010*, Washington DC: EIA, 2010; International Energy Agency, *World Energy Outlook 2009*, Paris: OECD/IEA, 2009; International Energy Agency, *Cleaner Coal in China*, Paris: OECD/IEA, 2009.

27 Shealy and Dorian, *Growing Chinese Energy Demand*.

28 International Energy Agency, *World Energy Outlook 2007*, Paris: OECD/IEA, 2007, pp. 335–6; International Energy Agency, *Cleaner Coal in China*; World Bank, *Economically, Socially and Environmentally Sustainable Coal Mining Sector in China*, Washington DC: World Bank, 2008.

29 International Energy Agency, *World Energy Outlook 2007*, pp. 339–40.

30 A. Sagawa and K. Koizumi, *Trends of Exports and Imports of Coal by China and its Influence on Asian Markets*, Tokyo: Institute of Energy Economics Japan, 2008.

31 International Energy Agency, *World Energy Outlook 2007*; International Energy Agency, *Cleaner Coal in China*; J. Blas, 'China lights thermal coal price fire', *Financial Times*, 14 January 2010, 36.

32 'China to face coal oversupply between 2011 and 2012 – industry expert', *Interfax China Energy Weekly*, IX (26), 8–14 July 2010, 6.

33 National Development and Reform Commission, *China's Medium and Long Term Energy Conservation Plan.*
34 *BP Statistical Review of World Energy 2010*, London: BP, 2010.
35 Andrews-Speed, *Energy Policy and Regulation*, pp. 297–319.
36 P. Horsnell, *Oil in Asia. Markets, Trading, Refining and Deregulation*, Oxford: Oxford University Press, 1997; P. Andrews-Speed, X. Liao and R. Dannreuther, *The Strategic Impact of China's Energy Needs*, International Institute for Strategic Studies, London, Adelphi Paper no. 346, 2002; B. D. Cole, *"Oil for the Lamps of China"– Beijing's 21st-century search for energy'*, McNair Paper 67, Institute for National Strategic Studies, Washington DC, 2003.
37 International Energy Agency, *World Energy Outlook 2007*, pp. 323–5.
38 'China to have major oil refining overcapacity by 2015 – expert', *Interfax China Energy Weekly*, IX (23), 17–23 June 2010, 10.
39 U.S. Energy Information Administration, *Projections of International Liquids Production to 2030.* Available at: www.eia.doe.gov/oiaf/ieo/pdf/ieopol.pdf (accessed 12 November 2007); International Energy Agency, *World Energy Outlook 2007*, p. 357; N. Berrah, F. Feng, R. Priddle and L. Wang, *Sustainable Energy in China. The Closing Window of Opportunity*, Washington DC: World Bank, 2007, p. 189.
40 International Energy Agency, *World Energy Outlook 2007.*
41 A. Chen, 'China to add 1.8 mln bbls African crude to reserves', Reuters Beijing, 23 March 2009.
42 M. Urquhart, 'China's strategic oil reserve plan', Reuters Beijing Newsroom, 30 December 2009. Available at: www.sify.com/finance/factbox-china-s-strategic-oil-reserve-plan-news-economy-jm4r4cjjbdd.html (accessed 10 January 2010).
43 International Energy Agency, *Developing China's Natural Gas Market. The Energy Policy Challenges*, Paris: OECD/IEA, 2002.
44 International Energy Agency, *World Energy Outlook 2007.*
45 N. Higashi, *Natural Gas in China. Market Evolution and Strategy*, International Energy Agency, Working Paper Series, Paris: OECD/IEA, 2009.
46 J.X. Liao, *The Politics of Oil Behind Sino-Japanese Relations: Beyond Energy Cooperation*, Stockholm: Institute for Security and Development Policy, 2008.
47 D. Girdis, S. Tavoulareas and R. Tomkins, *Liquefied Natural Gas in China. Options for Markets, Institutions and Finance*, Washington DC: World Bank, 2000.
48 Girdis, Tavoulareas and Tompkins, *Liquefied Natural Gas in China*; A. Miyamoto and C. Ishiguro, *Pricing and Demand for LNG in China: Consistency between LNG and Pipeline Gas in a Fast Growing Market*, Oxford: Oxford Institute for Energy Studies, Report NG 9, 2006.
49 Andrews-Speed, *Energy Policy and Regulation.*
50 Miyamoto and Ishiguro, *Pricing and Demand for LNG in China.*
51 International Energy Agency, *World Energy Outlook 2007*, p. 333; Higashi, *Natural Gas in China.*
52 E.S. Downs, *China's Quest for Energy Security*, Santa Monica, RAND Report MR-1244-AF, 2000; International Energy Agency, *China's Worldwide Quest for Energy*, Paris: OECD/IEA, 2000; Andrews-Speed, Liao and Dannreuther, *The Strategic Impact of China's Energy Needs;* J.X. Liao, 'A silk road for oil: Sino-Kazakh energy diplomacy', *Brown Journal of World Affairs*, 12, 2006, 39–51; K. Sheives, 'China turns west: Beijing's contemporary strategy towards central Asia', *Pacific Affairs*, 79, 2006, 205–24.
53 'CNPC awarded licenses for Sino-Turkmenistan natural gas project', *Interfax China Energy Weekly*, VI (32), August 2007, 16.
54 L. Eder, P. Andrews-Speed and A. Korzhubaev, 'Russia's evolving energy policy for its eastern regions, and implications for oil and gas cooperation between Russia and China', *Journal of World Energy Law and Policy*, 2, 2009, 219–41.

55 A. Chen, 'Reforms needed as China plans unconventional gas push', Reuters Beijing, 7 May 2010.
56 'CB boom', *China Business Weekly*, Beijing, 22–8 October 2007, 3; 'China to produce 500 m cu m of coal-bed methane this year', Xinhua News Agency, Beijing, 9 November 2007; D. Luo and Y. Dai, 'Economic evaluation of coalbed methane production in China', *Energy Policy*, 37, 2009, 3883–9.
57 U.S. Energy Information Administration, *International Statistics 2007*, Washington DC: EIA, 2007.
58 International Energy Agency, *World Energy Outlook 2007*.
59 *BP Statistical Review of World Energy 2009*, London: BP, 2009.
60 Shealy and Dorian, *Growing Chinese Energy Demand*.
61 International Energy Agency, *China's Power Sector Reforms. Where to Next?*, Paris: OECD/IEA, 2006.
62 International Energy Agency, *World Energy Outlook 2007*.
63 National Development Reform Commission, *Natural Gas Utilisation Policy*, Beijing: NDRC, 2007 (in Chinese).
64 International Energy Agency, *World Energy Outlook 2007*.
65 International Energy Agency, *World Energy Outlook 2007*; *BP Statistical Review of World Energy 2010*, London: BP, 2010.
66 State Planning Commission. *'95 Energy Report of China*, Beijing: State Planning Commission, 1995.
67 'Pressing ahead, atomically' *Beijing Review*, 27 September 2007, 28–30; 'Nuclear Power in China'. Available at: www.world-nuclear.org/info/inf63.html (accessed 26 February 2010).
68 J.A. Cherni and J. Kentish, 'Renewable energy policy and electricity market reforms in China', *Energy Policy*, 35, 2007, 3616–29; A. Lema and K. Ruby, 'Between fragmented authoritarianism and policy coordination: creating a Chinese market for wind energy', *Energy Policy*, 35, 2007, 3879–90.
69 Z. Zhang, 'Towards an effective implementation of clean development mechanism projects in China', *Energy Policy*, 34, 2006, 3691–701; M. Resnier, C. Wang, P. Du and J. Chen, 'The promotion of sustainable development in China through the optimization of a tax/subsidy plan among HFC and power generation CDM projects', *Energy Policy*, 35, 2007, 4529–44.
70 M. Yang, 'China's energy efficiency target 2010', *Energy Policy*, 36, 2008, 561–70.
71 National Development and Reform Commission, *China's National Climate Change Programme*, Beijing: NDRC, 2007.
72 'China earmarks 1.33 bn dollars for energy efficiency, discharge reduction', Xinhua News Agency, Beijing, 27 July 2007.
73 J. Lin, 'Energy conservation investment'.
74 *Implementation Plan for the Programme of One Thousand Enterprises Energy Conservation Action* issued by the National Development and Reform Commission, Beijing, 7 April 2006 (in Chinese).
75 W. Chandler and H. Gwin, *Financing Energy Efficiency in China*, Washington DC: Carnegie Endowment for International Peace, 2008.
76 P. Andrews-Speed, 'China's ongoing energy efficiency drive: origins, progress and prospects', *Energy Policy*, 37, 2009, 1331–44.
77 K. He *et al*, 'Oil consumption and CO2 emissions in China's road transport: current status, future trends, and policy implications', *Energy Policy*, 33, 2005, 1499–507; Z. Shen, 'Energy saving potential of China's car industry', *International Petroleum Economics*, 14 (8), 2006, 28–35 (in Chinese); M.P. Walsh, 'Can China control the side effects of motor vehicle growth?' *Natural Resources Forum*, 31, 2007, 21–34.
78 Shealy and Dorian, *Growing Chinese Energy Demand*; Rosen and Houser, *China Energy*.

79 G. Dyer, 'China increases taxes on big cars', *Financial Times*, 23 March 2008, 37; 'China orders curbs on government departments' car use', Xinhua News Agency, Beijing, 24 November 2007; 'China subsidizes green vehicles in pilot programme', Xinhua News Agency Beijing, 17 February 2009; K. Bradsher, 'China said to plan strict mileage rules', *New York Times*, 28 May 2009.

80 'China's State Council solicits opinions on rules for energy saving buildings', Xinhua News Agency, Beijing, 3 July 2007.

81 E. Graham-Harrison, 'China calls a halt to luxury public buildings', Reuters, Beijing, 18 April 2007.

82 'Chinese cabinet calls for tighter supervision of new construction work', Xinhua News Agency, Beijing, 21 November 2007; Y. Hu, 'Reining in real estate', *China Daily Business Weekly*, Beijing, 22–28 October 2007, 7.

83 'China to monitor government office buildings' energy conservation', Xinhua News Agency, Beijing, 27 October 2007.

84 'East China city says no air conditioning in offices under 33 degrees Celsius', Xinhua News Agency, Beijing, 24 June 2007.

85 'Rise in coal prices continued at Qinghuangdao port last week', *Interfax China Energy Weekly*, VII (27), 10–16 July 2008, 30–31; 'Coal prices stable at Qingdao port last week', *Interfax China Energy Weekly*, IX (25), 1–7 July 2010, 21.

86 'China raises gasoline prices 7 pc in response to high oil cost', *South China Morning Post*, 23 March, 2005; 'Oil prices raised, subsidies promised', *China Daily*, 27 March, 2006.

87 'China shocks with 18 pct fuel price rise', Reuters, Beijing, 20 June 2008.

88 A. Chen and J. Bai, 'China's gas price hike a small step towards reform', Reuters, Beijing, 1 June 2010; 'NDRC urges China's coal producers to cap prices', *Interfax China Energy Weekly*, IX (24), 24–30 June 2010, 4; 'China may delay electricity price increase to later this year', Bloomberg News, 30 June 2010.

89 'More details unveiled on proposed reform of fuel tax', Xinhua News Agency Beijing, 7 December 2008; 'China explains details of new oil pricing mechanism', Xinhua News Agency Beijing, 8 May 2009; 'China raises fuel prices', Xinhua News Agency Beijing, 29 June 2009.

90 'China's unit GDP energy consumption cut revised to 5.2%', Xinhua News Agency Beijing, 25 December 2009.

91 'China's energy efficiency improved in 2009', Xinhua News Agency Beijing, 1 March 2010.

92 'China's energy intensity increases by 3.2 percent in Q1', *Interfax China Energy Weekly*, IX (22), 10–16 June 2010, 4.

93 National Bureau of Statistics, *China Statistical Yearbook* 2009, Beijing: China Statistics Press, 2009.

94 *BP Statistical Review of World Energy 2010*.

95 J. Pan, W. Peng and others, *Rural Electrification in China, 1950–2004*, Stanford University, Program on Energy and Sustainable Development, Working Paper no. 60, 2006.

96 World Bank, 'India's Growth and Economy: analysis and quick facts, 2006'. Available at: www.web.worldbank.org/WBSITE/EXTERNAL/COUNTRIES/SOUTHASIAEXT/0,contentMDK:21136175~pagePK:2865106~piPK:2865128~t heSitePK:223547,00.html (accessed 3 September 2009).

97 V. Smil, *China's Past, China's Future. Energy, Food, Environment*, New York: RoutledgeCurzon, 2004; E.C. Economy, *The River Runs Black. The Environmental Challenges to China's Future*, Ithaca: Cornell University Press, 2004.

98 US Energy Information Administration, *International Energy Annual Outlook 2006*, Washington DC: EIA, 2006.

99 P. Andrews-Speed and X. Ma, 'Energy production and social marginalisation in China', *Journal of Contemporary China*, 17, 2008, 247–72.

3 The wider context of China's energy policy

1 For a discussion on how such changes have affected thinking on energy policy, see D. Helm (ed.), *The New Energy Paradigm*, Oxford: Oxford University Press, 2007.

2 See for example: J.H. Kalicki and D.L. Goldwyn, *Energy and Security. Toward a New Foreign Policy Strategy*, Baltimore: Johns Hopkins University Press, 2005; B. Barton, C. Redgwell, A. Ronne and D.N. Zillman (eds), *Energy Security. Managing Risk in a Dynamic Legal and Regulatory Environment*, Oxford: Oxford University Press, 2004; Roland Dannreuther, *International Security. The Contemporary Agenda*, Cambridge: Polity Press, 2007, pp. 79–99; A. Goldthau and J.M. Witte (eds),*Global Energy Governance. The New Rules of the Game*, Berlin: Global Public Policy Institute, 2010.

3 A.A. Neiderberger, C.U. Brunner and D. Zhou, 'Energy efficiency in China: impetus for a global climate policy breakthrough?', Woodrow Wilson International Center for Scholars, *China Environment Series*, Issue 8, 2006, 85–6; M. Meidan, P. Andrews-Speed and X. Ma, 'Shaping China's energy policy: actors and processes', *Journal of Contemporary China*, 18, 2009, 591–616 .

4 See, for example: R.C. Lieberman, 'Ideas, institutions, and political order: explaining political change', *American Political Science Review*, 96, 2002, 697–712; D. North, *Understanding the Process of Economic Change*, Princeton: Princeton University Press, 2005; D. Beland, 'Ideas and social policy: an institutionalist perspective', *Social Policy and Administration*, 39, 2005, 1–18; A. Greif, *Institutions and the Path to the Modern Economy. Lessons from Medieval Trade*, Cambridge: Cambridge University Press, 2006.

5 Christian Constantin, 'Understanding China's energy security', *World Political Science Review* 3 (3), 2007, article no.2. Available at: www.bepress.com/wpsr/vol3/iss3/art2 (accessed 15 July 2008).

6 J.K. Fairbank and E.O.Reischauer, *China. Tradition and Transformation*, Sydney: Allen & Unwin, 1989; W. Rodzinski, *The Walled Kingdom. A History of China from 2000 BC to the Present*, Glasgow: HarperCollins, 1991; J. Spence, *The Search for Modern China*, London: Century Hutchinson, 1990.

7 J.P. Dorian, *Minerals, Energy and Economic Development in China*, Oxford: Clarendon Press, 1994, pp. 56–62; K. Lieberthal, *Governing China. From Revolution through Reform*, New York: W.W. Norton, 1995, pp. 76–7; C. Brammall, *Chinese Economic Development*, London: Routledge, 2009, pp. 153, 363.

8 Dorian, *Minerals, Energy and Economic Development*, pp. 35–6.

9 T. Kambara and C. Howe, *China and the Global Energy Crisis. Development and Prospects for China's Oil and Natural Gas*, Cheltenham: Edward Elgar, 2007, pp. 17–23.

10 K. Woodard, *The International Energy Relations of China*, Stanford: Stanford University Press, 1980, pp. 13–25.

11 R.C. Keith, 'China's resource diplomacy and national energy policy', in R.C. Keith (ed.) *Energy, Security and Economic Development in East Asia*, New York: St Martin's Press, 1986, pp. 1–78.

12 P. Andrews-Speed, *Energy Policy and Regulation in the People's Republic of China*, The Hague: Kluwer Law, 2004.

13 Constantin, 'Understanding China's energy security'; D. Zweig and S. Ye, 'A crisis is looming: China's energy challenge in the eyes of university students', *Journal of Contemporary China* 17, 2008, 273–96.

14 Andrews-Speed, *Energy Policy and Regulation*.

15 E. Economy, *The River Runs Black. The Environmental Challenge to China's Future*, Ithaca, N.Y.: Cornell University Press, 2004, pp. 30–6; J. Miller, 'Daoism and Ecology', in R.S. Gottlieb (ed.) *The Oxford Handbook of Religion and*

Ecology, Oxford: Oxford University Press, 2006, pp. 283–309.; C.A. Ronan, *The Shorter Science and Civilisation in China: 1*, Cambridge: Cambridge University Press, 1978, p. 222.

16 C.A. Ronan, *The Shorter Science and Civilisation in China: 5*, Cambridge: Cambridge University Press, 1995, p. 190.

17 M. Elvin, 'The Environmental Legacy of Imperial China', in R.L. Edmonds (ed.) *Managing the Chinese Environment*, Oxford: Oxford University Press, 1998, pp. 9–32; Economy, *The River Runs Black*, pp. 36–43.

18 K.A. Wittfogel, *Oriental Despotism: A Comparative Study of Total Power*, New Haven: Yale University, Press, 1957.

19 E. Benvenisti, 'Asian traditions and contemporary international law on the management of natural resources', *Chinese Journal of International Law*, 7, 2008, 273–83.

20 C.A. Ronan, *The Shorter Science and Civilisation in China: 4*, Cambridge: Cambridge University Press, 1994, pp. 3–19; P. Golas, *Joseph Needham. Science and Civilisation in China. Volume V, Part 13, Mining*, Cambridge: Cambridge University Press, 1999, p. 425.

21 Golas, *Joseph Needham. Science and Civilisation in China* pp. 417–27.

22 Woodard, *The International Energy Relations of China*, pp. 13–19.

23 J. Shapiro, *Mao's War Against Nature: Politics and the Environment in Revolutionary China*, Cambridge: Cambridge University Press, 2001, p. 1.

24 P. Ho, 'Mao's war against nature? The environmental impact of the grain-first campaign', *The China Journal*, 50, 2003, 37–59.

25 Shapiro, *Mao's War Against Nature.*

26 Brammall, *Chinese Economic Development*, pp. 293, 549.

27 Dorian, *Minerals, Energy and Economic Development*, pp. 49–87; B. Naughton, *Growing out of the Plan. Chinese Economic Reform 1978–1993*, Cambridge: Cambridge University Press, 1996, pp. 26–33.

28 Andrews-Speed, *Energy Policy and Regulation*, pp. 259–80.

29 J. Pan and W. Peng, *Rural Electrification in China, 1950–2004*, Stanford University, Program on Energy and Sustainable Development, Working Paper no. 60, 2006.

30 World Bank, *China – Power Sector Reform: Toward Competition and Improved Performance*, Report No. 12929-CHA, Washington DC: World Bank, 1994; S. Shao, Z. *et al* (eds), *China. Power Sector Regulation in a Socialist Market Economy*, Discussion Paper no. 361, Washington DC: World Bank, 1997; N. Berrah, R. Lamech and J. Zhao, *Fostering Competition in China's Power Markets*. World Bank Discussion Paper no. 416, Washington DC: World Bank, 2001.

31 Andrews-Speed, *Energy Policy and Regulation.*

32 P. Andrews-Speed. and Z. Cao, 'Prospects for privatisation in China's energy sector' in S. Green and G.S. Liu (eds) *Exit the Dragon? Privatization and State Ownership in China*, London: Royal Institute for International Affairs, 2005, pp. 196–213.

33 P. Andrews-Speed, 'Power sector reform in China', in *China: Defining the Boundary between the Market and the State*, Paris: OECD, 2009, pp. 229–66.

34 N. Lardy, *Integrating China into the Global Economy*, Washington DC: Brookings Institution Press, 2002.

35 Andrews-Speed, *Energy Policy and Regulation*; Andrews-Speed, 'Power sector reform in China'; International Energy Agency, *Cleaner Coal in China*, Paris: OECD/IEA, 2009, p. 40; H.H. Wang, *China's Oil Industry and Market*, Amsterdam: Elsevier, 1999.

36 P. Andrews-Speed, X. Liao and R. Dannreuther, *The Strategic Implications of China's Energy Needs*, London, International Institute for Strategic Studies,

Adelphi Paper no. 346, 2002; K. Lieberthal and M. Herberg, 'China's Search for Energy Security: implications for US Policy', *NBR Analysis*, 17, 2006, 5–42; X. Ma and P. Andrews-Speed, 'The overseas activities of China's national oil companies: rationale and outlook', *Minerals and Energy*, 21, 2006, 1–14; E.S. Downs, *China's Quest for Energy Security*, Santa Monica, RAND Report MR-1244-AF, 2000; J. Mitchell and G. Lahn, *Oil for Asia*, London: Chatham House, Briefing Paper, 2007.

37 Constantin, 'Understanding China's energy security'.
38 R. Ferris Jr. and H. Zhang, 'Environmental law in the People's Republic of China', in K.A. Day (ed.) *China's Environment and the Challenge of Sustainable Development*, Armonk, N.Y.: M.E. Sharpe, 2005, pp. 66–101; Economy, *The River Runs Black*, pp. 91–128; X. Ma and L. Ortolano, *Environmental Regulation in China. Institutions, Enforcement and Compliance*, Lanham, MD: Rowman & Littlefield, 2000, pp. 115–31.
39 D.S.G. Goodman, 'The new middle class', in M. Goldman and R. MacFarquar (eds), *The Paradox of China's Post-Mao Reforms*, Cambridge, Mass.: Harvard University Press, 1999, pp. 241–61; V. Smil, *China's Past China's Future. Energy Food, Environment*, New York, RoutledgeCurzon, 2004, p. 144.
40 Economy, *The River Runs Black*, pp. 129–75; K. Gough, *Emerging Civil Society in China*, Stockholm: SIDA, 2004; D. Thompson and X. Lu, 'China's evolving civil society: from environment to health?', Woodrow Wilson International Center for Scholars, *China Environment Series*, Issue 8, 2006, 27–39.
41 Y.S. Lee, 'Public environmental consciousness in China: early empirical evidence', in K.A. Day (ed.) *China's Environment and the Challenge of Sustainable Development*, Armonk, N.Y.; M.E. Sharpe, 2005, pp. 35–65.
42 Lee, 'Public environmental consciousness in China'; Zweig and Ye, 'A crisis is looming'.
43 Andrews-Speed, 'Power sector reform in China'.
44 International Energy Agency, *World Energy Outlook 2007*, Paris: OECD/IEA, 2007, pp. 317–61.
45 T. Wang and J. Watson, *China's Energy Transition. Pathways for Low Carbon Development*, Sussex Energy Group, Tyndall Centre, Sussex University, 2009.
46 D.H. Rosen and T. Houser, *China Energy: A Guide for the Perplexed*, Washington DC: Peterson Institute for International Economics, 2007; P. Andrews-Speed, 'China's ongoing energy efficiency drive: origins, progress and prospects', *Energy Policy*, 37, 2005, 1331–44.
47 Rosen and Houser, *China Energy*; Andrews-Speed, 'China's ongoing energy efficiency drive'.
48 Andrews-Speed, *Energy Policy and Regulation*, pp. 169–83.
49 P. Nolan, *China and the Global Business Revolution*, Basingstoke: Palgrave, 2001, pp. 501–85; K.S. Gallaghar, *China Shifts Gear. Automakers, Oil, Pollution and Development*, Cambridge, Mass.: MIT Press, 2006; World Bank, *An Overview of China's Transport Sector – 2007*, Washington DC; World Bank, 2007, pp. 15–20; M. Parkash, *Promoting Environmentally Sustainable Transport in the People's Republic of China*, Manila: Asian Development Bank, 2008, p. 33.
50 Andrews-Speed, 'China's ongoing energy efficiency drive'.
51 Andrews-Speed, *Energy Policy and Regulation*; Andrews-Speed, 'China's ongoing energy efficiency drive'.
52 B. Naughton, *The Chinese Economy. Transitions and Growth* (Cambridge, Mass.: MIT Press, 2007), p. 389; Brammall, *Chinese Economic Development*, p. 371.
53 Rosen and Houser, *China Energy*.
54 C.L. Weber *et al*, 'The contribution of Chinese exports to climate change, *Energy Policy*, 36, 2008, 3572–77.

4 Inside China's energy policy

1 V. Smil, 'Energy development in China. The need for a coherent policy', *Energy Policy*, 9, 1981, 113–26; P. Andrews-Speed, *Energy Policy and Regulation in the People's Republic of China*, The Hague: Kluwer Law, 2004; K.G. Lieberthal and M. Oksenberg, *Policy Making in China. Leaders, Structures and Processes*, Princeton, NJ: Princeton University Press, 1988; E.S. Downs, 'The Chinese energy security debate', *The China Quarterly*, 177, 2004, 21–41; E. Downs, *The Energy Security Series: China*, Washington: The Brookings Foreign Policy Studies, 2006.

2 See for example: C. Mitchell, *The Political Economy of Sustainable Energy*, Basingstoke: Palgrave Macmillan, 2008; W. Ascher, *Bringing in the Future. Strategies for Farsightedness and Sustainability in Developing Countries*, Chicago: University of Chicago Press, 2009.

3 See for example: K. Lieberthal, *Governing China. From Revolution through Reform*, New York: W.W.Norton, 1995, pp. 159–63; P. Andrews-Speed, X. Liao and R. Dannreuther, *The Strategic Implications of China's Energy Needs*, London, International Institute for Strategic Studies, Adelphi Paper no. 346, 2002, p. 47.

4 X. Liao, *Chinese Foreign Policy Think Tanks and China's Policy Towards Japan*, Hong Kong: Chinese University Press, 2006, pp. 201–5; Lieberthal and Oksenberg, *Policy Making in China*.

5 Lieberthal and Oksenberg, *Policy Making in China*; Andrews-Speed, *Energy Policy and Regulation*.

6 T. Kambara and C. Howe, *China and the Global Energy Crisis. Development and Prospects for China's Oil and Natural Gas*, Cheltenham: Edward Elgar, 2007, pp. 46, 97.

7 Andrews-Speed, *Energy Policy and Regulation*; Downs, *The Energy Security Series: China*.

8 Andrews-Speed, *Energy Policy and Regulation*.

9 Downs, *The Energy Security Series: China*; B. Kong, 'Institutional insecurity', *China Security*, Summer 2006, 64–8; M. Meidan, P. Andrews-Speed and X. Ma, 'Shaping China's energy security – actors and processes', *Journal of Contemporary China*, 18, 2009, 591–616.

10 Downs, *The Energy Security Series: China*.

11 Downs, *The Energy Security Series: China*; D.H. Rosen and T. Houser, *China Energy: A Guide for the Perplexed*, Washington DC: Peterson Institute for International Economics, 2007.

12 Kong, 'Institutional insecurity'.

13 A. Chen and E. Graham-Harrison, 'China reshuffles energy, little change seen', Reuters China Energy Update, 11 March 2008; Y. Zheng and Z. Wang, *China's National People's Congress 2008: New Administration, Personnel Reshuffling and Policy Impacts*, The University of Nottingham: China Policy Institute, Briefing Series, 38, March 2008.

14 T. Wang, 'Chinese government specifies functions of National Energy Administration', Interfax China Energy Weekly, VII (29), 30 July 2008, 4–5; E. Downs, 'China's "new" energy administration', China Business Review.Com, November–December 2008, 42–5.

15 Meidan, Andrews-Speed and Ma, 'Shaping China's energy security'.

16 Andrews-Speed, Liao and Dannreuther, *The Strategic Implications*, p. 49; Downs, 'The Chinese energy security debate'.

17 Downs, 'The Chinese energy security debate'; C. Constantin, 'Understanding China's energy security', *World Political Science Review*, 3 (3), (2007), article no.2. Available at: www.bepress.com/wpsr/vol3/iss3/art2 (accessed 15 July 2008); Meidan, Andrews-Speed and Ma, 'Shaping China's energy security'.

18 C.P.W.Wong, C. Heady and W.T. Woo, *Fiscal Management and Economic Reform in the People's Republic of China*, Hong Kong: Oxford University Press, 1995; B. Naughton, *The Chinese Economy. Transitions and Growth*, Cambridge, Mass.: MIT Press, 2007, pp. 91–8.

19 Andrews-Speed, *Energy Policy and Regulation*, pp. 79–118, 139–52.

20 J. Zhang, *Catch-up and Competitiveness in China – The Case of Large Firms in the Oil Industry*, London: RoutledgeCurzon, 2004.

21 Y.C. Xu, *Electricity Reform in China, India and Russia. The World Bank Template and the Politics of Power*, Cheltenham: Edward Elgar, 2004; International Energy Agency, *China Power Sector Reforms. Where to Next?*, Paris: OECD/IEA, Paris, 2006; R. Pittman and V.Y. Zhang, *Electricity Restructuring in China: The Elusive Quest for Competition*, Antitrust Division, U.S. Department of Justice, Washington DC, 2008.

22 E. Thomson, *The Chinese Coal Industry: An Economic History*, London: RoutledgeCurzon, 2003; World Bank, *Economically, Socially and Environmentally Sustainable Coal Mining Sector in China*, Washington DC: World Bank, 2008.

23 P. Andrews-Speed and Z. Cao, 'Prospects for privatisation in China's energy sector', in S. Green and G.S. Liu (eds) *Exit the Dragon? Privatization and State Ownership in China*, London: Royal Institute for International Affairs, pp. 196–213.

24 Andrews-Speed, *Energy Policy and Regulation*.

25 See, for example, G. White, 'The dynamics of civil society in Post-Mao China', in B. Hook (ed.) *The Individual and the State in China*, Oxford: Clarendon Press, 1996, pp. 196–221; T. Brook and B.M. Frolic, *Civil Society in China*, Armonk: M.E. Sharpe, 1997.

26 J.H. Chung, H. Lai and M. Xia, 'Mounting challenges to governance in China: surveying collective protestors, religious sects and criminal organisations', *The China Journal* 56, 2006, 1–31.

27 X. Zhang and R. Baum, 'Civil society and the anatomy of a rural NGO', *The China Journal*, 52, 2004, 97–107; J. Unger and A. Chan, 'The internal politics of an urban Chinese working community: a case study of employee influence on decision-making at a state-owned factory', *The China Journal* 52, 2004, 1–24.

28 D.D.H. Yang, 'Civil society as an analytical lens for contemporary China', *China: An International Journal*, 2 (1), 2004, 1–27; Y. Lu, *Environmental Governance and Civil Society in China*, London, Chatham House Briefing Paper ASP BP 05/04, August 2005; Z. He, *Institutional Barriers to the Development of Civil Society in China*, Discussion Paper 15, China Policy Institute, University of Nottingham, February 2007; R. Baum, 'Political implications of China's information revolution: the media, the minders and their message', in C. Li (ed.) *China's Changing Political Landscape. Prospects for Democracy*, Washington DC: Brookings University Press, 2008, pp. 161–84.

29 K. Gough, *Emerging Civil Society in China*, Stockholm: SIDA, 2004; D. Thompson and X. Lu, 'China's evolving civil society: from environment to health', Woodrow Wilson International Center for Scholars, *China Environment Series* 8 (2006), 27–39.

30 G. Chan, 'China's compliance in global environmental affairs', *Asia Pacific Viewpoint*, 45, 2004, 69–86; Downs, 'The Chinese energy security debate'; G. Yang, 'Environmental NGOs and Institutional Dynamics in China', *The China Quarterly*, 181, 2005, 46–66.

31 J. Chen, *Chinese Law. Towards an Understanding of Chinese Law, Its Nature and Development*, The Hague: Kluwer Law International, 1999, p. 113.

32 Interview with senior government official involved in the drafting process, Beijing, August 2008.

33 Lieberthal, *Governing China*, 83–121.

34 P. Nolan, *China's Rise, Russia's Fall. Politics, Economics and Planning in the Transition from Stalinism*, London: MacMillan Press, 1995, pp. 34, 46–7.

35 J. Domes, *The Government and Politics of the PRC. A Time of Transition*, Boulder: Westview Press, 1985, pp. 195–206; C.P.W. Wong, 'People's Republic of China', in P.B. Rana and N. Hamid (eds) *From Centrally Planned to Market Economies: The Asian Approach. Volume 2: People's Republic of China and Mongolia*, Hong Kong: Oxford University Press, 1996, pp. 167–83.

36 Lieberthal and Oksenberg, *Policy Making in China*; K. Lieberthal, 'Introduction: the "Fragmented Authoritarianism" Model and Its Limitations', in K. Lieberthal and D. Lampton (eds) *Bureaucracy, Politics, and Decision Making in Post-Mao China*, Berkeley: University of California Press, 1992, pp. 3–31; J. Fewsmith, 'The new shape of elite politics', *The China Journal*, 45, 2001, 83–93; D. Shambaugh, *China's Communist Party. Atrophy and Adaptation*, Washington DC: Woodrow Wilson Center Press, 2008.

37 B. Naughton, 'China's economic think-tanks: their changing role in the 1990s', *China Quarterly*, 178, 2002, pp. 625–35.

38 Nolan, *China's Rise, Russia's Fall*, pp. 156–66.

39 Constantin, 'Understanding China's energy security'.

40 L. Dittmer, 'The changing nature of elite power politics', *The China Journal*, 45, 2001, 53–67; L. Dittmer, 'Leadership change and Chinese political development', *The China Quarterly*, 176, 2003, 903–25; F.C. Teiwes, 'Normal politics with Chinese characteristics', *The China Journal*, 45, 2001, 69–82.

41 E. Perry, 'Studying Chinese politics: farewell to revolution, *The China Journal*, 57, 2007, 1–22.

42 L.W. Pye, *The Spirit of Chinese Politics*, Cambridge, Mass.: Harvard University Press, 1992, p. 237; L.W. Pye, 'Jiang Zemin's style of rule: go for stability, monopolize power and settle for limited effectiveness', *The China Journal*, 45, 2001, 45–51.

43 S.L. Shirk, *The Political Logic of Economic Reform in China*, Berkeley: University of California Press, 1993, pp. 99–103; Fewsmith, 'The new shape of elite politics'.

44 Shirk, *The Political Logic of Economic Reform*, p. 105.

45 Kenneth Lieberthal, 'Introduction: the "Fragmented Authoritarianism"'; Lieberthal, *Governing China*, p. 82.

46 Shirk, *The Political Logic of Economic Reform*, p. 106; Lieberthal and Oksenberg, *Policy Making in China*, pp. 151–60; M. Xia, *The Dual Developmental State. Development Strategy and Institutional Arrangements for China's Transition*, Aldershot: Ashgate, 2000, pp. 214–18.

47 Liao, *Chinese Foreign Policy Think Tanks*.

48 S. Tsang, 'Consultative Leninism: China's new political framework', *Journal of Contemporary China*, 18, 2009, 865–80.

49 B. Kong, 'China's energy decision-making: becoming more like the United States', *Journal of Contemporary China*, 18, 2009, 789–812.

50 Andrews-Speed, *Energy Policy and Regulation*; Kong, 'Institutional insecurity'; Downs, *The Energy Security Series: China*.

51 Downs, 'China's "new" energy administration'.

52 Andrews-Speed, *Energy Policy and Regulation*, pp. 190–91.

53 Kong, 'Institutional insecurity'; B. Wang, 'An imbalanced development of coal and electricity industries in China', *Energy Policy*, 35, 2007, 4959–68; P. Andrews-Speed, 'China: oil prices, subsidies and rebates – where do we go from here?', Centre for Energy, Petroleum and Mineral Law and Policy, University of Dundee, 9 April, 2008. Available at: www.dundee.ac.uk/cepmlp/gateway/index.php?news=29168 (accessed 2 June 2010).

54 Andrews-Speed, *Energy Policy and Regulation*, pp. 185–201.

55 Andrews-Speed, *Energy Policy and Regulation*, pp. 79–103.

56 P. Andrews-Speed, 'Marginalisation in the energy sector: the case of township and village coal mines', in H.X. Zhang, B. Wu and R. Saunders (eds) *Marginalisation in China*, Aldershot: Ashgate, 2007, pp. 55–80.

57 X. Ma, *National Oil Company Reform from the Perspective of its Relationship with Government: The Case of China*, Unpublished Ph.D. Thesis, Centre for Energy, Petroleum and Mineral Law and Policy, University of Dundee, August 2008.

58 Kong, 'Institutional insecurity'; P. Andrews-Speed, 'Power sector reform in China', in *OECD Reviews of Regulatory Reform - China - Defining the Boundary between the Market and the State*, Paris: OECD, 2009, pp. 229–66.

59 Kong, 'China's energy decision-making'.

60 Andrews-Speed, *Energy Policy and Regulation*, pp. 119–37.

61 National Development Reform Commission, *China Gas Utilisation Policy*, Beijing: National Development Reform Commission, 2007 (in Chinese).

62 Smil, 'Energy Development in China'; Kambara and Howe, *China and the Global Energy Crisis*, p. 33.

63 Constantin, 'Understanding China's energy security'.

64 Andrews-Speed, *Energy Policy and Regulation*, pp. 169–83.

65 Downs, *The Energy Security Series: China*.

66 H.H. Wang, *China's Oil Industry and Market*, Amsterdam: Elsevier, 1999, pp. 12, 223; Downs, *The Energy Security Series: China*; Kong, 'China's energy decision-making'.

67 P. Andrews-Speed, 'China's draft Energy Law: a new beginning or more of the same?', Centre for Energy, Petroleum and Mineral Law and Policy, University of Dundee, 3 January 2008. Available at: www.dundee.ac.uk/cepmlp/gateway/index.php?news=29113 (accessed 7 January 2010).

68 B.W. Hogwood and L.A. Gunn, *Policy Analysis for the Real World*, Oxford: Oxford University Press, 1984; W. Parsons, *Public Policy. An Introduction to the Theory and Practice of Policy* Analysis, Aldershot: Edward Elgar, 1995.

69 See for example: Mitchell, *The Political Economy of Sustainable Energy*; G.C. Unruh, 'Understanding carbon lock-in', Energy Policy, 28, 2000, 817–30; International Energy Agency, *Deploying Renewables – Principles for Effective Policies*, Paris: OECD/IEA, 2008; L.J. Lundqvist and A. Biel (eds) *From Kyoto to the Town Hall. Making International and National Climate Policy Work at the Local Level*, London: Earthscan, 2007; I. Scrase and G. MacKerron, 'Lock-In', in I. Scrase and G. MacKerron (eds) *Energy for the Future: A New Agenda*, Basingstoke: Palgrave MacMillan, 2009, pp. 89–100; P. Andrews-Speed, The Institutions of Energy Governance in China', Notes de l'IFRI, Paris: Institut francais des relations internationales, 2010.

70 E. Economy, *The River Runs Black. The Environmental Challenge to China's Future*, Ithaca, N.Y.: Cornell University Press, 2004; X. Ma and L. Ortolano, *Environmental Regulation in China. Institutions, Enforcement and Compliance*, Lanham, MD: Rowman & Littlefield, 2000; Andrews-Speed, *Energy Policy and Regulation*.

71 J. Nygrad and X. Guo, *Environmental Management of China's Township and Village Industrial Enterprises*, Washington DC: World Bank, 2001; Economy, *The River Runs Black*; Ma and Ortolano, *Environmental Regulation in China*; Andrews-Speed, *Energy Policy and Regulation*; C. Gang, *The Politics of China's Environmental Protection. Problems and Progress*, Singapore: World Scientific Publishing, 2009.

72 Andrews-Speed, 'Marginalisation in the energy sector'.

73 Andrews-Speed, *Energy Policy and Regulation*.

74 Lieberthal and Oksenberg, *Policy Making in China*, pp. 151–60; Lieberthal, *Governing China*, pp. 208–14; Shambaugh, *China's Communist Party*.

75 Lieberthal, *Governing China*, pp. 226–30; L. Cheng, 'Jiang Zemin's successors: the rise of the fourth generation of leaders in the PRC, *The China Quarterly*, 161, 2000, 1–40; S. Heilmann, 'Regulatory innovation by Leninist means: Communist Party supervision in China's financial industry', *The China Quarterly*, 181, 2005, 1–21.

76 Documents of the 17th National Congress of the Communist Party of China (2007), Beijing: Foreign Languages Press, 2007, pp. 217–19.

77 International Energy Agency, *Energy Policies of IEA Countries. 2006 Review*, Paris: OECD/IEA, 2006, pp. 24–5.

78 D. Helm, 'The new energy paradigm, in D. Helm (ed.) *The New Energy Paradigm*, Oxford: Oxford University Press, 2007, pp. 9–35; D. Helm, 'Climate change policy: why has so little been achieved?', in D. Helm and C. Hepburn (eds) *The Economics and Politics of Climate Change*, Oxford: Oxford University Press, 2009, pp. 9–35.

79 V. Smil, 'Energy Development in China'; S. Nakajima, 'China's energy problems: present and future', *The Developing Economies*, 20, 1982, 472–98 .

80 *BP Statistical Review of World Energy 2008*, London: BP, 2008.

5 China's growing presence in the international oil and gas arena

1 T. Kambara and C. Howe, *China and the Global Energy Crisis. Development and Prospects for China's Oil and Natural Gas*, Cheltenham: Edward Elgar, 2007, pp. 12–14; R.W. Hardy, *China's Oil Future: A Case of Modest Expectations*, Colorado: Westview Press, 1978, p. 10.

2 Kambara and Howe, *China and the Global Energy Crisis*, pp. 13,19.

3 *BP Statistical Review of World Energy 2009*, London: BP, 2009.

4 H.H. Wang, *China's Oil Industry and Market*, Amsterdam: Elsevier, 1999, p. 230.

5 Wang, China's Oil Industry and Market, p. 232; J.P. Dorian, *Minerals, Energy and Economic Development in China*, Oxford: Clarendon Press, 1994, p. 151.

6 R.W. Hardy, *China's Oil Future: A Case of Modest Expectations*, Colorado: Westview Press, 1978, p. 103; A.D. Barnett, *China's Economy in Global Perspective*, Washington DC: The Brookings Institution: 1981, pp. 372–7.

7 S.S. Harrison, *China, Oil, and Asia: Conflict Ahead?*, New York: Columbia University Press 1977.

8 Hardy, *China's Oil Future*, pp. 1–12.

9 K. Woodard, 'Development of China's petroleum industry: an overview', in F. Fesharaki and D. Fridley (eds) *China's Petroleum Industry in the International Context*, Boulder: Westview Press, 1986, pp. 93–125; *BP Statistical Review of World Energy 2009*, London: BP, 2009.

10 Hardy, *China's Oil Future*, pp. 10, 47.

11 Woodard, 'Development of China's petroleum industry'; Dorian, *Minerals, Energy and Economic Development*, p. 145.

12 X. Liao, *Chinese Foreign Policy Think Tanks and China's Policy Towards Japan*, Hong Kong: The Chinese University Press, 2006, p. 203.

13 Woodard, 'Development of China's petroleum industry'; Kambara and Howe, *China and the Global Energy Crisis*, pp. 60–3.

14 Wang, *China's Oil Industry and Market*, pp. 227–66; Dorian, *Minerals, Energy and Economic Development*, pp. 134–84.

15 P. Andrews-Speed, 'China's search for energy security', *Asian Wall Street Journal* 10 December 2002, A 11.

16 The academic and policy literature on security of energy supply is cyclical in its volume, depending on the degree of threat to energy supplies. A peak in output in the 1970s and early 1980s was followed by a lull in the 1990s. Twenty-first century writings include: P. Horsnell, *The Probability of Oil Market Disruption:*

With an Emphasis on the Middle East, James A. Baker III Institute for Public Policy, Rice University, 2000; M. Lynch, *Blood or Gold? Politics, Economics and Energy Security*, The Emirates Occasional Papers no. 47, Dubai: The Emirates Centre for Strategic Studies and Research, 2002; V. Constantini and F. Gracceva, *Oil Security: Short- and Long-Term Policies*, INDES Working Papers no. 7, Brussels: Centre for European Policy Studies, 2004; B. Barton *et al* (eds) *Energy Security: Managing Risk in a Dynamic Legal and Regulatory Environment*, Oxford: Oxford University Press, 2004; J.H. Kalicki and D.L. Goldwyn (eds) *Energy and Security: Toward a New Foreign Policy Strategy*, Washington, DC: Woodrow Wilson Center Press/The Johns Hopkins University Press, 2005.

17 International Energy Agency, *World Energy Investment Outlook. Insights 2003*, Paris: OECD/IEA, 2003.

18 S. Pirani, J. Stern and K. Yafimava, *The Russo-Ukrainian Gas Dispute of January 2009: A Comprehensive Assessment*, Oxford: Oxford Institute for Energy Studies, 2009.

19 *BP Statistical Review of World Energy 2009*.

20 International Energy Agency, *Oil Supply Security. The Emergency Response Potential of IEA Countries in 2007*, Paris: OECD/IEA, 2007.

21 H. Geller, J. DeCicco, S. Laitner and C. Dyson, 'Twenty years after the embargo. US oil import dependence and how it can be reduced', *Energy Policy*, 22, 1994, 471–85; J. Deutch, A. Lauvergeon and W. Prawiraatmadja, *Energy Security and Climate Change*, Triangle Papers no. 61, 2007, Trilateral Commission, Washington DC, Paris, Tokyo; International Energy Agency, *Energy Security and Climate Policy. Assessing the Interactions*, Paris: OECD/IEA, 2007; D. Helm (ed.), *The New Energy Paradigm*, Oxford: Oxford University Press, 2007.

22 International Energy Agency, *China's Worldwide Quest for Energy Security*, Paris: OECD/IEA, 2000; E.S. Downs, *China's Quest for Energy Security*, Santa Monica, RAND Report MR-1244-AF, 2000; S. Gao, 'China', in P.B. Stares (ed.) *Rethinking Energy Security in Asia*, Tokyo: Japan Center for International Exchange, 2000, pp. 43–58; P. Andrews-Speed, X. Liao and R. Dannreuther, *The Strategic Impact of China's Energy Needs*, International Institute for Strategic Studies, Adelphi Paper no. 346, 2002.

23 C. Tian, 'Review of China's Oil Imports and Exports in 2008', *International Petroleum Economics* 17(3), 2009, 31–9 (in Chinese).

24 *BP Statistical Review of World Energy 2009*; N. Higashi, *Natural Gas in China. Market Evolution and Strategy*, International Energy Agency, Working Paper Series, Paris: OECD/IEA, 2009.

25 P. Andrews-Speed, ' Asia's energy demand and implications for the oil-producing countries of the Middle East', in *Energy Security in the Gulf: Challenges and Prospects*, Abu Dhabi: Emirates Center for Strategic Studies and Research, in press.

26 L. Eder, P. Andrews-Speed and A. Korzhubaev, 'Russia's evolving energy policy for its eastern regions, and implications for oil and gas cooperation between Russia and China', *Journal of World Energy Law and Business*, 2, 2009, 219–41.

27 P. Andrews-Speed, 'Is China becoming the banker for the international resources sector?', Centre for Energy Petroleum and Mineral Law and Policy, University of Dundee, 13 March 2009. Available at: www.dundee.ac.uk/cepmlp/gateway/index.php?news=29619 (accessed 25 September 2009).

28 'Chinese, Kazakh state oil firms purchase Kazakh oil, gas company', Xinhua News Agency Beijing, 24 April 2009; J. Anderlini and I. Gorst, 'CIC takes 11% stake in Kazakh oil group', *Financial Times*, 1 October 2009, 22.

29 'China slashes Iraq debt for oil deals', Upstreamonline.com newswire, 10 November 2009.

30 B. Blanchard, 'China's risky steps with Myanmar pipelines', Reuters Analysis, 4 February 2010.

31 Andrews-Speed, Liao and Dannreuther, *The Strategic Impact*, p. 62.

32 Eder, Andrews-Speed and Korzhubaev, 'Russia's evolving energy policy'; 'Russia's Gazprom expects to cut gas deal with China in 2011', Xinhua China News Agency, 22 January 2010; 'More on China-Russia pipeline to be completed in 2010', Xinhua News Agency Beijing, 7 March 2010; 'China-Russia oil pipeline to start operating 31 October', Xinhua News Agency, Beijing, 14 June 2010.

33 J.X. Liao, 'A silk road for oil. Sino-Kazakh energy diplomacy', *Brown Journal of World Affairs*, 12 (2), 2006, 39–51.

34 'Kazakhstan starts first phase of gas pipeline to China', *Interfax China Energy Weekly*, VIII (48), 16 December 2009, 7–8.

35 'Construction of Sino-Burma oil-and-gas pipelines to begin in September 2009', Xinhua New Agency, Beijing, 16 June 2009; J. Malhotra, 'Myanmar's pipelines confirm China's place in the Bay of Bengal', Business Standard, New Delhi, 29 June 2009. Available at: www.business-standard.com/india/news/myanmar-pipelines-confirm-china%5Cs-place-in-baybengal/362405/ (accessed 20 August 2009); 'CNPC gets exclusive operating rights for China-Burma pipeline', Xinhua News Agency Beijing, 22 December 2009.

36 D. Zha, 'Energy interdependence', *China Security*, Summer 2006, 2–16.

37 Downs, *China's Quest for Energy Security*, pp. 21–3.

38 X. Ma and P. Andrews-Speed, 'The overseas activities of China's national oil companies: rationale and outlook', *Minerals and Energy*, 21, 2006, 1–14.

39 Downs, *China's Quest for Energy Security*; Andrews-Speed, Liao and Dannreuther, *The Strategic Impact*, 34; A.M. Jaffe and S.W. Lewis, 'Beijing's Oil Diplomacy', *Survival* 44 (1) (2002), 115–34.

40 J. Mitchell and G. Lahn, *Oil for Asia*, Chatham House Briefing Paper EEDP BP 07/01, London, 2007; K.W. Paik *et al*, *Trends in Asian NOC Investment Abroad*, Chatham House Working Background Paper, London, 2007.

41 Ma and Andrews-Speed, 'The overseas activities of China's national oil companies'.

42 Ma and Andrews-Speed, 'The overseas activities of China's national oil companies'.

43 E. Downs, 'China's NOCs: lessons learned from adventures abroad', in *Fundamentals of the Global Oil and Gas Industry 2008*, London: Petroleum Economist, 2008, pp. 27–31.

44 FACTS Global Energy, *An Update of China's Overseas Oil and Gas Investment*, China Energy Series, Oil Edition, Issue 53, December 2008.

45 'CNPC to speed up oil assets buy plan', *China Daily*, 12 August 2009, 13; J. Lau and G. Dyer, 'China's top oil producer expands war chest', *Financial Times*, 10 September 2009, 22.

46 'PetroChina to invest 60 bn dollars overseas over 10 years', Xinhua News Agency, Beijing, 20 May 2010.

47 'Iran, CNPC sign $4.7 billion South Pars deal', Platts Oilgram, 4 June 2009, 1; 'Chinese firms to boost Iran's refinery output', Press TV news, Tehran, 12 July 2009; A. Chen, 'CNPC in Iran gas deal, beefs up Tehran', Reuters Beijing, 11 February 2010; J. Blas, 'Petrol cut-off ignites debate on Tehran sanctions', *Financial Times*, 8 March 2010, 9.

48 W. MacNamara, 'Addax takeover to take Sinopec into Iraq', *Financial Times*, 25 June 2009, 17.

49 A. Chen, 'BP, CNPC signs Iraq's first big post-invasion oil deal', Reuters Beijing, 4 November 2009; 'Petrochina to participate in developing Iraqi oilfield', Xinhua News Agency Beijing, 27 January 2010; H. Hafidh, 'China companies expected to close on Iraqi oil deals', Dow Jones Newswires, 4 March 2010; 'Chinese oil firm signs oilfield service contract in Iraq', Xinhua News Agency, Beijing, 17 May 2010.

50 A. Chen, 'Iraq could blacklist Sinopec after Addax deal', Reuters Beijing, 25 August 2009.
51 S. Tucker and J. Webber, 'CNOOC in $3bn Bridas deal', *Financial Times*, 15 March 2010, 15; 'China's Sinopec to buy into oil blocks', Reuters Beijing, 14 April 2010; 'Chinese firm signs oil deal with Venezuela', Xinhua News Agency, Beijing, 19 April 2010; M. Johnson and A. Ward, 'Sinochem buys stake in Brazil oilfield', *Financial Times*, 22 May 2010.
52 'China's oil sands push', Petroleum Economist online, October 2009; 'Total sells 10% interest in Canada's Northern Lights to Sinopec'. Available at: www. bloomberg.com/apps/news?pid=newsarchive&sid=az.qFmEo_FSc&refer=canada (accessed 2 May 2010); 'Sinopec to pay $4.65 billion in oil sands deal', Reuters Business and Financial News, 12 April 2010.
53 P. Smith, 'Shell and PetroChina in Arrow bid', *Financial Times*, 9 March 2010, 25.
54 J. Anderlini and I. Gorst, 'CIC takes 11% stake in Kazakh oil group', *Financial Times*, 1 October 2009, 22; 'China Investment Corporation, Russian oil firm start joint venture', *South China Morning Post*, 16 October 2009.
55 B. Kong, *China's International Petroleum Policy*, Santa Barbara: Praeger Security International, 2010, pp. 65–7.
56 Bo Kong, *China's International Petroleum Policy*, p. 66.
57 Bo Kong, *China's International Petroleum Policy*, p. 93.
58 FACTS Global Energy, *China's Overseas Oil and Gas Investment: Recent Developments*, China Energy Series, Gas edition, Issue 33, December 2009.
59 CNPC website. Available at: www.cnpc.com.cn/en/aboutcnpc/ourbusinesses/ explorationproduction (accessed 10 June 2010).
60 PFC Energy, *Chinese NOCs: Global Expansion Drivers*, National Oil Company Strategies Service, 5 April 2010.
61 FACTS Global Energy, *China's Overseas Oil and Gas Investment: Recent Developments*, December 2009.
62 B. Kong, *China's International Petroleum Policy*, pp. 69–75.

6 Strategies and driving forces behind the internationalisation of China's oil industry

1 P. Andrews-Speed, X. Liao and R. Dannreuther, *The Strategic Impact of China's Energy Needs*, International Institute for Strategic Studies, Adelphi Paper no. 346, 2002, pp. 33–6, 45–69; E. Downs, 'The Chinese energy security debate', *The China Quarterly*, 177, 2004, 21–41; X. Ma and P. Andrews-Speed, 'The overseas activities of China's national oil companies: rationale and outlook', *Minerals and Energy*, 21, 2006, 1–14; K. Lieberthal and M. Herberg, 'China's search for energy security: implications for US policy', *NBR Analysis*, 17, 2006, 5–42; J. Mitchell and G. Lahn, *Oil for Asia*, Chatham House Briefing Paper EEDP BP 07/01, London, 2007; T. Houser, 'The roots of Chinese oil investment abroad', *Asia Policy*, 5, 2008, 141–66.
2 P. Horsnell, *Oil in Asia. Markets, Trading, Refining and Deregulation*, Oxford: Oxford University Press, 1997, p. 53.
3 H.H. Wang, *China's Oil Industry and Market*, Amsterdam: Elsevier, 1999, pp. 121–40.
4 S.W. Lewis, *Chinese NOCs and World Energy Markets: CNPC, Sinopec and CNOOC*, James A. Baker III Institute for Public Policy, Rice University, March 2007; X. Xu, *Chinese NOC's Overseas Strategies: Background, Comparison and Remarks*, James A. Baker III Institute for Public Policy, Rice University, March 2007; Mitchell and Lahn, *Oil for Asia*; Houser, 'The roots of Chinese oil investment abroad'; FACTS Global Energy, *An Update of China's Overseas Oil and Gas Investment*, China Energy Series, Oil edition, Issue 53, December 2008.

5 L. Jakobson and D. Zha, 'China and the worldwide search for oil security', *Asia-Pacific Review*, 13 (2), 2006, 60–73; E. Downs, *The Energy Security Series: China*, Washington DC: The Brookings Foreign Policy Studies, December 2006; P.C. Evans and E.S. Downs, *Untangling China's Quest for Oil through State-backed Financial Deals*, The Brookings Institution, Policy Brief 154, Washington DC: The Brookings Institution, 2006; Mitchell and Lahn, *Oil for Asia*; B. Kong, *China's International Petroleum Policy*, Santa Barbara: Praeger Security International, 2010, pp. 67–9.

6 E. Downs, 'China's NOCs: lessons learned from adventures abroad', in *Fundamentals of the Global Oil and Gas Industry 2008*, London: Petroleum Economist, 2008, pp. 27–31.

7 Ma and Andrews-Speed, 'The overseas activities of China's national oil companies'; Kong, *China's International Petroleum Policy*, p. 92.

8 Houser, 'The roots of Chinese oil investment abroad'.

9 X. Ma, *National Oil Company Reform from the Perspective of its Relationship with Government: The Case of China*. Unpublished Ph.D. Thesis, Centre for Energy, Petroleum and Mineral Law and Policy, University of Dundee, August 2008.

10 J. Lau and G. Dyer, 'China's top oil producer expands war chest', *Financial Times*, 10 September 2009, 22.

11 Jakobson and Zha, 'China and the worldwide search for oil security'; M. Chan-Fiscel and R. Lawson, 'Bankrolling the "Going Out" strategy: China's financing of African aid and trade and implications for African debt and development', in M. Kitissou (ed.) *Africa in China's global strategy*, London: Adonis and Abbey, 2007, pp. 1–31; Kong, *China's International Petroleum Policy*, pp. 69–75, 87–9.

12 A. Vines *et al*, *Thirst for African Oil. Asian National Oil Companies in Nigeria and Angola*, London: Chatham House, 2009.

13 P. Andrews-Speed, 'China's energy role in the Middle East and prospects for the future, in *The New Energy Silk Road. The Growing Asia-Middle East Nexus*, Seattle: National Bureau of Asian Research, 2009, pp. 13–28.

14 Lewis, *Chinese NOCs and World Energy Markets*; International Crisis Group, *China's Thirst for Oil*, Asia Report no. 153, 9 June 2008.

15 Downs, *The Energy Security Series: China*; International Crisis Group, *China's Thirst for Oil*; Kong, *China's International Petroleum Policy*, pp. 93–4.

16 S. Tonnesson and A. Kolas, 'Energy security in Asia: China, India, Oil and peace', Report to the Norwegian Ministry of Foreign Affairs, International Peace Research Institute, Oslo, April 2006; G. Sachdeva, 'India's attitude towards China's growing influence in Central Asia', *China and Eurasia Forum Quarterly*, 4 (3), 2006, 23–34; C.J. Rusko and K. Sasikumar, 'India and China: from trade to peace, *Asian Perspective*, 31 (4), 2007, 99–123.

17 Ma and Andrews-Speed, 'The overseas activities of China's national oil companies'; Lieberthal and Herberg, 'China's search for energy security'; Houser, 'The roots of Chinese oil investment abroad'.

18 International Energy Agency, *China's Worldwide Quest for Energy Security*, Paris: OECD/IEA, 2000; E.S. Downs, *China's Quest for Energy Security*, Santa Monica, RAND Report MR-1244-AF, 2000; Andrews-Speed, Liao and Dannreuther, *The Strategic Impact*; A.M. Jaffe and S.W. Lewis, 'Beijing's oil diplomacy', *Survival*, 44, 2002, 115–34; J.Y.S. Cheng, 'A Chinese view of China's energy security', *Journal of Contemporary China*, 17, 2008, 297–317.

19 I. Taylor, *China and Africa. Engagement and Compromise*, Abingdon: Routledge, 2006, pp. 42, 69.

20 Andrews-Speed, Liao and Dannreuther, *The Strategic Impact*; Jaffe and Lewis, 'Beijing's oil diplomacy'; G. Christoffersen, 'The dilemmas of China's energy governance: recentralization and regional cooperation', *The China and Eurasia*

Forum Quarterly, 3 (3), 2005, 55–79; D. Zha, 'China's energy security: domestic and international issues', *Survival*, 48, 2006, 179–90; Jakobson and Zha, 'China and the worldwide search for oil security'; Kong, *China's International Petroleum Policy*, pp. 128–32.

21 Downs, *The Energy Security Series: China.*
22 'Beijing takes more active role in coordinating NOC activity', Reuters Beijing, 9 April 2010.
23 M.Y. Wang, 'The motivations behind China's government-initiated industrial investments overseas', *Pacific Affairs*, 2, 2002, 187–206.
24 S. Zhao, 'China's search for energy security: cooperation and competition in Asia Pacific', *Journal of Contemporary China*, 17, 2008, 207–27.
25 See Chapter 7 in this book for further discussion on collaboration.
26 L. Odgaard, *Maritime Security between China and Southeast Asia*, Aldershot: Ashgate, 2002; R.E. Ebel, *China's Energy Future. The Middle Kingdom Seeks its Place in the Sun*, Washington DC: The CSIS Press, 2005, 55–8; C.J. Pehrson, *String of Pearls: Meeting the Challenge of China's Rising Power Across the Littoral*, Carlisle, PA; Strategic Studies Institute, 2006; I. Storey, 'Securing Southeast Asia's sea lanes: a work in progress', Asia Policy, 6, 2008, 95–127; B.D. Cole, 'The energy factor in Chinese maritime strategy', in G.B. Collins *et al* (eds) *China's Energy Strategy. The Impact on Beijing's Maritime Policies*, Annapolis: Naval Institute Press, 2008, pp. 336–51; J. Lamont and A. Kazmin, 'Fear of influence', *Financial Times*, 13 July 2009, 7.
27 D. Yang, *China's Offshore Investment. A Network Approach*, Cheltenham: Edward Elgar, 2005, p. 197.
28 See, for example: Wang, 'The motivations behind China's government-initiated industrial investments'; Yang, *China's Offshore Investment*; P.J. Buckley *et al*, 'The determinants of Chinese outward foreign direct investment', *Journal of International Business Studies*, 38, 2007, 499–518; D.W. Yiu, C.M. Lau and G.D. Bruton, 'International venturing by emerging economy firms; the effects of firm capabilities, home country networks, and corporate entrepreneurship', *Journal of International Business Studies*, 38, 2007, 519–40.
29 Downs, *The Energy Security Series: China*; Ma and Andrews-Speed, 'The overseas activities of China's national oil companies'; Mitchell and Lahn, *Oil for Asia*; Houser, 'The roots of Chinese oil investment abroad'; Kong, *China's International Petroleum Policy*, pp. 37–41.
30 Ma, *National Oil Company Reform*; Kong, *China's International Petroleum Policy*, pp. 75–87.
31 Andrews-Speed, Liao and Dannreuther, *The Strategic Impact*.
32 Lieberthal and Herberg, 'China's search for energy security'.
33 Chinese sources that made this argument between 1995 and 2001 are large in number and include: State Planning Commission, *'95 Energy Report of China*, Beijing: State Planning Commission, 1995; F. Ai and others, 'An analysis of the oil problem and related policies', *Strategy and Management*, 6, 1995, 103–11 (in Chinese); B. An, 'Situations of the oil market in the Middle East and the concept of China's use of Middle East energy resources', *West Asia and Africa*, 4, 1996, 63–5 (in Chinese); C. Yang, 'Utilising international oil and gas resources in order to improve China's energy structure', *Energy of China*, 1998 (11), 12–16 (in Chinese); W. Jia *et al*, *The Development Strategy for China's Oil Industry 1996–2010*, Beijing: China Planning Publishing House, 1999 (in Chinese); L. Li and L. Li, 'On developing China's large transnational corporations in the oil industry', *China's Industrial Economy*, 2000, no.2, 44–8 (in Chinese); Z. Zhang, 'Ten major steps necessary for the development of China's refining industry in the 21st century', *International Petroleum Economics*, 8 (1), 2000, 37–9 (in Chinese); L. Hu, 'Strengthen the guarantee system or oil security in China', *China*

Energy, 2000, no.5, 15–17 (in Chinese); H. Chen, 'China's oil security strategy should be based on "Going Out"', *Review of Economic Research*, 25, 2001, 2–5 (in Chinese). Also see Kong, *China's International Petroleum Policy*, pp. 44–6.

34 J. Zhang, *Catch-up and Competitiveness in China. The Case of Large Firms in the Oil Industry*, London: RoutledgeCurzon, 2004, p. 3.

35 Ma and Andrews-Speed, 'The overseas activities of China's national oil companies'.

36 Andrews-Speed, Liao and Dannreuther, *The Strategic Impact*, pp. 45–70; Zhao, 'China's global search for energy security'.

37 G. Dyer, D. Pilling and H. Sender, 'A strategy to straddle the planet', *Financial Times*, 17 January 2011.

38 Andrews-Speed, Liao and Dannreuther, *The Strategic Impact*; Lieberthal and Herberg, 'China's search for energy security'; Downs, *The Energy Security Series: China*; Houser, 'The roots of Chinese oil investment abroad'.

39 Downs, 'The Chinese energy security debate'; A.M. Jaffe and K.B. Medlock III, 'China and Northeast Asia', in J.H. Kalicki and D.L. Goldwyn (eds) *Energy and Security: Toward a New Foreign Policy Strategy*, Washington, DC: Woodrow Wilson Center Press/The Johns Hopkins University Press, 2005, pp. 267–89; Houser, 'The roots of Chinese oil investment abroad'.

40 J.D. Pollack, 'Energy insecurity with Chinese and American characteristics: implications for Sino-American relations', *Journal of Contemporary China*, 17, 2008, 229–45.

41 J. Hellstrom, 'China's emerging role in Africa: a strategic overview', *FOI Studies in African Security*, May 2009; E.S. Downs, 'The fact and fiction in Sino-African energy relations', *China Security*, 3 (3), 2007, 42–68; International Crisis Group, *China's Thirst for Oil*; T. Houser and R. Levy, 'Energy security and China's UN diplomacy', *China Security*, 4 (3), 2008, 63–73; Kong, *China's International Petroleum Policy*, pp. 137–40.

42 Mitchell and Lahn, *Oil for Asia*; Erica Downs, 'China's NOCs: lessons learned from adventures abroad', in *Fundamentals of the Global Oil and Gas Industry 2008*, London: Petroleum Economist, 2008, pp. 27–31; Houser, 'The roots of Chinese oil investment abroad'.

43 For example in Kazakhstan: C.E. Ziegler, 'Competing for markets and influence: Asian national oil companies in Eurasia', *Asian Perspective*, 32, 2008, 129–63.

44 C. Alden, *China in Africa*, London: Zed Books, 2007, p. 45.

45 Kong, *China's International Petroleum Policy*, pp. 111–14.

46 *Guidelines on Fulfilling Social Responsibility by Central Enterprises*, State-owned Assets Supervision and Administration Commission, Beijing, 29 December 2007.

47 J. Wu, 'New office to audit assets outside China', *China Daily*, 21 August 2008, 2.

48 'Green rules eye Chinese firms abroad, *China Daily*, 29 May 2009; 'Green norms for overseas projects soon', *People's Daily*, 9 July 2010.

49 See this book, Chapters 9 and 10.

50 Ma and Andrews-Speed, 'The overseas activities of China's national oil companies'; Mitchell and Lahn, *Oil for Asia*; Ziegler, 'Competing for markets and influence'.

51 Taylor, *China and Africa*, pp. 197–206; Alden, *China in Africa*, p. 31; Chan-Fishel and Lawson, 'Bankrolling the "Going Out" strategy'; M. Meidan, 'China's Africa policy: business now, politics later', *Asian Perspective*, 30 (4), 2006, 69–93; I. Campos and A. Vines, 'Angola and China. A pragmatic partnership', Chatham House Working Paper, London: Chatham House, 2008.

52 Andrews-Speed, 'China's energy role in the Middle East'.

53 J.X. Liao, 'A silk road for oil. Sino-Kazakh energy diplomacy', *Brown Journal of World Affairs*, 12 (2), 2006, 39–51.

54 'China to build $8bn oil refinery in Nigeria', BBC News Online 6 July 2010. Available at: www.news.bbc.co.uk/1/hi/business/10527308 (accessed 10 July 2010); 'Nigeria, China to spend $23 billion building oil refineries', Bloomberg Businessweek (www.businessweek.com), 12 July 2010.

55 L. Eder, P. Andrews-Speed and A. Korzhubaev, 'Russia's evolving energy policy for its eastern regions, and implications for oil and gas cooperation between Russia and China', *Journal of World Energy Law and Business*, 2, 2009, 219–41.

56 See this book, Chapter 10; 'Kazakh senators push to end sales of assets to China', *Interfax China Energy Weekly*, VIII (45), 25 November 2009, 6; T. Erdbrink, 'Iranians wary of deeper ties with China', *Washington Post*, 14 April 2010.

7 Integration, the West and international energy policy

1 X. Xu, *Chinese NOC's Overseas Strategies: Background, Comparison and Remarks*, James A. Baker III Institute for Public Policy, Rice University, March 2007.

2 Quoted in E.S. Downs, *The Energy Security Series: China*, The Brookings Foreign Policy Studies, Washington DC: The Brooking Institution, 2006, p. 13.

3 It is interesting in this regard to contrast the extensive nature of the IR theoretical debate over China and Asia as compared to the Middle East, which remains largely untouched by significant IR theoretical debates. This can be seen most vividly in the leading IR journal, *International Security*.

4 J.J. Mearsheimer, *The Tragedy of Great Power Politics*, New York: Norton, 2001, p. 402.

5 R. Gilpin, *War and Change in World Politics*, Princeton: Princeton University Press, 1981, p. 187. Gilpin is the classic exponent of this view. But see also A.F.K Organski and J. Kugler, *The War Ledger*, Chicago: Chicago University Press, 1980; and F. Zakaria, *From Wealth to Power: The Unusual Origins of America's World Role*, Princeton: Princeton University Press, 1998.

6 For an analysis that reveals the difficulties in past attempts to incorporate rising powers, see M.D. Swaine and A.J. Tellis, *Interpreting China's Grand Strategy: Past, Present and Future*, Santa Monica: RAND, 2000.

7 See P.H. Gries, *China's New Nationalism: Pride, Politics and Diplomacy*, Berkeley: University of California Press, 2004, pp. 43–53; A.J. Nathan and R.S. Ross, *The Great Wall and Empty Fortress: China's Search for Security*, New York: Norton, 1997.

8 A.L. Friedberg, 'The future of US-China relations: is conflict inevitable?', *International Security*, 30 (2), 2005, p. 12.

9 For the classic statement on European integration, see E.B. Haas, *The Uniting of Europe: Political, Economic and Social Forces*, London: Stevens, 1958.

10 R.N. Rosecrance, *The Rise of the Trading State*, New York: Basic Books, 1986.

11 A key text in this regard is R.O. Keohane, *After Hegemony: Cooperation and Discord in the World Political Economy*, Princeton: Princeton University Press, 1984. See also J.R. O'Neal and B.M. Russett, *Triangulating Peace: Democracy, Interdependence, and International Organizations*, New York: W.W. Norton, 2001.

12 For the realist traditions, see A.I. Johnston, *Cultural Realism: Strategic Culture and Grand Strategy in Chinese History*, Princeton: Princeton University Press, 1995. For the process of socialisation into more liberal norms, see A.I. Johnston, 'International structures and Chinese foreign policy' in S.S. Kim (ed.) *China and the World: Chinese Foreign Policy Faces the New Millennium*, Boulder, CO: Westview Press, 1998; and A.I. Johnston, 'Is China a status quo power?', *International Security*, 27 (4), 2003, 5–56.

13 As of 2009, China had over 6,000 troops on such operations, more than any other Permanent Member of the Security Council.

14 M.D. Swayne and A.I. Johnston, 'China and arms control institutions', in E. Economy and M. Oksenberg (eds), *China Joins the World: Progress and Prospects*, New York: Council on Foreign Relations, 1999, Ch. 3.

15 Wu Yingchun, as quoted in Y. Deng, *China's Struggle for Status: The Realignment of International Relations*, Cambridge: Cambridge University Press, 2008, p. 50.

16 See A.I. Johnston, 'Chinese middle class attitudes towards international affairs: Nascent liberalization?', *China Quarterly*, 179, 2004, 603–28; M. Pei, 'Creeping democratization in China', *Journal of Democracy*, 6 (4), 1995, 64–79; and E. Economy, 'Don't break the engagement', *Foreign Affairs*, 83 (3), 2004, 96–109.

17 J. Mann, *The China Fantasy*, New York: Viking, 2007.

18 E.D. Mansfield and J. Snyder, 'Democratization and the danger of war', *International Security*, 20 (1), 1995, 5–38. As applied to China, see A. Waldron, 'How would democracy change China?', *Orbis*, 2, 2004, 247–61.

19 S.M Lipset, 'Some social requisites of democracy: economic development and political legitimacy', *The American Political Science Review*, 53 (1), 1959, 69–105.

20 For an overview of the 'China threat' debate, see D. Roy, 'Hegemon on the horizon? China's threat to East Asian security', *International Security*, 19 (1), 1994, 149–68.

21 E. S. Downs and P.C. Saunders, 'Legitimacy and the limits of nationalism: China and the Diadyu island', *International Security*, 23 (3), 1998/9, 114–46. See also A. Goldstein, *Rising to the Challenge: China's Grand Strategy and International Security*, Stanford: Stanford University Press, 2005; and R.S. Ross, 'Beijing as a conservative power', *Foreign Affairs*, 76 (2), 1997, 33–44.

22 For an application of the 'security dilemma' to China and East Asia, see T.J. Christensen, 'China, the US-Japan alliance and the security dilemma in East Asia', *International Security*, 23 (4), 1999, 49–80.

23 See, for example, the work of Qin Yaqing, vice president of China's Foreign Affairs University, who has been the leading Chinese constructivist and who has called for the China peacefully 'fusing into the international society'.

24 B.S. Glaser and E.S. Medeiros, 'The changing ecology of foreign policy making in China: the ascension and demise of the theory of peaceful rise', *China Quarterly* 190, 2007, 291–310. Although it could also be added that 'the emphasis on peaceful' was also potentially seen within certain circles to undermine China's deterrence strategy in relation to Taiwan.

25 R. Aron, *Peace and War: A Theory of International Relations*, London: Weidenfeld and Nicolson, 1966, pp. 99–104.

26 F. Fukuyama, *The End of History and the Last Man*, London: Hamish Hamilton, 1992.

27 See, for example, J.M. Goldgeier and M. McFaul, 'A tale of two worlds: core and periphery in the post-Cold War era', *International Organization*, 46 (2), 1992, 467–91; G.J. Ikenberry, *After Victory: Institutions, Strategic Restraint and the Rebuilding of Order after Major Wars*, Princeton: Princeton University Press, 2001.

28 R. Cooper, *The Breaking of Nations: Order and Chaos in the Twenty-First Century*, London: Atlantic Books, 2003.

29 R. Foot, *Rights Beyond Borders: The Global Community and the Struggle over Human Rights in China*, Oxford: Oxford University Press, 2000; G. Rozman, 'China's quest for great power identity', *Orbis*, 43 (3), 1999, 383–402; and L.W. Pye, 'China: not your typical superpower', *Problems of Post-Communism*, July/August, 1996, 3–15.

30 For reviews on the 'resource curse', see M.L. Ross, 'The political economy of the resource curse', *World Politics*, 51 (2), 1999, 297–322; and P. Stevens, 'Resource impact: curse or blessing: a literature review', *CEPMLP Internet Journal*, 13(4), 2003. Available at: www.dundee.ac.uk/cepmlp/journal/html/Vol13/vol13-14.html (accessed 10 August 2010).

31 F. Leverett and P. Noel, 'The new axis of oil', *The National Interest*, Summer 2006, 62–70

32 J.I. Lieberman, 'China-US energy policies: a choice of cooperation or collision', 30 November 2005. Available at: www.cfr.org/publication/9335/chinaus_energy-policies.html (accessed 10 September 2009).

33 Speech before sixth ASEM meeting, Helsinki, 10–11 September 2006.

34 US Department of Energy, *Section 1837: National Security Review of International Energy Requirements*, February 2006.

35 J.T. Dreyer, 'Sino-American energy cooperation', *Journal of Contemporary China*, 16, 2007, 46176. For further analyses on China-US energy cooperation (or competition), see F. Leverett, 'Managing China-US energy competition in the Middle East', *The Washington Quarterly*, 29 (1), 2005–06, 187–201; and D. Zha and W. Hu, 'Promoting energy partnership in Beijing and Washington', *The Washington Quarterly*, 30(4), 2007, 105–15.

36 See EU websites, for example: www.ec.europa.eu/environment/climat/china.htm (accessed on 2 July 2010).

37 Joint Statement by the National Energy Administration of the People's Republic of China and the International Energy Agency, Paris, 14 October 2009. Available at: www.iea.org/journalists/ministerial2009/joint_statement_cn.pdf (accessed on 14 February 2010).

38 G. Kessler, 'US says China must address its intentions: how its power is used is of concern', *Washington Post*, 22 September 2005.

39 *New York Times*, 7 July 2005.

40 For a good overview of the UNOCAL incident and linking it to other US-China crises, see S.L. Shirk, *China: Fragile Superpower*, Oxford: Oxford University Press, 2007, pp. 249–51.

41 S. Walt, 'International Relations: one world, many theories', *Foreign Policy*, 110, 1998, 29–46; J.L. Gaddis, 'International Relations Theory and the end of the Cold War', *International Security*, 17 (3), 1992–3, 5–58; and R. Dannreuther, *International Security: the Contemporary Agenda*, Polity: Cambridge, 2007, pp. 34–54.

42 P.J. Katzenstein and R. Sil, 'Rethinking Asian security: A case for analytical eclecticism' in J.J. Suh, P.J. Katzenstein and A. Carlson, *Rethinking Security in East Asia: Identity, Power and Efficiency*, Stanford: Stanford University Press, 2004, pp. 1–33.

43 Friedberg, 'The future of US-China relations'.

44 For an overview of the 'new institutionalism', see K. Thelen, 'Historical institutionalism in comparative politics', *Annual Review of Political Studies*, 2, 1999, pp. 369–404. For seminal texts, see D.C. North, *Institutions, Institutional Change and Economic Performance*, Cambridge: Cambridge University Press, 1990; and P. Pierson, *Politics in Time: History, Institutions, and Social Analysis*, Princeton: Princeton University Press, 2004.

45 For a seminal constructivist contribution, see A. Wendt, *Social Theory of International Politics*, Cambridge: Cambridge University Press, 1999. For an example of constructivist theory applied to China, see A.I. Johnston and P. Evans, 'China's engagement with multilateral security institutions' in I.A. Johnston and R.S. Ross (eds), *Engaging China: The Management of an Emerging Power*, New York: Routledge, 1999, pp. 235–72.

46 A good assessment of the insights provided by applying systems theory to IR, see R. Jervis, *Systems Effects: Complexity in Political and Social Life*, Princeton: Princeton University Press, 1997. The following analysis has, in part, been inspired by Jervis's recommendation to utilise such a systems approach to China's rise, as see in 'Correspondence: thinking systemically about China', *International Security*, 31 (2), 2006, 206–8.

47 R. Jervis, 'Cooperation under the security dilemma', *World Politics*, 30 (2), 1978, 167–94.

8 The revisionist alternative: energy and the Sino-Russian axis

1 The difficulties of 'hard balancing' are reflected in the fact that US projected defence spending for 2009 is US$711billion, which exceeds the military expenditure of the next thirty countries combined and China and Russia each spend less than 10 per cent of the US military budget. On the prospects for 'soft balancing', see R.A. Pape, 'Soft balancing against the United States', *International Security*, 30 (1), 2005, 7–45; and T.V. Paul, 'Soft balancing in the age of US primacy', *International Security*, 30 (1), 2005, 46–71. For a critique of the viability of soft balancing, see S.G. Brooks and W.C. Wohlforth, 'Hard times for soft balancing', *International Security*, 30(1), 2005, 72–108.

2 For example, Robert Kagan argues that the 'axis of democracy' is increasingly being countered by the 'association of autocracies' in R. Kagan, *The Return of History and End of Dreams*, London: Atlantic Books, 2008.

3 F. Leverett and P. Noel, 'The new axis of oil', *National Interest*, July 2006. Available at: www.nationalinterest.org/General.aspx?id=92&id2=12336 (accessed 22 September 2009).

4 For the convergence thesis, see P. Ferdinand, 'Russia and China: converging responses to globalization', *International Affairs*, 83 (4), 2007, 655–800; R. Menon, 'The strategic convergence between Russia and China', *Survival*, 39 (2), 1997, 101–25; and M. Leonard, *Divided World: the Struggle for Primacy in 2020*, London: Centre for European Reform, 2007.

5 B. Lo, *Axis of Convenience: Moscow, Beijing and the New Geopolitics*, Washington DC: Brookings Institution Press, 2008. For a similarly nuanced approach, see J-P. Cabestan *et al*, *La Chine et la Russie: Entre Convergence et Mefiance*, Paris: UNICOMM, 2008.

6 Lo, *Axis of Convenience*, p. 49.

7 See, for example, N. Ferguson, 'Leading historian issues warning of new Cold War', *Sunday Herald*, 6 September 2008; and A. Cohen, 'The Russia-China Friendship and Cooperation Treaty: a strategic shift in Eurasia?', *Heritage Foundation Backgrounder*, 1459, 18 July 2001. For the ways in which Russia under Putin is perceived to have become increasingly more hostile to the West and thus closer to China, see E. Lucas, *The New Cold War: How the Kremlin Menaces both Russia and the West*, London: Bloomsbury, 2008.

8 A. Kuchins, 'Russia and China: the ambivalent embrace', *Current History*, 106, 2007, p. 327.

9 A. Lukin, *The Bear Watches the Dragon: Russian Perceptions of China and the Evolution of Russia-Chinese Relations Since the Eighteenth Century*, Armonk NY: M.E. Sharpe, 2003, pp. 16–25.

10 Lukin, *The Bear Watches the Dragon*, p. 69.

11 Quoted in R. Menon, 'The limits of Chinese-Russian partnership', *Survival*, 51(3), 2009, 102. Mao made these comments in September 1964 at a meeting with the Japanese Socialist Party.

12 G. Rozman, 'Russia in Northeast Asia: in search of a strategy' in R. Levgold (ed.), *Russian Foreign Policy in the 21st Century and the Shadow of the Past*, New York: Columbia University Press, 2007, p. 362. For a more accurate and far less alarmist assessment of Chinese immigration into Russia, see V. Portyakov, 'Russian vector in the Chinese global Chinese migration', *Far Eastern Affairs*, 34 (1), 2006, 47–61.

13 For an excellent account of the settlement of the border issues, see Cabestan *et al*, *La Chine et La Russie*, pp. 35–42.

14 A. Kozyrev, 'Transfiguration of Kafkaesque metamorphosis', *Nezavisimaya gazeta*, 20 August 1993. Chinese concerns about Russia's pro-western leanings can be seen in H. Zhao, 'New frame of Sino-Russian-US triangular relations' in *Post-Cold War World*, Shanghai: Shanghai Institute of International Studies, 2000, pp. 155–8.

15 Y. Primakov, *Russian Crossroads: Towards the New Millennium*, New Haven: Yale University Press, 2004, p. 71.

16 Menon, 'The limits of Chinese-Russian partnership', pp. 107–10.

17 Ferdinand, 'Russia and China: converging response to globalization', p. 663. For a good general account, see R. Wade, *Governing the Market: Economic Theory and the Role of Government in East Asian Modernization*, Princeton: Princeton University Press, 1995.

18 K.W. Paik, 'Sino-Russian oil and gas development cooperation: the reality and implications', *The Journal of Energy and Development*, 22 (2), 1998, 275–84; P. Andrews-Speed, 'Natural gas in East Siberia and the Russian Far East: a view from the Chinese corner', *Cambridge Review of International Affairs*, 12 (1), 1998, 77–95.

19 G. Rozman, 'Sino-Russian relations in the 1990s: a balance sheet', *Post-Soviet Affairs*, 14(2), 1998, 93–111; and D. Kerr, 'Problems in Sino-Russian economic relations', *Europe-Asia Studies*, 50 (7), 1998, 1133–56.

20 L. Eder, P. Andrews-Speed and A. Korzhubaev, 'Russia's evolving energy policy for its eastern regions, and implications for oil and gas cooperation between Russia and China', *Journal of World Energy Law and Policy*, 2 (3), 2009, 219–41.

21 Eder *et al*, 'Russia's evolving energy policy'; P. Andrews-Speed, X. Liao and R. Dannreuther, *Strategic Implications of China's Energy Needs* Adelphi Paper no. 346, Oxford: Oxford University Press, 2002, p. 64.

22 Cabestan *et al*, *La Chine et La Russie*, p. 88; Andrews-Speed, 'Natural gas in East Siberia'.

23 C. Locatelli, 'The Russian oil industry between public and private governance: obstacles to international oil companies' investment strategies', *Energy Policy*, 34, 2006, 1975–85; and V. Milov, L.L. Coburn and I. Damchenko, 'Russia's energy policy, 1992–2005', *Eurasian Geography and Economics*, 47 (3), 2006, 285–313.

24 'Gazprom and Rosneft have displaced private and large western oil companies in the East of Russia', *Nezavisimaya gazeta*, 11 September 2007; and Eder *et al*, 'Russia's evolving energy policy'.

25 The reason for the shift to the north of lake Baikal was to avoid purported negative environmental impact on the region. See L. Buzynski, 'Oil and territory in Putin's relations with China and Japan', *The Pacific Review*, 19 (3), 2006, 287–303; Lo, *Axis of Convenience*, pp 143–6.

26 Eder *et al*, 'Russia's evolving energy policy'.

27 K. Golubkova, 'Russian court starts TNK-BP's Kovytka bankruptcy', Reuters News Update, 21 June 2010.

28 Y. Bin, 'The Russian-Chinese oil politik', *Comparative Connections*, 5 (3), 2003, p. 139; and Lo, *Axis of Convenience*, p. 144.

29 See, for example, L. Wang, 'Russia's eastern energy diplomacy and Sino-Russian energy cooperation', *Xiandai Guoji Guanxi*, 8, 2006, pp. 8–20. See also G. Christofferson, 'The dilemmas of China's energy governance: recentralization and regional cooperation, *The China and Eurasia Forum Quarterly*, 3 (3), 2005, 56–60.

30 Moscow was, in this regard, concerned about the precedent set by the Blue Stream gas pipeline to Turkey, which had given Turkey certain monopoly powers to dictate terms. See L. Goldstein and V. Kozyrev, 'China, Japan and the scramble for Siberia', *Survival*, 48 (1), 2006, p. 171.

31 D. Baturin, 'Slavneft will not be given to the Chinese communists', *Kommersant*, 16 December 2002.

32 'Chinese leaders throw their weight behind East-West gas pipeline', *Gas Matters*, October 2004, pp. 3–4.

33 Andrews-Speed *et al*, *The Strategic Implications of China's Energy Needs*, pp. 53–7.

34 Eder *et al*, 'Russia's evolving energy policy'.

35 P. Andrews-Speed, 'China's overseas oil investments, host country perspectives', *CEMPLP Gateway*, 12 October 2009. Available at: www.dundee.ac.uk/cepmlp/gateway/index.php?news=30264 (accessed 10 May 2010).

36 Eder *et al*, 'Russia's evolving energy policy'.

37 A. Rasizade, 'Entering the old "Great Game" in Central Asia', *Orbis*, 47(1), 2003; L. Kleveman, *The New Great Game: Blood and Oil in Central Asia*, New York: Grove Press, 2004; and S. Atal, 'The new Great Game', *The National Interest*, Fall 2005.

38 For an excellent review of Russia's complex energy diplomacy towards Europe, see D. Helm, 'The Russian dimension and Europe's external energy policy', 3 September 2007. Available at: www.dieterhelm.co.uk/publications/Russian_dimension.pdf> (accessed 12 May 2010).

39 For details of China's investments into Kazakhstan, see J.X. Liao, 'A silk road for oil: Sino-Kazakh energy diplomacy', *Brown Journal of World Affairs*, 12 (2), 2006, 39–51.; Cabestan *et al*, *La Chine et La Russie*, pp. 127–33; and Z. Saurbek, 'Kazakh-Chinese energy relations: economic pragmatism or political cooperation?', *China and Eurasia Forum Quarterly*, 56 (1), 2008, 79–93.

40 For a more extended discussion of this, see E. Wilson, 'Astana's love-in with Beijing', *Far East Economic Review*, June 2007, 42–5.

41 International Energy Agency, *Perspectives on Caspian Oil and Gas Development*, Paris: IEA/OECD, 2009, pp. 21–3. See also M. Lanteigne, 'China's energy security and Eurasian diplomacy: the case of Turkmenistan', *Politics*, 27 (3), 2007, 147–55.

42 P. Andrews-Speed *et al*, *The Strategic Implications of China's Energy Needs*, p. 58.

43 'Gazprom squeezed by central Asian contracts', *Eurasianet.org*, 24 March 2009. Available at: www.eurasianet.org/departments/insightb/articles/eav032409d.shtml (accessed 6 May 2010).

44 See, for example, *Rossiya-Kitai: Perspektivy rasvitiya vzaimootnosheniii v kontekste mirovogo krizisa*, Moscow: Centre of Political Information, 2008, p. 17. See also S.J. Blank, 'The Eurasian energy triangle: China, Russia and the Central Asian states', *Brown Journal of World Affairs*, 12 (2), 2006, 59–60.

45 Lo, *Axis of Convenience*, pp. 112–13.

46 S. Yenikeyeff, *Kazakhstan's Gas: Export Markets and Export Routes*, Oxford: Oxford Institute for Energy Studies, 2008, p. 16.

47 K. Sheives, 'China turns West: Beijing's contemporary strategy towards Central Asia', *Pacific Affairs*, 79 (2), 2006, p. 212.

48 For a good overview of the SCO, see C-P. Chung, 'China and the institutionalization of the Shanghai Cooperation Organization', *Problems of Post-Communism*, 53 (5), 2006, 3–14.

49 Menon, 'The limits of Chinese-Russian partnership', pp. 118–19; Lo, *Axis of Convenience*, p. 109.

50 H. Wang, 'SCO energy club: defining China's position', *International Petroleum Economics*, 15 (6), 2007, 1–5.

51 Trade with Turkey is at about $40bn as against $3bn with Iran. For further analysis of Russia's diplomatic engagement in the Middle East, see R. Dannreuther, 'Russia and the Middle East: towards a new Cold War?', *Europe-Asia Studies* (forthcoming 2010).

52 For an extensive analysis, see R.W. Garver, *China and Iran: Ancient Partners in a Post-Imperial World*, Seattle: University of Washington Press, 2006.
53 'Iran's major oil customers and energy partners', *Alexander's Gas and Oil Connections*, 14, 7 August 2009.
54 F. Leverett and H. Leverett, 'Iran strategy', *New York Times*, 29 September 2009.
55 J. Garver, F. Leverett and H.M. Leverett, *Moving (Slightly) Closer to Iran: China's Shifting Calculus for Managing its 'Persian Gulf Dilemma'*, Washington DC: Reischauer Center for East Asian Studies, 2009, p. 46.
56 P. Andrews-Speed, 'China's energy role in the Middle East and prospects for the future' in *The New Energy Silk Road: The Growing Asia-Middle East Energy Nexus*, Seattle: National Bureau of Asian Research, 2009, pp. 13–18.

9 Hegemony, oil and Asian regional politics

1 A classic expression of this is hegemonic stability theory, which sees the causes for the prosperity and peace of the late nineteenth century and the post-World War II period as due to the stabilising influence of British and then US hegemony. It was when such hegemony is lost, and great power competition arises, that conflict and war arises. For the classic statement, see C.P. Kindleberger, *The World in Depression, 1929–39*, Berkeley: University of California Press, 1973. For important restatements within IR, see R. Gilpin, *The Political Economy of International Relations*, Princeton: Princeton University Press, 1987 and W.C. Wohlforth, 'The stability of a unipolar world', *International Security*, 24 (1), 1991, 5–41.
2 See R. Foot, 'Chinese strategies in a US-hegemonic global order: accommodating and hedging', *International Affairs*, 82 (1), 2006, 79–83.
3 Although there is at times recognition that the 'public goods' provided by US hegemony are beneficial to China, this does not undermine the general view of the negative impact of US hegemony. See R. Chen, 'China perceives America: perspectives of international relations experts', *Journal of Contemporary China*, 12, 2003, 285–97; and S. Blum, 'Chinese views of US hegemony', *Journal of Contemporary China* 12, 2003, 239–64.
4 P. Andrews-Speed, 'China's energy role in the Middle East and prospects for the future', *The New Energy Silk Road: The Growing Asia-Middle East Energy Nexus*, Seattle: National Bureau of Asian Research, 2009, pp. 13–18.
5 J.V. Mitchell and P. Stevens, *Ending Dependence: Hard Choices for Oil Exporting States*, London: Chatham House, 2008.
6 For this period of Chinese engagement, see Y. Shichor, *The Middle East in China's Foreign Policy, 1949–1977*, Cambridge: Cambridge University Press, 1979; and L.C. Harrison, *China Considers the Middle East*, London: I. B. Tauris, 1993.
7 For a good review, see Y. Shichor, 'Competence and incompetence: the political economy of China's relations with the Middle East', *Asian Perspective*, 30(4), 2006, pp. 45–50.
8 See Y. Shichor, 'Mountains out of molehills: arms transfers in Sino-Middle Eastern relations', *Middle East Review of International Affairs*, 4 (3), 2000, 68–79.
9 J. Calabrese, 'China and the Persian Gulf: energy and security', *Middle East Journal*, 52 (1), 1998, p. 364. For more general survey, see G.M. Steinberg, 'Chinese policies on arms control and proliferation in the Middle East', *China Report*, 34, 1998, 381–400.
10 Y. Shichor, 'Decision-making in triplicate: China and the three Iraqi wars' in A. Scobell and L. Wortzel (eds), *Chinese Decisionmaking under Stress*, Carlisle: Strategic Studies Institute, US Army War College, 2005, pp. 185–222.
11 J.K. Douglas, M.B. Nelson and K. Schwartz, 'Fuelling the dragon's flame: how China's energy demands affect its relationships in the Middle East', *US-China Economic and Security Review Commission*, 14 September 2006, pp. 15–18.

12 C. Zambelis and B. Gentry, 'China through Arab eyes: American influence in the Middle East', *Parameters*, 38(1), 2008, 60–72.

13 For an analysis of this, see F. Leverett and J. Bader, 'Managing China-US energy competition in the Middle East', *The Washington Quarterly*, 29 (1), 2005–06, p. 191.

14 D. Dombey and H. Morris, 'Clinton turns the tables on Tehran over sanctions', *Financial Times*, 19 May 2010. For broader discussion on Iran's stance towards Iranian nuclear proliferation, see International Crisis Group, *The Iran Nuclear Issue: the View from Beijing*, 17 February 2010. Available at: www.crisisgroup.org/en/publication-type/media-releases/2010/asia/the-iran-nuclear-issue-the-view-from-beijing.aspx (accessed 17 May 2010).

15 S.P. Matthews, 'China's new energy focus: strategic partnership with Saudi Arabia', 2008, p. 5. Available at: www.bakerbotts.com/files/Publication/8dd9a398-bd08-4c27-9309-44436ff39c81/Presentation/PublicationAttachment/86d1ad0a-fe3c-46c4-a2e6-4499134a953b/ChinasNewEnergy.pdf (accessed 17 May 2010).

16 J-F. Seznec, 'Saudi Arabia's relations with China and Asia and prospects for the future', *NBR Research Conference Report*, Washington: National Bureau of Asian Research, October 2009, pp. 41–52.

17 Leverett and Bader, 'Managing China-US Energy Competition', p. 18.

18 Andrews-Speed, 'China's energy role', p. 26.

19 'China now largest investor in Iraq oil and gas', *Middle East Economic Digest*, 17 March 2010.

20 K. Wu *et al*, 'Oil in Asia and the Pacific: production, consumption, imports and policy options', *Asia Pacific Issues*, 85, August 2008, p. 2.

21 'China's overseas oil and gas investments: An update', *Facts Global Energy*, 39, September 2007, p. 11.

22 M. Lanteigne, 'China's maritime security and the "Malacca Dilemma"', *Asian Studies*, 4 (2), 2008, p. 144. There are some disputes whether Hu actually used this term but it certainly has acquired a prominence due to its purported use by him.

23 X. Zhang, 'Southeast Asia and energy: gateway to stability', *China Security*, 3 (2), 2007, p. 19; J.H. Ho, 'The Security of sea lanes in Southeast Asia', *Asian Survey*, 46 (4), 2006, pp. 559–60.

24 For an overview of Chinese analysts' fears of this, see G. Collins, A. Erickson and L. Goldstein, 'Chinese naval analysts consider the energy question', in *Maritime Implications of China's Energy Strategy: Interim Report*, Newport RI: Chinese Maritime Studies Institute, 2006.

25 For a good analysis of this, see J. Lee, 'China's ASEAN invasion', *The National Interest*, May/June 2007, p. 41.

26 M. Klare, *Resource Wars: the New Landscape of Global Conflict*, New York: Henry Holt, 2001, pp. 109–27.

27 R.D. Kaplan, 'Center stage for the 21st century: rivalry in the Indian Ocean', *Foreign Affairs*, 88 (2), 2009, 16–32. The Fulda Pass was the main potential invasion route of the Soviet army into western Europe.

28 Lei Wu and Shen Qinyu, 'Will China go to war over oil?', *Far Eastern Economic Review*, 169 (3), 2006, 38–40.

29 For an extensive analysis of this, see G.B. Collins and W.S. Murray, 'No oil for the lamps of China?', *Naval War College Review*, 61 (2), 2008, 79–95.

30 See J. Kurzantlick, *Charm Offensive: How China's Soft Power is Transforming the World*, New Haven: Yale University Press, 2007.

31 A.I. Johnston, 'China's militarized interstate dispute behavior, 1949–1992: A first cut at the data', *China Quarterly*, 153, 1998, p. 2.

32 For an assessment of the major current sources of conflict and cooperation, see Francois Godement, 'China and India: rivals always, partners sometimes',

China Analysis, November 2009, pp. 1–2. Available at: www.ecfr.eu/content/entry/ecfr_and_asia_centre_publish_latest_issue_of_china_analysis/ (accessed on 25 May 2010).

33 B.K. Singh, 'Energy security and India-China cooperation', *International Association for Energy Newsletter*, 2010. Available st: www.iaee.org/en/publications/newsletterdl.aspx?id=92 (accessed 26 May 2010).

34 S. Tonnesson and A. Kolas, *Energy security in Asia: China, India, oil and peace*, Oslo: International Peace Research Institute, 2006.

35 For an analysis of this sense of losing out to China, see M. Lall, 'India-Myanmar relations – Geopolitics and energy in the light of the balance of power', *ISAS Working Paper*, 29, 2 January 2008, pp. 27–8.

36 Tonnesson and Kolas, *Energy Security in Asia*, p. 83.

37 For the inherent problems of gas transit pipelines, see P. Stevens, *Transit Troubles: Pipelines as a Source of Conflict*, London: Royal institute of International Affairs, 2009.

38 Zhang, 'Southeast Asia and Energy', p. 23.

39 S. Fazl-e-Haider, 'Pakistan, Iran sign gas pipeline deal', *Asia Times*, 27 May 2009. See also H. Lai, 'Security of China's energy imports' in H. Lai (ed.), *Asian Energy Security: The Maritime Dimension*, Basingstoke: Palgrave Macmillan, 2009, pp. 60–63.

40 'China's navy: drive for modernization', *Strategic Comments* 14 (1), 2008, pp. 1–2. For the geopolitical ambitions of many of the younger Chinese naval officers, see T. Yoshihara and J. Holmes, 'Command of the sea with Chinese characteristics', *Orbis*, 49 (4), 2005, 677–94.

41 R.A Bitzinger, 'Aircraft carriers: China's emerging maritime ambition', *RSIS Commentaries*, 7 April 2009.

42 B. Simpfendorfer, 'China's historic return to the Gulf, *Foreign Policy*, 2 April 2010; and 'Chinese navy's new strategy in action', *IISS Strategic Comments*, 16(6), 2010.

43 C.J. Pehrson, *String of Pearls: Meeting the Challenge of China's Rising Power Across the Littoral*, Carlisle, PA; Strategic Studies Institute, 2006. The phrase 'String of pearls' was first coined by the US defence contractor, Booz-Allen-Hamilton.

44 A. Selth, 'Burma's Coco Islands: rumours and realities in the Indian Ocean', *SEARC Working Papers*, 101, November 2008.

45 For more extensive analyses of these disputes, see C. Schofield, 'Dangerous ground: a geopolitical overview of the South China Sea' in S. Bateman and R. Emmers (ed.), *Security and International Politics in the South China Sea: Towards a Cooperative Management Regime*, London: Routledge, 2009; R. Drifte, 'Japanese-Chinese territorial disputes in the East China Sea – between military confrontation and economic cooperation', Working paper, Asia Research Centre, London School of Economics and Political Science, 2008. Available at: www.eprints.lse.ac.uk/20881/ (accessed 10 May 2010).

46 Z. Keyuan, 'Joint development in the South China Sea: a new approach', *International Journal of Marine and Coastal Law*, 21(1), 2006, 83–109. While Chinese estimates are in the order of 105–213 billion barrels of oil, the more sober US Energy Information Administration estimate is of 7 billion barrels.

47 J.X. Liao, 'Sino-Japanese energy security and regional stability: the case of the East China Sea gas exploration', *East Asia*, 25 (1), 2008, p. 59.

48 'China and Japan reach principled consensus on the East China Sea issue', Embassy, Chinese Foreign Ministry, 18 June 2008. Available at: www.spedr.com/247ux (accessed 20 May 2010).

49 'Chinese Foreign Minister Yang Jiechi meets the press on East China Sea issue', 24 June 2008. Available at: www.spedr.com/2iku3 (accessed 20 May 2010).

50 E.S. Medeiros, *China's International Behaviour: Activism, Opportunism and Diversification*, Santa Monica: RAND Corporation, 2009, pp. 130–31.
51 Lee, 'China's ASEAN invasion', p. 46.
52 E. Goh, 'Great powers and hierarchical order in Southeast Asia: analyzing regional security strategies', *International Security*, 32 (3), 2007/8, 113–57.
53 R. Emmers, 'Changing power distribution in the South China Sea: implications for conflict management and avoidance', Working paper 183, S. Rajaratnam School of International Studies, September 2009.
54 The 2009 incident over the US surveillance ship *Impeccable* in the South China Sea provides a recent example of this. See M. Valencia, 'The *"Impeccable* incident"*: truth and consequences', *China Security* 5 (2), 2009, 22–8; and Ji Guoxing, 'The legality of the *"Impeccable* incident"', *China Security*, 5 (2), 2009, 16–21.

10 The neo-imperialist temptation: Africa and Latin America

1 On the aid provided to Africa during this period, see D. Brautigam, *Chinese Aid and African Development: Exporting Green Revolution*, London: Macmillan, 1998. For more general accounts of this period, see J. Cooley, *East Wind over Africa: Red China's African Offensive*, New York: Walker, 1965; and C. Johnson, *Communist China and Latin America, 1959–1967*, New York: Columbia University Press, 1970.
2 S. Van Evera, 'Why Europe matters and the third world does not: American grand strategy after the cold war', *Journal of Strategic Studies*, 13 (2), 1990, 1–51.
3 G.S. Paz, 'Rising China's offensive in Latin America and the US reaction', *Asian Perspective*, 30 (4), 2006, p. 96.
4 See, for example, D. Mahtani, 'The new scramble for Africa's resources', *Financial Times Special Report*, 28 January 2008; 'A new scramble', *The Economist*, 27 November 2004; M. Klare and D. Volman, 'The African "gold rush" and American national security', *Third World Quarterly*, 27 (4), 2006, 609–28.
5 For a good analysis of this deal and the controversy it created, see P. Lee, 'China has a copper headache', *Asia Times*, 11 March 2010. Available at: www.atimes.com/atimes/China_Business/LC11Cb03.html (accessed 7 July 2010).
6 A. Russell, '"Dream come true" for Standard', *Financial Times*, 26 October 2007.
7 V. Foster *et al*, 'Building bridges: China's growing role as infrastructure financier for Sub-Saharan Africa', *World Bank Report*, July 2008, p. ix.
8 Dependency theory was, in particular, developed in Latin America. For classic statements, see A. Emmanuel, *Unequal Exchange: A Study of the Imperialism of Trade*, New York: Monthly Review Press, 1972; T. Dos Santos, 'The structure of dependence', *American Economic Review*, 60 (1), 1970, 231–6; and A.G. Frank, *Dependent Accumulation and underdevelopment*, London: Macmillan, 1978.
9 *Business Day*, 6 January 2007, quoted in I. Taylor, *China's New Role in Africa*, Boulder: Lynne Rienner, 2009, p. 2.
10 The classic statement is J. Gallagher and R. Robinson, 'The Imperialism of free trade', *The Economic History Review*, 6 (1), 1953, 1–15. See also J. Gallagher and R. Robinson, *Africa and the Victorians: The Official Mind of Imperialism*, Basingstoke: Macmillan, 1961.
11 For an in-depth and up-to-date analysis of the aid and development support provided by China to Africa, see D. Brautigam, *The Dragon's Gift: The Real Story of China in Africa*, Oxford: Oxford University Press, 2009.
12 *People's Daily*, 26 April 2006.

13 'Kagame attacks West's "exploiters"', *Financial Times*, 12 February 2010.
14 D. Moya, *Dead Aid: Why Aid Is Not Working And How There Is A Better Way For Africa*, London: Allen Lane, 2009.
15 For an analysis of this, see J. Casteneda, 'Latin America's left turn', *Foreign Affairs*, 85 (3), 2006, 28–43.
16 For examples of this, see on Latin America, J. T. Dreyer, 'From China with love: P.R.C. overtures with Latin America', *Brown Journal of World Affairs*, 12 (2), 2006, 85–98; for Africa, see Klare and Volman, 'The African "gold rush" and D. Morris, 'The chance to go deep: U.S. energy interests in West Africa', *American Foreign Policy Interests*, 28 (3), 225–38.
17 See M. Naim, 'Rogue aid', *Foreign Policy*, 159, 2007, 94–5; and A. Halff, 'Africa on my mind: the panda menace', *The National Interest*, July–August 2007, 35–41. For a good overview of the issues of governance and human rights, see I. Taylor, 'Governance in Africa and Sino-African relations: contradictions or confluence?', *Politics*, 27 (3), 139–46.
18 E. Reeves, *China, Darfur and the Olympics: Tarnishing the Torch?*, New York: Dream for Darfur, 2007.
19 S. Raine, *China's African Challenges*, London: Routledge, 2009, pp. 138–141.
20 'China 2008', *OECD Investment Policy Reviews*, 2008. Available at: www.oecd.org.dataoecd/25/11/41792683.pdf (accessed 12 May 2009). In Latin America, it is a similar story with China's estimated US $25–30 billion dwarfed by the EU investments of $620 billion and the United States of US $350 billion.
21 For a good analysis of this, see E.S. Downs, 'The fact and fiction of Sino-African energy relations', *China Security*, 3 (3), 2007, 43–7. Downs estimates that Chinese NOCs have just 8 per cent of the combined commercial value of IOCs investments in African oil and 3 per cent of all companies invested in African oil.
22 D. Large, 'China and the contradictions of "non-interference" in Sudan', *Review of African Political Economy*, 105, 2008, p. 95.
23 An example of this is Sinopec's entry into Gabon's upstream development after Total had declined the offer; see M. Meidan, 'China's Africa policy: business now, politics later', *Asian Perspective*, 30 (4), 2006, 79–81.
24 Taylor, *China's New Role in Africa*, p. 50.
25 In Sudan, it is not only Russia but also the US and the UK who have historically been more significant arms exporters. See J. Hellstrom, 'China's emerging role in Africa: a strategic overview', *FOI Studies in African Security*, May 2009, p. 15.
26 In 2009, it is estimated Chinese NOCs spent a record $32 billion as against India ONGC's single investment of $2.1 billion. See R. Katakey and J. Duce, 'India loses to China in Africa-to-Kazakhstan-to-Venezuela oil', *Bloomberg*, 29 June 2009. Available at: www.bloomberg.com/news/2010-06-30/india-losing-to-china-in-africa-to-kazakhstan-to-venezuela-oil-purchases.html (accessed 7 July 2010).
27 For the policymaking structure for China in Africa, see B. Gill and J. Reilly, 'The tenuous hold of China Inc. in Africa', *The Washington Quarterly*, 30 (3), 2007, 37–53.
28 C. Alden, *China in Africa*, London: Zed Books, 2007, p. 58.
29 R. McGregor, 'China's diplomacy "hijacked" by big companies', *Financial Times*, 16 March 2008; see also International Crisis Group, 'China's thirst for oil', *Asia Report*, 153, 9 June 2008, p. 3.
30 Raine, *China's African Challenges*, pp. 164–6; B. Gill and C-H. Huang, 'China's expanding role in peacekeeping', 2 February 2009. Available at: www.csis.org/media.csis/pubs/pac0907.pdf (accessed 3 January 2010).
31 J.G. Frynas, 'Corporate social responsibility in the oil and gas sector, *Journal of World Energy Law and Business*, 2 (3), 2009, 178–95.
32 B. Alier, *Southern Sudan: Too Many Agreements Dishonoured*, Reading: Ithaca Press, 1990, p. 263.

33 'Fact sheet nine: the main international oil companies present in Sudan'. Available at: www.understandingsudan.org (accessed 10 August 2010).

34 Large, 'China and the contradictions of 'non-interference' in Sudan', p. 96.

35 The historical links include the symbolic connection of 'Chinese' Gordon, who was involved in fighting Taipeng rebels in China before becoming Governor General of Sudan and then being killed in Khartoum in 1885.

36 Raine, *China's African Challenges*, p. 184.

37 Chinese analysts have expressed dismay that this continuing support for Total shows a lack of respect to what China has done for the country. See Downs, *Fact and Fiction of Sino-African Energy Relations*, p. 62.

38 This was seen in the two resolutions passed in 2004 and 2005 – UNSCR 1556 and 1591 respectively – where China negotiated to weaken the resolutions before then abstaining on them.

39 Small Arms Survey, 'Arms, oil and Darfur: the evolution of relations between China and Sudan', *Sudan Issue Brief*, 7, 2007, 1–11.

40 Brautigam, *The Dragon's Gift*, p. 281.

41 'China told Sudan to adopt UN's Darfur plan – Envoy', *Sudan Tribune*, 7 February 2007.

42 L. Polgreen, 'China, in new role, uses ties to press Sudan on troubled Darfur', *International Herald Tribune*, 23 February 2008.

43 C-H. Huang, 'China's evolving perspective on Darfur: significance and policy implications', *Pacnet NewsLetter*, 25 July 2007.

44 A former US ambassador described the government in Equatorial Guinea as 'an ongoing family criminal organisation', as quoted in R. Soares De Oliviera, *Oil and Politics in the Gulf of Guinea*, London: Hurst, 2007, p. 224.

45 L. Palacios, 'Latin America as energy supplier' in R. Roett and G. Paz (eds), *China's Expansion into the Western Hemisphere: Implications for Latin America and the United States*, Washington DC: Brookings Institution Press, 2008, p. 105.

46 Y. Liu, 'Venezuela's oil nationalization tests China's oil companies', *Xinhua News Agency*, 11 June 2007.

47 For the report, see US Government Accountability Office, *Issues Related to Potential Reductions in Venezuelan Oil Production*, Report to the Chairman, Committee on Foreign Relations, US Senate (GAO-06-668), June 2006.

48 W. Ratliff, 'Beijing's pragmatism meets Hugo Chavez,' *Brown Journal of World Affairs*, 12 (2), 2006, p. 77.

49 W. Ratliff, 'In search of a balanced relationship: China, Latin America, and the United States', *Asian Politics and Policy*, 1 (1), 2009, p. 17.

50 This agreement followed two years of negotiations that began with the state-to-state agreement in May 2008. This earlier agreement included the joint construction of a refinery in China that was not included in the 2010 agreement.

51 A. Trombly, 'China eyes Venezuelan and Brazilian oil', *Council on Hemispheric Affairs*, 10 March 2010. Available at: www.coha.org/china-eyes-venezuelan-and-brazilian-oil (accessed 5 May 2010).

52 A. Gabuyev and A. Gritskova, 'Russia is changing its priorities in relations with Venezuela', *Kommersant*, 22 July 2008.

53 Ambassdor Ju Yijie in an interview in late 2005, as quoted in Ratliff, 'Beijing's Pragmatism', p. 79.

54 'Venezuela increases oil exports to China by 21 percent', *Reuters*, 13 April 2010.

55 A. Vines, L. Wong, M. Weimer and I. Campus, *Thirst for African Oil: Asian National Oil Companies in Nigeria and Angola*, London: Royal Institute for International Affairs, 2009, pp. 46–8.

56 'Angola was China's largest crude supplier in March', *Financial Times*, 29 April 2010.

57 For an extensive analysis of this, see Vines *et al*, *Thirst for Oil*, part 2.

58 Downs, *The Fact and Fiction of Energy Relations*, p. 57.
59 For a good analysis, see Brautigam, *The Dragon's Gift*, pp. 273–7.
60 B. Faucon and S. Su, 'The hostility towards workers cools Angola-China relationship', *Wall Street Journal*, 10 August 2010.
61 C.I. Obi, 'Enter the dragon? Chinese oil companies and resistance in the Niger Delta', *Review of African Political Economy*, 117, 2008, 417–34.
62 Vines *et al*, *Thirst for African Oil*, p. 22.
63 T. Burgis, 'Nigeria feels pull from east and west', *Financial Times*, 29 September 2009.
64 T. Olusegun, 'New refinery planned for Lagos Free Trade Zone', *IPS News*, 18 July 2010. Available at: www.ipsnews.net/news.asp?idnews=52190 (accessed on 10 August 2010); and T. Burgus, 'China in $23bn Nigeria oil deal', *Financial Times*, 15 May 2010.

Bibliography

Ai, F., 'An analysis of the oil problem and related policies', *Strategy and Management*, 6, 1995, 103–11 (in Chinese).

Alden, C., *China in Africa*, London: Zed Books, 2007.

Alier, B., *Southern Sudan: Too Many Agreements Dishonoured*, Reading: Ithaca Press, 1990.

An, B., 'Situations of the oil market in the Middle East and the concept of China's use of Middle East energy resources', *West Asia and Africa*, 4, 1996, 63–5 (in Chinese).

Andrews-Speed, P., 'Natural gas in East Siberia and the Russian Far East: A view from the Chinese corner', *Cambridge Review of International Affairs*, 12(1), 1998, 77–95.

Andrews-Speed, P., *Energy Policy and Regulation in the People's Republic of China*, London: Kluwer Law, 2004.

Andrews-Speed, P., 'Marginalisation in the energy sector: the case of township and village coal mines', in H.X. Zhang, B. Wu and R. Saunders (eds), *Marginalisation In China*, Aldershot: Ashgate, 2007, pp. 55–80.

Andrews-Speed, P., 'China's energy role in the Middle East and prospects for the future', in *The New Energy Silk Road. The Growing Asia-Middle East Nexus*, Seattle: National Bureau of Asian Research, 2009, pp. 13–28.

Andrews-Speed, P., 'China's ongoing energy efficiency drive: origins, progress and prospects', *Energy Policy*, 37, 2009, 1331–44.

Andrews-Speed, P., 'Power sector reform in China', in *China: Defining the Boundary between the Market and the State*, Paris: OECD, 2009, pp. 229–66.

Andrews-Speed, P., *The Institutions of Energy Governance in China*, Notes de l'IFRI, Paris: Institut francais des relations internationales, 2010. Available at: www.ifri.org/index.php?page=detail-contribution&id=5842&id_provenance=97

Andrews-Speed, P., 'Asia's energy demand and implications for the oil-producing countries of the Middle East', in *Energy Security in the Gulf: Challenges and Prospects*, Abu Dhabi: Emirates Center for Strategic Studies and Research, in press.

Andrews-Speed, P. and Z. Cao, 'Prospects for privatisation in China's energy sector', in S. Green and G.S. Liu (eds) *Exit the Dragon? Privatization and State Ownership in China*, London: Royal Institute for International Affairs, 2005, pp. 196–213.

Andrews-Speed, P. and X. Ma, 'Energy production and social marginalisation in China', *Journal of Contemporary China*, 17, 2008, 247–72.

Andrews-Speed, P., X. Liao and R. Dannreuther, *The Strategic Implications of China's Energy Needs*, London: International Institute for Strategic Studies, Adelphi Paper no. 346, 2002.

Aron, R., *Peace and War: A Theory of International Relations*, London: Weidenfeld and Nicolson, 1966.

Ascher, W., *Bringing in the Future. Strategies for Farsightedness and Sustainability in Developing Countries*, Chicago, IL: University of Chicago Press, 2009.

Asian Development Bank, *Governance and Sound Development Management*, Manila: Asian Development Bank, 1995.

Atal, S., 'The new Great Game', *The National Interest*, Fall 2005.

Barnett, A.D., *China's Economy in Global Perspective*, Washington DC: The Brookings Institution, 1981.

Barton, B., C. Redgwell, A. Ronne and D.N. Zillman (eds), *Energy Security. Managing Risk in a Dynamic Legal and Regulatory Environment*, Oxford: Oxford University Press, 2004.

Baum, R., 'Political implications of China's information revolution: the media, the minders and their message', in C. Li (ed.) *China's Changing Political Landscape. Prospects for Democracy*, Washington DC: Brookings University Press, 2008, pp.161–84.

Baum, R. and A. Shevchenko, 'The state of the state', in M. Goldman and R. MacFarquhar (eds) *The Paradox of China's Post-Mao Reforms*, Cambridge, Mass.: Harvard University Press, 1999, pp. 333–60.

Beland, D., 'Ideas and social policy: an institutionalist perspective', *Social Policy and Administration*, 39, 2005, 1–18.

Benvenisti, E., 'Asian traditions and contemporary international law on the management of natural resources', *Chinese Journal of International Law*, 7, 2008, 273–83.

Berrah, N., F. Feng, R. Priddle and L. Wang, *Sustainable Energy in China. The Closing Window of Opportunity*, Washington DC: World Bank, 2007.

Berrah, N., R. Lamech and J. Zhao, *Fostering Competition in China's Power Markets*, World Bank Discussion Paper no. 416, Washington DC: World Bank, 2001.

Bin Y., 'The Russian-Chinese oil politik', *Comparative Connections*, 5(3), 2003, 137–46.

Bitzinger, R.A., 'Aircraft carriers: China's emerging maritime ambition', *RSIS Commentaries*, 7 April 2009.

Blank, S.J., 'The Eurasian energy triangle: China, Russia and the Central Asian states', *Brown Journal of World Affairs*, 12 (2), 2006, 53–68.

Blum, S., 'Chinese views of US hegemony', *Journal of Contemporary China*, 12, 2003, 239–64.

Blum, S.D., *Lies that Bind. Chinese Truth, Other Truths*, Lanham, MD: Rowman & Littlefield, 2007.

Bosworth, B. and S. Collins, *Accounting for Growth: Comparing China and India*, Cambridge, Mass.: National Bureau of Economic Research, Working Paper 12943, 2007.

Brammall, C., *Chinese Economic Development*, London: Routledge, 2009.

Brautigam, D., *Chinese Aid and African Development: Exporting Green Revolution*, London: Macmillan, 1998.

Brautigam, D., *The Dragon's Gift: The Real Story of China in Africa*, Oxford: Oxford University Press, 2009.

Brook, T. and B.M. Frolic, *Civil Society in China*, Armonk, NY: M.E. Sharpe, 1997.

Brooks S.G. and W.C. Wohlforth, 'Hard times for soft balancing', *International Security*, 30(1), 2005, 72–108.

Buckley, P.J., L.J. Clegg, A.R. Cross, X. Liu, H. Voss and P. Zheng, 'The determinants of Chinese outward foreign direct investment', *Journal of International Business Studies*, 38, 2007, 499–518.

Burns, J.P., 'Governance and civil service reform', in Howell, J. (ed.) *Governance in China*, Lanham: Rowman & Littlefield, 2004, pp. 37–57.

Buzynski, L., 'Oil and territory in Putin's relations with China and Japan', *The Pacific Review*, 19(3), 2006, 287–303.

Cabestan, J-P., S. Colin, I. Facon and M. Meidan, *La Chine et la Russie: Entre Convergence et Méfiance*, Paris: UNICOMM, 2008.

Calabrese, J., 'China and the Persian Gulf: energy and security', *Middle East Journal*, 52(1), 1998, 351–66.

Campos I. and A. Vines, *Angola and China. A Pragmatic Partnership*, Chatham House Working Paper, London: Chatham House, 2008.

Casteneda, J., 'Latin America's left turn', *Foreign Affairs*, 85(3), 2006, 28–43.

Chan-Fiscel, M. and R. Lawson, 'Bankrolling the "Going Out" strategy: China's financing of African aid and trade and implications for African debt and development', in M. Kitissou (ed.) *Africa in China's global strategy*, London: Adonis and Abbey, 2007, pp. 1–31.

Chan, G., 'China's compliance in global environmental affairs', *Asia Pacific Viewpoint*, 45, 2004, 69–86.

Chandler, W. and H. Gwin, *Financing Energy Efficiency in China*, Washington DC: Carnegie Endowment for International Peace, 2008.

Chen, H., 'China's oil security strategy should be based on "Going Out"', *Review of Economic Research*, 25, 2001, 2–5 (in Chinese).

Chen, J., *Chinese Law. Towards an Understanding of Chinese Law, Its Nature and Development*, The Hague: Kluwer Law International, 1999.

Chen, R., 'China perceives America: perspectives of international relations experts', *Journal of Contemporary China*, 12, 2003, 285–97.

Chen, Z., 'Study on estimating demand and supply in China's energy market in the 11th Five-Year Plan period', *Energy of China*, 28(5), 2006, 16–23 (in Chinese).

Cheng, J.Y.S., 'A Chinese view of China's energy security', *Journal of Contemporary China*, 17, 2008, 297–317.

Cheng, L., 'Jiang Zemin's successors: the rise of the fourth generation of leaders in the PRC', *The China Quarterly*, 161, 2000, 1–40.

Cheng, T.J. and C.M. Tsai, 'Powering rent seeking in the electricity industry', in T.K. Ngo and Y. Wu (eds) *Rent Seeking in China*, Abingdon: Routledge, 2009, 117–44.

Cherni, J.A. and J. Kentish, 'Renewable energy policy and electricity market reforms in China', *Energy Policy*, 35, 2007, 3616–29.

Chinese Academy of Social Sciences, *Energy Development Report of China 2006*, Beijing: Social Sciences Academy Press, 2006.

Chinese Academy of Social Sciences, *Energy Development Report of China 2008*, Beijing: Social Sciences Academy Press, 2008.

Chiu, B. and M.K. Lewis, *Reforming China's State-owned Enterprises and Banks*, Cheltenham: Edward Elgar, 2006.

Christensen, T.J., 'China, the US-Japan alliance and the security dilemma in East Asia', *International Security*, 23(4), 1999, 49–80.

Christoffersen, G., 'The dilemmas of China's energy governance: recentralization and regional cooperation', *The China and Eurasia Forum Quarterly*, 3(3), 2005, 55–79.

Chung, C-P, 'China and the institutionalization of the Shanghai Cooperation Organization', *Problems of Post-Communism*, 53(5), 2006, 3–14.

Chung, J.H., H. Lai and M. Xia, 'Mounting challenges to governance in China: surveying collective protestors, religious sects and criminal organisations', *The China Journal*, 56, 2006, 1–31.

Cole, B.D., *"Oil for the Lamps of China"– Beijing's 21st-Century Search for Energy*, Washington DC: McNair Paper 67, Institute for National Strategic Studies, 2003.

Cole, B.D., 'The energy factor in Chinese maritime strategy', in G.B. Collins, A.S. Erickson, L.J. Goldstein and W.S. Murray (eds) *China's Energy Strategy. The Impact on Beijing's Maritime Policies*, Annapolis, MD: Naval Institute Press, 2008, pp. 336–51.

Collins G.B. and W.S. Murray, 'No oil for the lamps of China?', *Naval War College Review*, 61(2), 2008, 79–95.

Collins, G., A. Erickson and L. Goldstein, 'Chinese naval analysts consider the energy question', *Maritime Implications of China's Energy Strategy: Interim Report*, Newport, RI: Chinese Maritime Studies Institute, 2006.

Collins, G.B., A.S. Erickson, L.J. Goldstein and W.S. Murray, *China's Energy Strategy. The Impact on Beijing's Maritime Policies*, Annapolis, MD: Naval Institute Press, 2008, pp. 336–51.

Constantin, C., 'Understanding China's energy security', *World Political Science Review*, 3(3), 2007, article no. 2. Available at: www.bepress.com/wpsr/vol3/iss3/art2.

Cooley, J., *East Wind over Africa: Red China's African Offensive*, New York: Walker, 1965.

Cooper, R., *The Breaking of Nations: Order and Chaos in the Twenty-First Century*, London: Atlantic Books, 2003.

Constantini, V. and F. Gracceva, *Oil Security: Short- and Long-Term Policies*, INDES Working Papers no. 7, Brussels: Centre for European Policy Studies, 2004.

Cox, R., 'The path-dependency of an idea: why Scandinavian welfare states remain distinct', *Social Policy and Administration*, 38, 2004, 204–19.

Dannreuther, R., *International Security. The Contemporary Agenda*, Cambridge: Polity Press, 2007.

Dannreuther, R., 'Russia and the Middle East: towards a new Cold War?', *Europe-Asia Studies* (forthcoming 2011).

Deng, Y. *China's Struggle for Status: The Realignment of International Relations*, Cambridge: Cambridge University Press, 2008.

Deutch, J., A. Lauvergeon and W. Prawiraatmadja, *Energy Security and Climate Change*, Triangle Papers, no. 61, Washington DC, Paris, Tokyo: Trilateral Commission, 2007.

Development Research Center, *Overview of the National Energy Strategy*, Beijing: State Council Development Research Center, 2004.

Dittmer, L., 'The changing nature of elite power politics', *The China Journal*, 45, 2001, 69–82.

Dittmer, L., 'Leadership change and Chinese political development', *The China Quarterly*, 176, 2003, 903–25.

Domes, J., *The Government and Politics of the PRC. A Time of Transition*, Boulder, CO: Westview Press, 1985.

Dorian, J.P., *Minerals, Energy and Economic Development in China*, Oxford: Clarendon Press, 1994.

Dos Santos, T., 'The structure of dependence', *American Economic Review*, 60(1), 1970, 231–6.

Douglas, J.K, M.B. Nelson and K. Schwartz, 'Fuelling the dragon's flame: how China's energy demands affect its relationships in the Middle East', *US-China Economic and Security Review Commission*, 14 September 2006.

Downs, E.S., *China's Quest for Energy Security*, RAND Report MR-1244-AF, Santa Monica: RAND, 2000.

Downs, E.S., 'The Chinese Energy Security Debate', *The China Quarterly*, 177, 2004, 21–41.

Downs, E.S., *The Energy Security Series: China*, The Brookings Foreign Policy Studies, Washington DC: The Brookings Institution, 2006.

Downs, E.S., 'The fact and fiction in Sino-African energy relations', *China Security*, 3(3), 2007, 42–68.

Downs, E.S., 'China's NOCs: lessons learned from adventures abroad', in *Fundamentals of the Global Oil and Gas Industry 2008*, London: Petroleum Economist, 2008, pp. 27–31.

Downs E.S. and P.C. Saunders, 'Legitimacy and the limits of nationalism: China and the Diadyu island', *International Security*, 23(3), 1998/9, 114–46.

Dreyer, J.T., 'From China with love: P.R.C. overtures with Latin America', *Brown Journal of World Affairs*, 12(2), 2006, 85–98.

Dreyer, J.T., 'Sino-American energy cooperation', *Journal of Contemporary China*, 16, 2007, 461–76.

Drifte, R., 'Japanese-Chinese territorial disputes in the East China Sea – between military confrontation and economic cooperation', Working paper, Asia Research Centre, London School of Economics and Political Science, 2008.

Ebel, R.E., *China's Energy Future. The Middle Kingdom Seeks its Place in the Sun*, Washington DC: The CSIS Press, 2005, 55–8.

Economy, E., 'Don't break the engagement', *Foreign Affairs*, 83(3), 2004, 96–109.

Economy, E., *The River Runs Black. The Environmental Challenge to China's Future*, Ithaca, N.Y.: Cornell University Press, 2004.

Eder, L., P. Andrews-Speed and A. Korzhubaev, 'Russia's evolving energy policy for its eastern regions, and implications for oil and gas cooperation between Russia and China', *Journal of World Energy Law and Policy*, 2, 2009, 219–41.

Elvin, M., 'The environmental legacy of Imperial China', in R.L. Edmonds (ed.), *Managing the Chinese Environment*, Oxford: Oxford University Press, 1998, pp. 9–32.

Emmanuel, A., *Unequal Exchange: A Study of the Imperialism of Trade*, New York: Monthly Review Press, 1972.

Emmers, R., 'Changing power distribution in the South China Sea: implications for conflict management and avoidance', Working Paper 183, S. Rajaratnam School of International Studies, September 2009.

Engel, C., 'Learning the law', *Journal of Institutional Economics*, 4, 2008, 275–97.

Evans, P.C. and E.S. Downs, *Untangling China's Quest for Oil through State-backed Financial Deals*, The Brookings Institution, Policy Brief 154, Washington DC: The Brookings Institution, 2006

FACTS Global Energy, *An Update of China's Overseas Oil and Gas Investment*, China Energy Series, Oil edition, Issue 53, December 2008.

FACTS Global Energy, *China's Overseas Oil and Gas Investment: Recent Developments*, China Energy Series, Gas edition, Issue 33, December 2009.

Fairbank, J.K. and E.O. Reischauer, *China. Tradition and Transformation*, Sydney: Allen & Unwin, 1989.

Feng, C., 'Democrats within the Communist Party since 1989', *Journal of Contemporary China*, 17, 2008, 673–88.

Ferdinand, P., 'Russia and China: converging responses to globalization', *International Affairs*, 83(4), 2007, 655–800.

Ferris, R., Jr. and H. Zhang, 'Environmental law in the People's Republic of China', in K.A. Day (ed.), *China's Environment and the Challenge of Sustainable Development*, Armonk, NY: M.E. Sharpe, 2005, pp. 66–101.

Fewsmith, J., 'The new shape of elite politics', *The China Journal*, 45, 2001, 83–93.

Fisher-Vanden, K., G.H. Jefferson, H. Liu, Q. Tao, 'What is driving China's decline in energy intensity?', *Resource and Energy Economics*, 26, 2004, 77–97.

Foot, R., *Rights Beyond Borders: the Global Community and the Struggle over Human Rights in China*, Oxford: Oxford University Press, 2000.

Foot, R., 'Chinese strategies in a US-hegemonic global order: accommodating and hedging', *International Affairs*, 82(1), 2006, 77–94.

Foster, V., W. Butterfield, C. Chen and N. Pushak, 'Building bridges: China's growing role as infrastructure financier for Sub-Saharan Africa', *World Bank Report*, July 2008.

Frank, A.G., *Dependent Accumulation and Underdevelopment*, London: Macmillan, 1978.

Friedberg, A.L., 'The future of US-China relations: is conflict inevitable?', *International Security*, 30(2), 2005, 7–45.

Frynas, J.G., 'Corporate social responsibility in the oil and gas sector', *Journal of World Energy Law and Business*, 2(3), 2009, 178–95.

Fukuyama, F., *The End of History and the Last Man*, London: Hamish Hamilton, 1992.

Gaddis, J.L., 'International relations theory and the end of the Cold War', *International Security*, 17(3), 1992–3, 5–58.

Gallaghar, K.S., *China Shifts Gear. Automakers, Oil, Pollution and Development*, Cambridge, Mass.: MIT Press, 2006.

Gallagher J. and R. Robinson, 'The imperialism of free trade', *The Economic History Review*, 6(1), 1953, 1–15.

Gallagher J. and R. Robinson, *Africa and the Victorians: The Official Mind of Imperialism*, Basingstoke: Macmillan, 1961.

Gang, C., *The Politics of China's Environmental Protection. Problems and Progress*, Singapore: World Scientific Publishing, 2009.

Gao, S., 'China', in P.B. Stares (ed.) *Rethinking Energy Security in Asia*, Tokyo: Japan Center for International Exchange, 2000, pp. 43–58.

Garver, J., F. Leverett and H.M. Leverett, *Moving (Slightly) Closer to Iran: China's Shifting Calculus for Managing its 'Persian Gulf Dilemma'*, Washington DC: Reischauer Center for East Asian Studies, 2009.

Garver, R.W., *China and Iran: Ancient Partners in a Post-Imperial World*, Seattle, WA: University of Washington Press, 2006.

Geller, H., J. DeCicco, S. Laitner and C. Dyson, 'Twenty years after the embargo. US oil import dependence and how it can be reduced', *Energy Policy*, 22, 1994, 471–85.

Gill B. and J. Reilly, 'The tenuous hold of China Inc. in Africa', *The Washington Quarterly*, 30(3), 2007, 37–53.

Gilpin, R., *War and Change in World Politics*, Princeton: Princeton University Press, 1981.

Gilpin, R., *The Political Economy of International Relations*, Princeton: Princeton University Press, 1987.

Girdis, D., S. Tavoulareas and R. Tomkins, *Liquefied Natural Gas in China. Options for Markets, Institutions and Finance*, Washington DC: World Bank, 2000.

Goh, E., 'Great powers and hierarchical order in Southeast Asia: analyzing regional security strategies', *International Security*, 32(3), 2007/8, 113–57.

Golas, P., *Joseph Needham. Science and Civilisation in China. Volume V, Part 13, Mining*, Cambridge: Cambridge University Press, 1999.

Goldgeier J.M. and M. McFaul, 'A tale of two worlds: core and periphery in the post-Cold War era', *International Organization*, 46(2), 1992, 467–91.

Goldman, M. and R. MacFarquhar, 'Dynamic economy, declining Party-State', in M. Goldman and R. MacFarquhar (eds) *The Paradox of China's Post-Mao Reforms*, Cambridge, Mass., Harvard University Press, 1999, pp. 3–29.

Goldstein L. and V. Kozyrev, 'China, Japan and the scramble for Siberia', *Survival*, 48(1), 2006, 163–78.

Goldstein, A., *Rising to the Challenge: China's Grand Strategy and International Security*, Stanford, CA: Stanford University Press, 2005.

Goldthau, A. and J.M. Witte (eds), *Global Energy Governance. The New Rules of the Game*, Berlin: Global Public Policy Institute, 2010.

Goodman, D.S.G., 'The new middle class', in M. Goldman and R. MacFarquar (eds), *The Paradox of China's Post-Mao Reforms*, Cambridge, Mass., Harvard University Press, 1999, pp. 241–61.

Gough, K., *Emerging Civil Society in China*, Stockholm: SIDA, 2004.

Grief, A., *Institutions and the Path to the Modern Economy. Lessons from Medieval Trade*, Cambridge: Cambridge University Press, 2006.

Gries, P.H., *China's New Nationalism: Pride, Politics and Diplomacy*, Berkeley, CA: University of California Press, 2004.

Haas, E.B., *The Uniting of Europe: Political, Economic and Social Forces*, London: Stevens, 1958.

Halff, A., 'Africa on my mind: the panda menace', *The National Interest*, July-August 2007, 35–41.

Halpbern, N.P., 'Information flows and policy coordination in the Chinese bureaucracy', in K.G. Lieberthal and D.M. Lampton (eds) *Bureaucracy, Politics, and Decision Making in Post-Mao China*, Berkeley, CA: University of California Press, 1992, pp. 125–48.

Han, Z.Y., Y. Fan, J.L. Jiao, J.S. Yan and Y.M. Wei, 'Energy structure, marginal efficiency and substitution rate', *Energy*, 32, 2007, 935–42.

Hang, L. and M. Tu, 'The impacts of energy prices on energy intensity', *Energy Policy*, 35, 2007, 2978–88.

Hardy, R.W., *China's Oil Future: A Case of Modest Expectations*, Colorado: Westview Press, 1978.

Harrison, L.C., *China Considers the Middle East*, London: I.B. Tauris, 1993.

Harrison, S.S., *China, Oil, and Asia: Conflict Ahead?*, New York: Columbia University Press, 1977.

He, K., H. Huo, Q. Zhang, D. He, F. An, M. Wang and M.P. Walsh, 'Oil consumption and CO2 emissions in China's road transport: current status, future trends, and policy implications', *Energy Policy*, 33, 2005, 1499–507.

He, Z., *Institutional Barriers to the Development of Civil Society in China*, Discussion Paper 15, China Policy Institute, University of Nottingham, February 2007.

Heilmann, S., 'Regulatory innovation by Leninist means: Communist Party supervision in China's financial industry', *The China Quarterly*, 181, 2005, 1–21.

Hellstrom, J., 'China's emerging role in Africa: a strategic overview', *FOI Studies in African Security*, May 2009.

Helm, D., 'The Russian dimension and Europe's external energy policy', 3 September 2007. Available at: www.dieterhelm.co.uk/publications/Russian_dimension.pdf

Helm, D., 'The new energy paradigm', in D. Helm (ed.), *The New Energy Paradigm*, Oxford: Oxford University Press, 2007, pp. 9–35.

Helm, D., 'Climate change policy: why has so little been achieved?', in D. Helm and C. Hepburn (eds) *The Economics and Politics of Climate Change*, Oxford: Oxford University Press, 2009, pp. 9–35.

Higashi, N., *Natural Gas in China. Market Evolution and Strategy*, International Energy Agency, Working Paper Series, Paris: OECD/IEA, 2009.

Ho, J.H., 'The security of sea lanes in Southeast Asia', *Asian Survey*, 46(4), 2006, 558–74.

Ho, P., 'Mao's war against nature? The environmental impact of the grain-first campaign', *The China Journal*, 50, 2003, 37–59.

Hogwood, B.W. and L.A. Gunn, *Policy Analysis for the Real World*. Oxford, Oxford University Press, 1984.

Horowitz, S. and C. Marsh, 'Explaining regional economic policies in China: interest groups, institutions, and identities', *Communist and Post-Communist Studies*, 35, 2002, 115–32.

Horsnell, P., *Oil in Asia. Markets, Trading, Refining and Deregulation*, Oxford: Oxford University Press, 1997.

Horsnell, P., *The Probability of Oil Market Disruption: With an Emphasis on the Middle East*, James A. Baker III Institute for Public Policy, Rice University, 2000.

Houser, T. and R. Levy, 'Energy security and China's UN diplomacy', *China Security*, 4(3), 2008, 63–73.

Houser, T., 'The roots of Chinese oil investment abroad', *Asia Policy*, 5, 2008, 141–66.

Hu, L., 'Strengthen the guarantee system or oil security in China', *China Energy*, 2000 (5), 15–17 (in Chinese).

Hu, Z., D. Moskovitz and J. Zhao, *Demand-Side Management in China's Restructured Power Industry*, ESMAP Report 314/5, Washington DC: World Bank, 2005.

Huang, C-H., 'China's evolving perspective on Darfur: significance and policy implications', *Pacnet NewsLetter*, 25 July 2007.

Ikenberry, G.J., *After Victory: Institutions, Strategic Restraint and the Rebuilding of Order after Major Wars*, Princeton, NJ: Princeton University Press, 2001.

International Crisis Group, 'China's thirst for oil', *Asia Report*, 153, 9 June 2008.

International Crisis Group, *The Iran Nuclear Issue: the View from Beijing*, 17 February 2010. Available at: www.crisisgroup.org/en/publication-type/media-releases/2010/asia/the-iran-nuclear-issue-the-view-from-beijing.aspx (accessed 17 May 2010).

International Energy Agency, *Developing China's Natural Gas Market. The Energy Policy Challenges*, Paris: OECD/IEA, 2002.

International Energy Agency, *World Energy Investment Outlook. Insights 2003*, Paris: OECD/IEA, 2003.

International Energy Agency, *World Energy Outlook 2004*, Paris, OECD/IEA, 2004.

International Energy Agency, *China's Power Sector Reforms. Where to Next?*, Paris: OECD/IEA, 2006.

International Energy Agency, *Energy Policies of IEA Countries. 2006 Review*, Paris: OECD/IEA, 2006.

International Energy Agency, *World Energy Outlook 2007*, Paris: OECD/IEA, 2007.

International Energy Agency, *Energy Security and Climate Policy. Assessing the Interactions*, Paris: OECD/IEA, 2007.

International Energy Agency, *Deploying Renewables – Principles for Effective Policies*, Paris: OECD/IEA, 2008.

International Energy Agency, *Cleaner Coal in China*, Paris: OECD/IEA, 2009.

International Energy Agency, *Perspectives on Caspian Oil and Gas Development*, Paris: IEA/OECD, 2009.

International Energy Agency, *World Energy Outlook 2009*, Paris: OECD/IEA, 2009.

Jackson, M.P. and B. Jiang, *Natural Gas in the Energy Futures of China and India*, Stanford University, Program on Energy and Sustainable Development, Working Paper no. 62, 2007.

Jaffe, A.M. and K.B. Medlock III, 'China and Northeast Asia', in J.H. Kalicki and D.L. Goldwyn (eds) *Energy and Security: Toward a New Foreign Policy Strategy*, Washington DC: Woodrow Wilson Center Press/The Johns Hopkins University Press, 2005, pp. 267–89.

Jaffe, A.M. and S.W. Lewis, 'Beijing's oil diplomacy', *Survival*, 44, 2002, 115–34.

Jakobson, L. and D. Zha, 'China and the worldwide search for oil security', *Asia-Pacific Review*, 13(2), 2006, 60–73.

Jenner, W.J.F., *The Tyranny of History. The Roots of China's Crisis*, London: Allen Lane, 1992.

Jervis R., *Systems Effects: Complexity in Political and Social Life*, Princeton, NJ: Princeton University Press, 1997.

Jervis, R., 'Correspondence: thinking systemically about China', *International Security*, 31(2), 2006, 206–8.

Jervis, R., 'Cooperation under the security dilemma', *World Politics*, 30(2), 1978, 167–94.

Ji G., 'The legality of the "*Impeccable* incident"', *China Security*, 5(2), 2009, 16–21.

Jia, W., Q. Xu, Y. Wang and X. Yang, *The Development Strategy for China's Oil Industry 1996–2010*, Beijing: China Planning Publishing House, 1999 (in Chinese).

Johnson, C., *Communist China and Latin America, 1959–1967*, New York: Columbia University Press, 1970.

Johnston, A.I., *Cultural Realism: Strategic Culture and Grand Strategy in Chinese History*, Princeton, NJ: Princeton University Press, 1995.

Johnston, A.I. 'China's militarized interstate dispute behavior, 1949–1992: a first cut at the data', *China Quarterly*, 153, 1998, 1–30.

Johnston, A.I., 'International structures and Chinese foreign policy' in S.S. Kim (ed.) *China and the World: Chinese Foreign Policy Faces the New Millennium*, Boulder, CO: Westview Press, 1998.

Johnston, A.I., 'Is China a status quo power?', *International Security*, 27(4), 2003, 5–56.

Johnston, A.I, 'Chinese middle class attitudes towards international affairs: Nascent liberalization?', *China Quarterly*, 179, 2004, 603–28.

Johnston A.I. and P. Evans, 'China's engagement with multilateral security institutions' in A.I. Johnston and R.S. Ross (eds), *Engaging China: The Management of an Emerging Power*, New York: Routledge, 1999, pp. 235–72.

Kagan, R., *The Return of History and End of Dreams*, London: Atlantic Books, 2008.

Kalicki, J.H. and D.L. Goldwyn, *Energy and Security. Toward a New Foreign Policy Strategy*, Baltimore, MD: Johns Hopkins University Press, 2005.

Kambara, T. and C. Howe, *China and the Global Energy Crisis. Development and Prospects for China's Oil and Natural Gas*, Cheltenham: Edward Elgar, 2007.

Kaplan, R., 'Center stage for the 21st century: rivalry in the Indian Ocean', *Foreign Affairs*, 88(2), 2009, 16–32.

Katzenstein P.J. and R. Sil, 'Rethinking Asian security: a case for analytical eclecticism' in J.J. Suh, P.J. Katzenstein and A. Carlson, *Rethinking Security in East Asia: Identity, Power and Efficiency*, Stanford, CA: Stanford University Press, 2004, pp. 1–33.

Keith, R.C., 'China's resource diplomacy and national energy policy', in R.C. Keith (ed.) *Energy, Security and Economic Development in East Asia*, New York: St Martin's Press, 1986, pp. 1–78.

Keohane, R.O., *After Hegemony: Cooperation and Discord in the World Political Economy*, Princeton, NJ: Princeton University Press, 1984.

Kerr, D., 'Problems in Sino-Russian economic relations', *Europe-Asia Studies*, 50(7), 1998, 1133–56.

Keyuan Z., 'Joint development in the South China Sea: a new approach', *International Journal of Marine and Coastal Law*, 21(1), 2006, 83–109.

Kindleberger, C. *The World in Depression, 1929–39*, Berkeley, CA: University of California Press, 1973.

Kingston, C. and G. Cabellero, G., 'Comparing theories of institutional change', *Journal of Institutional Economics*, 5, 2009, 151–80.

Klare M. and D. Volman, 'The African "gold rush" and American national security', *Third World Quarterly*, 27(4), 2006, 609–28.

Klare, M., *Resource Wars:The New Landscape of Global Conflict*, New York: Henry Holt, 2001.

Kleveman, L., *The New Great Game: Blood and Oil in Central Asia*, New York: Grove Press, 2004.

Kong, B., 'Institutional insecurity', *China Security*, Summer 2006, 64–8.

Kong, B., 'China's energy decision-making: becoming more like the United States', *Journal of Contemporary China*, 18, 2009, 789–812.

Kong, B., *China's International Petroleum Policy*, Santa Barbara, CA: Praeger, 2010.

Kuchins, A., 'Russia and China: the ambivalent embrace', *Current History*, 106, 2007, 321–7.

Kurzantlick, J., *Charm Offensive: How China's Soft Power is Transforming the World*, New Haven, CT: Yale University Press, 2007.

Lai, H., 'Security of China's energy imports', in H. Lai (ed.), *Asian Energy Security: The Maritime Dimension*, Basingstoke: Palgrave Macmillan, 2009.

Lall, M., 'India-Myanmar relations – geopolitics and energy in the light of the balance of power', *ISAS Working Paper*, 29, 2 January 2008.

Lam, W., 'China's political feet of clay', *Far Eastern Economic Review*, 172(8), 2009, 10–14.

Lampton, D.M., 'A plum for a peach: bargaining, interest, and bureaucratic politics in China', in K.G. Lieberthal and D.M. Lampton (eds) *Bureaucracy, Politics, and Decision Making in Post-Mao China*, Berkeley, CA: University of California Press, 1992, pp. 35–58.

Lanteigne, M., 'China's energy security and Eurasian diplomacy: the case of Turkmenistan', *Politics*, 27(3), 2007, 147–55.

Lanteigne, M., 'China's maritime security and the "Malacca Dilemma"', *Asian Studies*, 4(2), 2008, 143–61.

Lardy, N., *Integrating China into the Global Economy*, Washington DC: Brookings Institution Press, 2002.

Large, D., 'China and the contradictions of "non-interference" in Sudan', *Review of African Political Economy*, 105, 2008, 93–106.

Lee, J., 'China's ASEAN invasion', *The National Interest*, May/June 2007.

Lee, Y.S., 'Public environmental consciousness in China: early empirical evidence', in K.A. Day (ed.), *China's Environment and the Challenge of Sustainable Development*, Armonk, NY: M.E. Sharpe, 2005, pp. 35–65.

Lei W. and Shen Q., 'Will China go to war over oil?', *Far Eastern Economic Review*, 169(3), 2006, 38–40.

Lema, A. and K. Ruby, 'Between fragmented authoritarianism and policy coordination: creating a Chinese market for wind energy', *Energy Policy*, 35, 2007, 3879–90.

Leonard, M., *Divided World: The Struggle for Primacy in 2020*, London: Centre for European Reform, 2007.

Leung, G.C.K., 'China's oil use, 1990–2008', *Energy Policy*, 38, 2010, 932–44.

Leverett, F. and J. Bader, 'Managing China-US energy competition in the Middle East', *The Washington Quarterly*, 29(1), 2005/6, 187–201.

Leverett, F. and P. Noel, 'The new axis of oil', *The National Interest*, Summer 2006, 62–70.

Lewis, S.W., *Chinese NOCs and World Energy Markets: CNPC, Sinopec and CNOOC*, James A. Baker III Institute for Public Policy, Rice University, March 2007.

Li L. and L. Li, 'On developing China's large transnational corporations in the oil industry', *China's Industrial Economy*, 2000(2), 44–8 (in Chinese).

Liao, H., L. Fan and Y.M. Wei, 'What induced China's energy intensity to fluctuate: 1997–2006', *Energy Policy*, 35, 2007, 4640–49.

Liao, J.X., *Chinese Foreign Policy Think Tanks and China's Policy Towards Japan*, Hong Kong: Chinese University Press, 2006.

Liao, J.X., 'A silk road for oil: Sino-Kazakh energy diplomacy', *Brown Journal of World Affairs*, 12, 2006, 39–51.

Liao, J.X., 'Sino-Japanese energy security and regional stability: the case of the East China Sea gas exploration', *East Asia*, 25(1), 2008, 57–78.

Liao, J.X., *The Politics of Oil Behind the Sino-Japanese Energy Security Strategies*, Singapore: Institute for Security and Development Policy, 2008.

Liao, J.X., *The Politics of Oil Behind Sino-Japanese Relations: Beyond Energy Cooperation*, Stockholm: Institute for Security and Development Policy, 2008.

Lieberman, R.C., 'Ideas, institutions and political order: explaining political change', *American Political Science Review*, 96, 2002, 697–712.

Lieberthal, K.G., 'Introduction: the 'Fragmented Authoritarianism' model and its limitations', in K.G. Lieberthal and D.M. Lampton (eds) *Bureaucracy, Politics, and Decision Making in Post-Mao China*, Berkeley, CA: University of California Press, 1992, pp.1–30.

Lieberthal, K., *Governing China. From Revolution through Reform*, New York: W.W. Norton, 1995.

Lieberthal, K. and M. Herberg, 'China's search for energy security: Implications for US policy', *NBR Analysis*, 17(1), 2006, 5–42.

Lieberthal, K.G. and D.M. Lampton (eds), *Bureaucracy, Politics, and Decision Making in Post-Mao China*, Berkeley, CA: University of California Press, 1992.

Lieberthal, K.G. and M. Oksenberg, *Policy Making in China. Leaders, Structures and Processes*, Princeton, NJ: Princeton University Press, 1988.

Lin, J., 'Energy conservation investment: a comparison between China and the USA', *Energy Policy*, 35, 2007, 916–24.

Lin, J., N. Zhou, M. Levine and D. Fridley, 'Taking out 1 billion tons of CO_2: the magic of China's 11th Five-Year Plan', *Energy Policy*, 36, 2008, 954–79.

Lipset, S.M., 'Some social requisites of democracy: economic development and political legitimacy', *The American Political Science Review*, 53(1), 1959, 69–105.

Liu, M. and L. Zhu, 'A study on coordinated growth among industry structure adjustment, energy supply and consumption in China', *Energy of China*, 28(1), 2006, 11–14 (in Chinese).

Lo, B., *Axis of Convenience: Moscow, Beijing and the New Geopolitics*, Washington DC: Brookings Institution Press, 2008.

Locatelli, C., 'The Russian oil industry between public and private governance: Obstacles to international oil companies' investment strategies', *Energy Policy*, 34, 2006, 1975–85.

Lu, Y., *Environmental Governance and Civil Society in China*, London: Chatham House Briefing Paper ASP BP 05/04, August 2005.

Lucas, E., *The New Cold War: How the Kremlin Menaces both Russia and the West*, London: Bloomsbury, 2008.

Lukin, A. *The Bear Watches the Dragon: Russian Perceptions of China and the Evolution of Russia-Chinese Relations Since the Eighteenth Century*, Armonk, NY: M.E. Sharpe, 2003.

Lundqvist, L.J. and A. Biel (eds), *From Kyoto to the Town Hall. Making International and National Climate Policy Work at the Local Level*, London: Earthscan, 2007.

Luo, D. and Y. Dai, 'Economic evaluation of coalbed methane production in China', *Energy Policy*, 37, 2009, 3883–9.

Lynch, M., *Blood or Gold? Politics, Economics and Energy Security*, The Emirates Occasional Papers no. 47, Dubai: The Emirates Centre for Strategic Studies and Research, 2002.

Ma, C. and D.I. Stern, 'China's changing energy intensity trend: a decomposition analysis', *Energy Economics*, 30, 2008, 1037–53.

Ma, X., *National Oil Company Reform from the Perspective of its Relationship with Government: The Case of China*, Unpublished Ph.D. Thesis, Centre for Energy, Petroleum and Mineral Law and Policy, University of Dundee, 2008.

Ma, X. and P. Andrews-Speed. 'The overseas activities of China's national oil companies: rationale and outlook', *Minerals and Energy*, 21, 2006, 1–14.

Ma, X. and L. Ortolano, *Environmental Regulation in China. Institutions, Enforcement and Compliance*, Lanham, MD: Rowman & Littlefield, 2000.

Manion, M., 'When Communist Party candidates can lose, who wins? Assessing the role of local People's Congresses in the selection of leaders in China', *The China Quarterly*, 195, 2008, 607–30.

Mann, J., *The China Fantasy*, New York: Viking, 2007.

Mansfield E.D. and J. Snyder, 'Democratization and the danger of war', *International Security*, 20(1), 1995, 5–38.

McElroy, M.B., X. Lu, C.P. Nielsen, and Y. Wang, 'Potential for wind-generated electricity in China', *Science*, 325, 2009, 1378–80.

Mearsheimer, J.J., *The Tragedy of Great Power Politics*, New York: Norton, 2001.

Medeiros, E.S., *China's International Behaviour: Activism, Opportunism and Diversification*, Santa Monica: RAND Corporation, 2009, pp. 130–31.

Meidan, M., 'China's Africa policy: business now, politics later', *Asian Perspective*, 30(4), 2006, 69–93.

Meidan, M., P. Andrews-Speed and X. Ma, 'Shaping China's energy policy: actors and processes', *Journal of Contemporary China*, 18, 2009, 591–616.

Menon, R., 'The limits of Chinese-Russian partnership', *Survival*, 51(3), 2009, 99–130.

Menon, R., 'The strategic convergence between Russia and China', *Survival*, 39(2), 1997, 101–25.

Miller, J., 'Daoism and ecology', in R.S. Gottlieb (ed.) *The Oxford Handbook of Religion and Ecology*, Oxford: Oxford University Press, 2006, 283–309.

Milov, V., L.L. Coburn and I. Damchenko, 'Russia's energy policy, 1992–2005', *Eurasian Geography and Economics*, 47(3), 2006, 285–313.

Mitchell, C., *The Political Economy of Sustainable Energy*, Basingstoke: Palgrave MacMillan, 2008.

Mitchell, J.V., and P. Stevens, *Ending Dependence: Hard Choices for Oil Exporting States*, London: Chatham House, 2008.

Mitchell, J.V. and G. Lahn, *Oil for Asia*, Chatham House Briefing Paper, London: Chatham House, 2007.

Miyamoto, A. and C. Ishiguro, *Pricing and Demand for LNG in China: Consistency between LNG and Pipeline Gas in a Fast Growing Market*, Oxford: Oxford Institute for Energy Studies, Report NG 9, 2006.

Montinola, G., Y. Qian and B.R. Weingast, 'Federalism, Chinese style: the political basis for economic success', *World Politics*, 48, 1995, 50–81.

Morris, D., 'The chance to go deep: U.S. energy interests in West Africa', *American Foreign Policy Interests*, 28(3), 2006, 225–38.

Moya, D., *Dead Aid: Why Aid Is Not Working And How There Is A Better Way For Africa*, London: Allen Lane, 2009.

Naim, M., 'Rogue aid', *Foreign Policy*, 159, 2007, 94–5.

Nakajima, S., 'China's energy problems: present and future', *The Developing Economies*, 20, 1982, 472–98.

Nathan, A.J. and R.S. Ross, *The Great Wall and Empty Fortress: China's Search for Security*, New York: Norton, 1997.

National Bureau of Statistics, *China Statistical Yearbook 2006*, Beijing: China Statistics Press, 2006.

National Bureau of Statistics, *China Statistical Yearbook 2009*, Beijing: China Statistics Press, 2009.

National Congress of the Communist Party of China, *Documents of the 17th National Congress of the Communist Party of China (2007)*, Beijing, Foreign Languages Press.

National Development and Reform Commission, *China's Medium and Long Term Energy Conservation Plan*, Beijing: National Development Reform Commission, 2004.

National Development and Reform Commission, *Implementation Plan for the Programme of One Thousand Enterprises Energy Conservation Action* issued by the National Development and Reform Commission, Beijing, 7 April 2006 (in Chinese).

National Development Reform Commission, *China Gas Utilisation Policy*, Beijing: National Development Reform Commission, 2007.

Naughton, B., 'China's economic think tanks: their changing role in the 1990s', *China Quarterly*, 33, 2002, 625–35.

Naughton, B., *Growing out of the Plan. Chinese Economic Reform 1978–1993*, Cambridge: Cambridge University Press, 1996.

Naughton, B., *The Chinese Economy. Transitions and Growth*, Cambridge, Mass.: MIT Press, 2007.

Neiderberger, A.A., C.U. Brunner and D. Zhou, 'Energy efficiency in China: impetus for a global climate policy breakthrough?', Woodrow Wilson International Center for Scholars, *China Environment Series*, Issue 8, 2006, 85–6.

Nel W.P. and C.J. Cooper, 'A critical review of IEA's oil demand forecast for China', *Energy Policy*, 36, 2008, 1096–106.

Ngo, T.K., 'The politics of rent production', in T.K. Ngo and Y. Wu (eds) *Rent Seeking in China*, Abingdon: Routledge, 2009, pp. 1–21.

Nolan, P., *China's Rise, Russia's Fall. Politics, Economics and Planning in the Transition from Stalinism*, London: MacMillan Press, 1995.

Nolan, P., *China and the Global Business Revolution*, Basingstoke: Palgrave, 2001.

North, D.C., *Institutions, Institutional Change and Economic Performance*, Cambridge: Cambridge University Press, 1990.

North, D.C., *Understanding the Process of Economics Change*, Princeton, NJ: Princeton University Press, 2005.

Nygrad, J. and X. Guo, *Environmental Management of China's Township and Village Industrial Enterprises*, Washington DC: World Bank, 2001.

Obi, C.I., 'Enter the dragon? Chinese oil companies and resistance in the Niger Delta', *Review of African Political Economy*, 117, 2008, 417–34.

Odgaard, L., *Maritime Security between China and Southeast Asia*, Aldershot: Ashgate, 2002.

OECD, 'China 2008', *OECD Investment Policy Reviews*, 2008. Available at: www.oecd.org.dataoecd/25/11/41792683.pdf

Oksenberg, M., 'China's political system: challenges of the twenty-first century', *The China Journal*, 45, 2001, 21–35.

O'Neal, J.R. and B.M. Russett, *Triangulating Peace: Democracy, Interdependence, and International Organizations*, New York: W.W. Norton, 2001.

Organski A.F.K. and J. Kugler, *The War Ledger*, Chicago, IL: Chicago University Press, 1980.

Paik, K.W., 'Sino-Russian oil and gas development cooperation: the reality and implications', *The Journal of Energy and Development*, 22(2), 1998, 275–84.

Paik, K.W., V. Marcel, G. Lahn, J.V. Mitchell and E. Adylov, *Trends in Asian NOC Investment Abroad*, Chatham House Working Background Paper, London: Chatham House, 2007.

Palacios, L., 'Latin America as energy supplier', in R. Roett and G. Paz (eds), *China's Expansion into the Western Hemisphere: Implications for Latin America and the United States*, Washington DC: Brookings Institution Press, 2008.

Pan, J., W. Peng and others, *Rural Electrification in China, 1950–2004*, Stanford University, Program on Energy and Sustainable Development, Working Paper no. 60, 2006.

Pape, R.A., 'Soft balancing against the United States', *International Security*, 30(1), 2005, 7–45.

Parkash, M., *Promoting Environmentally Sustainable Transport in the People's Republic of China*, Manila: Asian Development Bank, 2008.

Parsons, W., *Public Policy. An Introduction to the Theory and Practice of Policy Analysis*, Aldershot: Edward Elgar, 1995.

Paul, T.V., 'Soft balancing in the age of US primacy', *International Security*, 30(1), 2005, 46–71.

Paz, G.S., 'Rising China's offensive in Latin America and the US reaction', *Asian Perspective*, 30(4), 2006, 96–112.

Pehrson, C.J., *String of Pearls: Meeting the Challenge of China's Rising Power Across the Littoral*, Carlisle, PA; Strategic Studies Institute, 2006.

Pei, M. 'Creeping democratization in China', *Journal of Democracy*, 6(4), 1995, 64–79.

Perry, E., 'Studying Chinese politics: farewell to revolution?', *The China Journal*, 57, 2007, 1–22.

Pierson, P., *Politics in Time: History, Institutions, and Social Analysis*, Princeton, NJ: Princeton University Press, 2004.

Pirani, S., J. Stern and K. Yafimava, *The Russo-Ukrainian Gas Dispute of January 2009: A Comprehensive Assessment*, Oxford: Oxford Institute for Energy Studies, 2009.

Pittman, R. and V.Y. Zhang, *Electricity Restructuring in China: The Elusive Quest for Competition*, Washington DC: Antitrust Division, US Department of Justice, 2008.

Pollack, J.D., 'Energy insecurity with Chinese and American characteristics: implications for Sino-American relations', *Journal of Contemporary China*, 17, 2008, 229–45.

Pollack, J.D., 'Structure and process in the Chinese military system', in K.G. Lieberthal and D.M. Lampton (eds) *Bureaucracy, Politics, and Decision Making in Post-Mao China*, Berkeley, CA: University of California Press, 1992, pp. 153–80.

Portyakov, V., 'Russian vector in the Chinese global Chinese migration', *Far Eastern Affairs*, 34(1), 2006, pp. 47–61.

Primakov, Y., *Russian Crossroads: Towards the New Millennium*, New Haven, CT: Yale University Press, 2004.

Pye, L.W., *The Spirit of Chinese Politics*, Cambridge Mass.: Harvard University Press, 1992.

Pye, L.W., 'China: not your typical superpower', *Problems of Post-Communism*, July/August, 1996, 3–15.

Pye, L.W., 'Jiang Zemin's style of rule: go for stability, monopolize power and settle for limited effectiveness', *The China Journal*, 45, 2001, 45–51.

Raine, S., *China's African Challenges*, London: Routledge, 2009.

Rasizade, A., 'Entering the old "Great Game" in Central Asia', *Orbis*, 47(1), 2003, 41–58.

Ratliff, W., 'Beijing's pragmatism meets Hugo Chavez', *Brown Journal of World Affairs*, 12(2), 2006, 75–83.

Ratliff, W., 'In search of a balanced relationship: China, Latin America, and the United States', *Asian Politics and Policy*, 1(1), 2009, 1–30.

Reeves, E., *China, Darfur and the Olympics: Tarnishing the Torch?*, New York: Dream for Darfur, 2007.

Resnier, M., C. Wang, P. Du and J. Chen, 'The promotion of sustainable development in China through the optimization of a tax/subsidy plan among HFC and power generation CDM projects', *Energy Policy*, 35, 2007, 4529–44.

Rodzinski, W., *The Walled Kingdom. A History of China from 2000 BC to the Present*, Glasgow: Harper Collins, 1991.

Ronan, C.A., *The Shorter Science and Civilisation in China: 1*, Cambridge: Cambridge University Press, 1978.

Ronan, C.A., *The Shorter Science and Civilisation in China: 4*, Cambridge: Cambridge University Press, 1994.

Ronan, C.A., *The Shorter Science and Civilisation in China: 5*, Cambridge: Cambridge University Press, 1995.

Rosecrance, R.N., *The Rise of the Trading State*, New York: Basic Books, 1986.

Rosen, D.H. and T. Houser, *China Energy: A Guide for the Perplexed*, Washington DC: Peterson Institute for International Economics, 2007.

Rosen, S., 'The victory of materialism: aspirations to join China's urban moneyed classes and the commercialization of education', *The China Journal*, 51, 2004, 27–51.

Ross, M.L., 'The political economy of the resource curse', *World Politics*, 51(2), 1999, 297–322.

Ross, R.S. 'Beijing as a conservative power', *Foreign Affairs*, 76(2), 1997, 33–44.

Roy D., 'Hegemon on the horizon? China's threat to East Asian security', *International Security*, 19(1), 1994, 149–68.

Rozman, G., 'Sino-Russian relations in the 1990s: a balance sheet', *Post-Soviet Affairs*, 14(2), 1998, 93–111.

Rozman, G., 'China's quest for great power identity', *Orbis*, 43(3), 1999, 383–402.

Rozman, G., 'Russia in Northeast Asia: in search of a strategy' in R. Levgold (ed.), *Russian Foreign Policy in the 21st Century and the Shadow of the Past*, New York: Columbia University Press, 2007.

Rusko, C.J. and K. Sasikumar, 'India and China: from trade to peace', *Asian Perspective*, 31(4), 2007, 99–123.

Sachdeva, G., 'India's attitude towards China's growing influence in Central Asia', *China and Eurasia Forum Quarterly*, 4(3), 2006, 23–34.

Sagawa, A. and K. Koizumi, *Trends of Exports and Imports of Coal by China and its Influence on Asian Markets*, Tokyo: Institute of Energy Economics Japan, 2008.

Sapio, F., 'Rent seeking, corruption and clientilism', in Ngo, T.K. and Y. Wu (eds) *Rent Seeking in China*, Abingdon: Routledge, 2009, pp. 22–42.

Saurbek, Z., 'Kazakh-Chinese energy relations: economic pragmatism or political cooperation?', *China and Eurasia Forum Quarterly*, 56(1), 2008, 79–93.

Schofield, C., 'Dangerous ground: a geopolitical overview of the South China Sea' in S. Bateman and R. Emmers (eds), *Security and International Politics in the South China Sea: Towards a Cooperative Management Regime*, London: Routledge, 2009.

Scrase, I. and G. MacKerron, 'Lock-in', in I. Scrase. and G. MacKerron (eds) *Energy for the Future: A New Agenda*, Basingstoke: Palgrave MacMillan, 2009, pp. 89–100.

Selth, A., 'Burma's Coco Islands: rumours and realities in the Indian Ocean', *SEARC Working Papers*, 101, November 2008.

Seznec, J.F., 'Saudi Arabia's relations with China and Asia and prospects for the future', *NBR Research Conference Report*, Washington: National Bureau of Asian Research, October 2009.

Shambaugh, D., *China's Communist Party. Atrophy and Adaptation*, Washington DC: Woodrow Wilson Center Press, 2008.

Shao S., Z. Lu, N. Berrah, B. Tenenbaum and J. Zhao (eds), *China. Power Sector Regulation in a Socialist Market Economy*, World Bank Discussion Paper no. 361, Washington DC: World Bank, 1997.

Shapiro, J., *Mao's War Against Nature: Politics and the Environment in Revolutionary China*, Cambridge: Cambridge University Press, 2001.

Shealy, M. and J.P. Dorian, *Growing Chinese Energy Demand. Is the World in Denial?*, Washington DC: Center for Strategic and International Studies, 2007.

Sheehan, P. and F. Sun, *Energy Use in China: Interpreting Changing Trends and Future Directions*, Centre for Strategic Economic Studies, Climate Change Working Paper no.13, Victoria University, Melbourne, 2007.

Sheives, K., 'China turns West: Beijing's contemporary strategy towards Central Asia', *Pacific Affairs*, 79(2), 2006, 205–24.

Shen, Z., 'Energy saving potential of China's car industry', *International Petroleum Economics*, 14(8), 2006, 28–35 (in Chinese).

Shevchenko, A., 'Bringing the party back in: the CCP and the trajectory of market transition in China', *Communist and Post-Communist Studies* 37, 2004, 161–85.

Shichor, Y., *The Middle East in China's Foreign Policy, 1949–1977*, Cambridge: Cambridge University Press, 1979.

Shichor, Y., 'Mountains out of molehills: arms transfers in Sino-Middle Eastern relations', *Middle East Review of International Affairs*, 4(3), 2000, 68–79.

Shichor, Y., 'Decision-making in triplicate: China and the three Iraqi wars' in A. Scobell and L. Wortzel (eds), *Chinese Decisionmaking under Stress*, Carlisle: Strategic Studies Institute, US Army War College, 2005.

Shichor, Y., 'Competence and incompetence: the political economy of China's relations with the Middle East', *Asian Perspective*, 30(4), 2006, 39–67.

Shirk, S.L., *China: Fragile Superpower*, Oxford: Oxford University Press, 2007.

Shirk, S.L., 'The Chinese political system and the political strategy of economic reform', in K.G. Lieberthal and D.M. Lampton (eds), *Bureaucracy, Politics, and Decision Making in Post-Mao China*, Berkeley, CA: University of California Press, 1992, pp. 59–90.

Shirk, S.L., *The Political Logic of Economic Reform in China*, Berkeley, CA: University of California Press, 1993.

Simpfendorfer, B., 'China's historic return to the Gulf', *Foreign Policy*, 2 April 2010.

Singh, B.K., 'Energy security and India-China cooperation', *International Association for Energy Newsletter*, 2010. Available at: www.iaee.org/en/publications/newsletterdl.aspx?id=92

Sinton, J.E., 'Accuracy and reliability of China's energy statistics', *China Economic Review*, 12, 2001, 373–83.

Sinton, J.E. and D.G. Fridley, 'What goes up: recent trends in China's energy consumption', *Energy Policy*, 28, 2000, 671–87.

Sinton, J.E., M.D. Levine and Q. Wang, 'Energy efficiency in China: accomplishments and challenges', *Energy Policy*, 26, 1988, 813–29.

Small Arms Survey, 'Arms, oil and Darfur: the evolution of relations between China and Sudan', *Sudan Issue Brief*, 7, 2007, 1–11.

Smil, V., 'Energy development in China. The need for a coherent policy', *Energy Policy*, 9, 1981, 113–26.

Smil, V., *China's Past China's Future. Energy Food, Environment*, New York: RoutledgeCurzon, 2004.

Soares de Oliviera, R., *Oil and Politics in the Gulf of Guinea*, London: Hurst, 2007.

Spence, J., *The Search for Modern China*, London: Century Hutchinson, 1990.

State Planning Commission, *'95 Energy Report of China*, Beijing: State Planning Commission, 1995.

Steenhof, P., 'Decomposition of electricity demand in China's industrial sector', *Energy Economics*, 28, 2006, 370–84

Steinberg, G.M., 'Chinese policies on arms control and proliferation in the Middle East', *China Report*, 34, 1998, 381–400.

Stevens, P., 'Resource impact: curse or blessing: a literature review', *CEPMLP Internet Journal*, 13(4), 2003. Available at: www.dundee.ac.uk/cepmlp/journal/html/Vol13/vol13-14.html

Stevens, P., *Transit Troubles: Pipelines as a Source of Conflict*, London: Royal institute of International Affairs, 2009.

Storey, I., 'Securing Southeast Asia's sea lanes: a work in progress', *Asia Policy*, 6, 2008, 95–127.

Swaine M.D. and A.I. Johnston, 'China and arms control institutions', in E. Economy and M. Oksenberg (eds), *China Joins the World: Progress and Prospects*, New York: Council on Foreign Relations, 1999.

Swaine M.D. and A.J. Tellis, *Interpreting China's Grand Strategy: Past, Present and Future*, Santa Monica, CA: RAND, 2000.

Taylor, I., *China and Africa. Engagement and Compromise*, Abingdon: Routledge, 2006.

Taylor, I., 'Governance in Africa and Sino-African relations: contradictions or confluence?', *Politics*, 27(3), 2007, 139–46.

Taylor, I., *China's New Role in Africa*, Boulder, CO: Lynne Rienner, 2009.

Teiwes, F.C., 'Normal politics with Chinese characteristics', *The China Journal*, 45, 2001, 69–82.

Thelen, K., 'Historical institutionalism in comparative politics', *Annual Review of Political Studies*, 2, 1999, 369–404.

Thompson, D. and X. Lu, 'China's evolving civil society: from environment to health ?', Woodrow Wilson International Center for Scholars, *China Environment Series*, Issue 8, 2006, 27–39.

Thomson, E., *The Chinese Coal Industry: An Economic History*, London: RoutledgeCurzon, 2003.

Tian, C., 'Review of China's oil imports and exports in 1999', *International Petroleum Economics*, 8(2), 2000, 5–9 (in Chinese).

Tian, C., 'Review of China's oil imports and exports in 2004', *International Petroleum Economics*, 13(3), 2005, 10–16 (in Chinese).

Tian, C., 'Review of China's oil imports and exports in 2008', *International Petroleum Economics*, 17(3), 2009, 31–9 (in Chinese).

Tonnesson S. and A. Kolas, *Energy security in Asia: China, India, Oil and Peace*, Oslo: International Peace Research Institute, 2006.

Tonnesson, S. and A. Kolas, *Energy Security in Asia: China, India, Oil and Peace*, Report to the Norwegian Ministry of Foreign Affairs, International Peace Research Institute, Oslo, April 2006.

Trombly, A., 'China eyes Venezuelan and Brazilian oil', *Council on Hemispheric Affairs*, 10 March 2010. Available at:www.coha.org/china-eyes-venezuelan-and-brazilian-oil

Tsai, L., 'Understanding the falsification of village income statistics', *The China Quarterly*, 196, 2008, 805–26.

Tsang, S., 'Consultative Leninism: China's new political framework', *Journal of Contemporary China*, 18, 2009, 865–80.

Unger, J. and A. Chan, 'The internal politics of an urban Chinese working community: a case study of employee influence on decision-making at a state-owned factory', *The China Journal*, 52, 2004, 1–24.

Unruh, G.C., 'Understanding carbon lock-in', *Energy Policy*, 28, 2000, 817–30.

US Department of Energy, *Section 1837: National Security Review of International Energy Requirements*, February 2006.

US Government Accountability Office, *Issues Related to Potential Reductions in Venezuelan Oil Production*, Report to the Chairman, Committee on Foreign Relations, US Senate (GAO-06-668), June 2006.

Valencia, M., 'The "*Impeccable* incident": truth and consequences', *China Security* 5(2), 2009, 22–8.

Van Evera, S., 'Why Europe matters and the third world does not: American grand strategy after the cold war', *Journal of Strategic Studies*, 13(2), 1990, 1–51.

Vines, A., L. Wong, M. Weimer and I. Campos, *Thirst for African Oil: Asian National Oil Companies in Nigeria and Angola*, London: Royal Institute for International Affairs, 2009.

Wade, R., *Governing the Market: Economic Theory and the Role of Government in East Asian Modernization*, Princeton, NJ: Princeton University Press, 1995.

Waldron A., 'How would democracy change China?', *Orbis*, 2, 2004, 247–61.

Walsh, M.P., 'Can China control the side effects of motor vehicle growth?', *Natural Resources Forum*, 31, 2007, 21–34.

Walt, S., 'International Relations: one world, many theories', *Foreign Policy*, 110, 1998, 29–46.

Wang, B., 'An imbalanced development of coal and electricity industries in China', *Energy Policy*, 35, 2007, 4959–68.

Wang, H., 'SCO energy club: defining China's position', *International Petroleum Economics*, 15(6), 2007, 1–5 (in Chinese).

Wang, H.H., *China's Oil Industry and Market*, Amsterdam: Elsevier, 1999.

Wang, L., 'Russia's eastern energy diplomacy and Sino-Russian energy cooperation', *Contemporary International Relations*, 8, 2006, 8–20 (in Chinese).

Wang, M.Y., 'The motivations behind China's government-initiated industrial investments overseas', *Pacific Affairs*, 2, 2002, 187–206.

Wang, T. and J. Watson, *China's Energy Transition. Pathways for Low Carbon Development*, Sussex Energy Group, University of Sussex, 2009.

Wank, D.L., 'Producing property rights: strategies, networks, and efficiency in urban China's nonstate firms', in J.C. Oi and A.G. Walder (eds) *Property Rights and Economic Reform in China*, Stanford, CA: Stanford University Press, 1999, pp. 248–72.

Weber, C.L., G.P. Peters, D. Guan and K. Hubecek, 'The contribution of Chinese exports to climate change', *Energy Policy*, 36, 2008, 3572–7.

Wedeman, A., 'The intensification of corruption in China', *The China Quarterly*, 180, 2004, 895–921.

Wendt, A., *Social Theory of International Politics*, Cambridge: Cambridge University Press, 1999.

White, G., 'The dynamics of civil society in Post-Mao China', in B. Hook (ed.) *The Individual and the State in China*, Oxford: Clarendon Press, 1996, pp. 196–221.

Wittfogel, K.A., *Oriental Despotism. A Comparative Study of Total Power*, New Haven, CT: Yale University Press, 1957.

Wohlforth, W.C., 'The stability of a unipolar world', *International Security*, 24(1), 1991, 5–41.

Wong, C.P.W., 'People's Republic of China', in P.B. Rana and N. Hamid (eds) *From Centrally Planned to Market Economies: The Asian Approach. Volume 2: People's Republic of China and Mongolia*, Hong Kong: Oxford University Press, 1996, pp. 167–83.

Wong, C.P.W., C. Heady and W.T. Woo, *Fiscal Management and Economic Reform in the People's Republic of China*, Hong Kong: Oxford University Press, 1995;

Woodard, K., *The International Energy Relations of China*, Stanford, CA: Stanford University Press, 1980.

Woodard, K., 'Development of China's petroleum industry: an overview', in F. Fesharaki and D. Fridley (eds) *China's Petroleum Industry in the International Context*, Boulder, CO: Westview Press, 1986, pp. 93–125.

World Bank, *Governance and Development*, Washington DC: World Bank, 1992.

World Bank, *China – Power Sector Reform: Toward Competition and Improved Performance*, Report No. 12929-CHA, Washington DC: World Bank, 1994.

World Bank, *An Overview of China's Transport Sector – 2007*, Washington DC: World Bank, 2007.

World Bank, *Economically, Socially and Environmentally Sustainable Coal Mining Sector in China*, Washington DC: World Bank, 2008.

Wright, T., 'Rents and rent seeking in the coal industry', in T.K. Ngo and Y.Wu (eds) *Rent Seeking in China*, Abingdon: Routledge, 2009, pp. 98–116.

Wu, K., F. Fesharaki, S.B. Westley and W. Prawiraatmadja, 'Oil in Asia and the Pacific: production, consumption, imports and policy options', *Asia Pacific Issues*, 85, August 2008.

Xia, M., *The Dual Developmental State. Development Strategy and Institutional Arrangements for China's Transition*, Aldershot: Ashgate, 2000.

Xu, X., *Chinese NOC's Overseas Strategies: Background, Comparison and Remarks*, James A. Baker III Institute for Public Policy, Rice University, March 2007.

Xu, Y.C., *Electricity Reform in China, India and Russia. The World Bank Template and the Politics of Power*, Cheltenham: Edward Elgar, 2004.

Yang, C., 'Utilising international oil and gas resources in order to improve China's energy structure', *Energy of China*, 1998(11), 12–16 (in Chinese).

Yang, D., *China's Offshore Investment. A Network Approach*, Cheltenham: Edward Elgar, 2005.

Yang, D.D.H., 'Civil society as an analytical lens for contemporary China', *China: An International Journal*, 2(1), 2004, 1–27.

Yang, G., 'Environmental NGOs and institutional dynamics in China', *The China Quarterly*, 181, 2005, 46–66.

Yang, H. and M. Zhang, 'Analysis of impact of energy-intensive products export on China's energy', *Energy of China* 29(1), 2007, 27–9 (in Chinese).

Yang, M., 'China's energy efficiency target 2010', *Energy Policy*, 36, 2008, 561–70.

Yenikeyeff, S., *Kazakhstan's Gas: Export Markets and Export Routes*, Oxford: Oxford Institute for Energy Studies, 2008.

Yiu, D.W., C.M. Lau and G.D. Bruton, 'International venturing by emerging economy firms; the effects of firm capabilities, home country networks, and corporate entrepreneurship', *Journal of International Business Studies*, 38, 2007, 519–40.

Yoshihara T. and J. Holmes, 'Command of the sea with Chinese characteristics', *Orbis*, Fall 2005, pp. 677–94

Zakaria, F., *From Wealth to Power: The Unusual Origins of America's World Role*, Princeton, NJ: Princeton University Press, 1998.

Zambelis C., and B. Gentry, 'China through Arab eyes: American influence in the Middle East', *Parameters*, 38(1), 2008, 60–72.

Zha, D., 'China's energy security: domestic and international issues', *Survival*, 48, 2006, 179–90.

Zha, D., 'Energy interdependence', *China Security*, Summer 2006, 2–16.

Zha D. and W. Hu, 'Promoting energy partnership in Beijing and Washington', *The Washington Quarterly*, 30(4), 2007, 105–15.

Zhang, J., *Catch-up and Competitiveness in China – The Case of Large Firms in the Oil Industry*, London: RoutledgeCurzon, 2004.

Zhang, X., 'Southeast Asia and energy: gateway to stability', *China Security*, 3(2), 2007.

Zhang, X. and R. Baum, 'Civil society and the anatomy of a rural NGO', *The China Journal*, 52, 2004, 97–107.

Zhang, Z., 'Ten major steps necessary for the development of China's refining industry in the 21st century', *International Petroleum Economics*, 8(1), 2000, 37–9 (in Chinese).

Zhang, Z., 'Towards an effective implementation of clean development mechanism projects in China', *Energy Policy*, 34, 2006, 3691–701.

Zhao, H., 'New frame of Sino-Russian-US triangular relations', in *Post-Cold War World*, Shanghai: Shanghai Institute of International Studies, 2000, pp. 155–8.

Zhao, S., 'China's search for energy security: cooperation and competition in Asia Pacific', *Journal of Contemporary China*, 17, 2008, 207–27.

Zheng, Y. and Z. Wang, *China's National People's Congress 2008: New Administration, Personnel Reshuffling and Policy Impacts*, The University of Nottingham, China Policy Institute, Briefing Series, Issue 38, March 2008.

Ziegler, C.E., 'Competing for markets and influence: Asian national oil companies in Eurasia', *Asian Perspective*, 32, 2008, 129–63.

Zweig, D. and S. Ye, 'A crisis is looming: China's energy challenge in the eyes of university students', *Journal of Contemporary China*, 17, 2008, 273–96.

Index

Topics relate to China, unless otherwise stated. Page references in *italic* type indicate relevant figures and tables.